IN THE FOOTSTEPS
OF SMUGGLERS

MY LIFE ON A BASQUE MOUNTAIN

GEORGINA HOWARD

Bradt GUIDES

First published in the UK in July 2024 by
Bradt Guides Ltd
31a High Street, Chesham, HP5 1BW, England
www.bradtguides.com

Print edition published in the USA by The Globe Pequot Press Inc,
PO Box 480, Guilford, Connecticut 06437-0480

Edited and project managed by Samantha Cook
Cover design by Claire Henley
Layout and typesetting by Ian Spick
Production managed by Sue Cooper, Bradt Guides & Zenith Media

ISBN: 9781804692110

British Library Cataloguing in Publication Data
A catalogue record for this book is available from the British Library

Digital conversion by www.dataworks.co.in
Printed in the UK by Zenith Media

Paper used for this product comes from sustainably managed forests, recycled
and controlled sources.

AUTHOR BIOGRAPHY

Originally from Birmingham, in the UK, Georgina Howard (w pyreneanexperience.com) studied European languages before heading to Copenhagen. Here she worked as a writer and trainer, her activities ranging from teaching English to the Inuit hunters and fishermen of Greenland to imparting intercultural awareness skills to Danish statisticians. After eight years, she moved to an isolated Basque hamlet in the Spanish Pyrenees, where she has now lived for more than two decades. In that time she has gained privileged insights into local culture and Basque mountain life, and set up her own idiosyncratic brand of walking, culture and language holidays at Pyrenean Experience. *In the Footsteps of Smugglers* is her first book for Bradt.

DEDICATION

This book is dedicated to all my wonderful friends in Britain, Denmark, Spain, France, Italy and Australia who asked me to stay – or told me to go – but who listened and cared. And to all my guests from around the world who bought into this crazy idea of mine, braving the ten hairpin bends up to my mountain hamlet and believing in me – at times before I even believed in myself.

And last – but by no means least – to all the amazing Basque farmers and shepherds of Ameztia who adopted my tiny family and gave us a home. This is your story and a tribute to your unwavering generosity and nobility of spirit. I bow my head in admiration and gratitude. This is your book, not mine.

Oh, and there is of course my Basque baby, Marion, now a young woman, my *raison d'être* who keeps me sane and drives me mad in equal proportion. Forgive me, my darling, for all these indiscretions about our life. I know you will. This is just one of the wonderful things about you – you always do.

ACKNOWLEDGEMENTS

Firstly, I would like to thank Mum and Dad for your constancy, for always believing that doors should be opened, and horizons extended – to you I am forever beholden. It all started with you.

Also my heartfelt thanks go to Mary and Barry Tomalin for your unconditional belief in me, for giving me the confidence to strive for my dreams, for that serendipitous walk and for your advice about 'not losing my voice'. To my friend Ian Swedlund, surfer and symphony orchestra musician: you showed me how to catch waves with my sentences and how to turn paragraphs into rhapsodies. Your instinct for balance and harmony can be found in every phrase. To you – as always – I am eternally indebted.

To Simon Robinson, my remarkable, unfailing friend and former editor who – despite a rather delicate moment with a snake on my garden wall – has stood firmly at my side, publishing my second book *Breaking the Language Barrier* in 2001 and picking up the gauntlet to see *In the Footsteps of Smugglers* through to the end as well. It wouldn't have been finished without you.

I am grateful to Diana Friedman for keeping my narrative on Planet Earth, and for your insightful creative writing seminars beneath the hibiscus tree, to Carol Ungar for your unwavering friendship, patience and no-frills honesty, to Krista Jones for deeply caring, your cups of tea and kindness, to Kel Portman, for pushing me to embrace further nuances and finer concepts, for indulging my passion for maps and buckling down over Christmas to draw the charming map of Ameztia in this book. Thanks to my outstanding friend and Basque teacher, Aurkene Andueza, who has inspired my love of the Basque language and has painstakingly corrected my misspelt Basque words again and again; and to my final proofreader, Ross Dickinson, who took on a text in five languages and embraced the intricacies without a flinch. Thanks too to Anna Moores for your warm and charming welcome into the Bradt fold and to Murray Stewart, stalwart friend and author of the award-winning Bradt guide to *The Basque Country and Navarre*. Thank you for always being there at the drop of a hat, for giving me the benefit of your research and for checking the narrative for validity and substance – a quality sadly not applicable to that celebratory 'chicken in a puddle' meal I cooked for you last year.

Finally my deep gratitude to Sam Cook, my brilliant editor, a complete stranger, to whom, apprehensively, I handed over the final version of this, my life's story. Thank you for embracing its spirit and idiosyncrasy, for your instinct for chronology and discrepancy, for your exactitude and grace, and for understanding where I was going better than I understood it myself.

NOTE

Although all events and people described in this book are real, some names of people and places have been changed in order to protect identities.

THE BASQUE COUNTRY: A QUESTION OF DEFINITION

For any proud Basque, 'the Basque Country' is a territorial entity consisting of the seven Basque-speaking provinces: Gipuzkoa (Guipuzcoa), Bizkaia (Vizcaya), Araba (Alava) and Nafarroa (Navarra) in Spain, and Nafarroa Beherea (Basse Navarre), Lapurdi (Labourd) and Zuberoa (Soule) in France. This territory is, however, defined uniquely by cultural and linguistic factors.

There was only one brief period in history, at the end of the first millennium, during which this 'Basque Country' did indeed exist as a unified political entity. This was under the rule of Sancho III, at which time it included other parts of Spain and France, too.

Although today this territory of the seven provinces does not *officially* exist, in the minds of most Basque people it does, unequivocally, and the term Euskal Herria, 'the Basque Country', is widely used among the Basques to describe their 'homeland'.

To complicate matters, there is an official 'Basque Country' (Euskadi), also referred to as the Basque Autonomous Community, which consists of just three of the seven Basque-speaking provinces: Gipuzkoa, Bizkaia and Araba, all located in Spain. This reduced version defines the Basque Country as understood by almost everyone who is not Basque. Together, these three provinces combine to form one of Spain's seventeen autonomous communities.

This story is set in Nafarroa (Navarra – or, in English, Navarre), which is part of the culturally and linguistically defined Basque Country (but not of the legal one) – and so, like the majority of the Basque Navarrese, when I refer to 'the Basque Country' in my narrative, I too refer to the linguistically defined Euskal Herria of Spain and France, rather than the more limited Spanish autonomous community of Euskadi.

BASQUE WORDS AND SPELLING

When it comes to Spanish/Basque words and terms, I have tended to adopt Basque usage, except when it comes to the larger towns of San Sebastián and Pamplona, which are internationally recognised by their Spanish names. Nafarroa is the Basque name for the Spanish autonomous community of Navarra; however, the wider English-speaking public is familiar with the name 'Navarre' and so this is the term that I have adopted throughout this book for the sake of simplicity.

Nevertheless, do please bear with me. The use of Basque terms within the book is a rough science. I live in a bilingual society and many Basque words have been adopted into the local Spanish vernacular (and vice versa). In daily conversation, these more ubiquitous Basque words often adopt the Spanish (Latin) plural 's', such as the word *pintxos* (tapas), while other terms, confined predominantly to the Basque language, sit more naturally with the original Basque plural 'k' – *puskak*, for example. It is also important to know that there are many versions of Basque and words, and spellings, can change from one mountain village to the next.

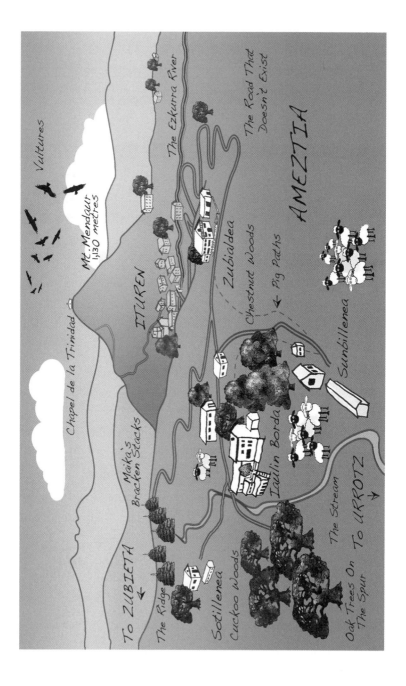

CONTENTS

The Basque Country – a Question of Definition...................... vi

Basque Words and Spelling vii

Prologue   My Life on a Basque Mountain xiii

PART I   **SCANDINAVIA** I

Chapter I   **Heading North** – The Wheelchair
in the Snow.. 2

PART 2   **THE BASQUE COUNTRY**................................. I I

Chapter 2   **Heading South** – Alice in Wonderland............ 12

Chapter 3   **Navarre and the Basques** – Heading into
the Beyond 20

*The two definitions of the 'Basque Country',
introduction to Navarre, the institution of the
Basque house, the Basque code of honour (*euskaldun
hitza*), Basque 'sheepherders' in America, Guernica,
the Spanish Civil War.*

Chapter 4   **Marketing** – Telephones and Witches 31

*Basque politics and ETA (1), Basque flags
and nationalism.*

Chapter 5   **The Baztan Valley** – Noble Peasants,
Pilgrims and Cider 41

*Baztan Valley lifestyle and landscapes in the
sixteenth century, Camino de Santiago, the Codex
Calixtinus, cider.*

Chapter 6 **Finding the Walks** – Chocolate Croissants, Maps and Cold Cups of Tea............................ 46
*Geography and topography, Basque mythology (1) (*lamiak*), smuggling tales (1), the WWII Comet Line resistance network (1).*

Chapter 7 **The Guests Arrive** – Mutiny in the Kitchen 60
Basque architecture, Spanish–English cultural differences.

Chapter 8 **People** – Sheiks and Silver Robots................. 72

Chapter 9 **A Basque Fiesta** – As Good as it Gets............ 80
ETA (2), Basque culture and fiestas.

Chapter 10 **A New Valley** – The Grandmother, the Miller and the Ostrich.............................. 89
Geography and topography.

PART 3 **MY BASQUE MOUNTAIN**................................. 95

Chapter 11 **A House with a View** – The Turtle on the Tap.. 96
Basque farms and farming life, Basque house names.

Chapter 12 **My Basque Village** – The Hello Kitty Fountain 110
Basque village life (1).

Chapter 13 **A Basque Baby** – A Fairy Godmother with an Axe.. 116
Basque village life (2) and local characters.

Chapter 14 **My Neighbours** – The Wellington Boot
in the Snow.. 124
*Basque community and solidarity, life under Franco
(1), wedding traditions, gravedigging, the annual
pig-killing (*matanza*).*

Chapter 15 **Local History** – Tin Cows and Tadpoles 136
*Spanish Inquisition in the Basque Country, popular
witches' tales, inheritance laws, life under Franco (2).*

Chapter 16 **The Seasons** – British Unpunctuality............ 148
*Mountain architecture, superstitions (*eguzkiloreak*),
haymaking, hunting, paganism, the winter festival
of the Joaldunak.*

Chapter 17 **Basque Borders and the Comet Line** – Eggnogs
and Petticoats.. 162
Smuggling (2), the Comet Line and resistance (2).

Chapter 18 **Mother and Baby** – Snakes, Toothpaste
Tubes and the Moon 180
*Farming traditions, planting by the moon,
traditional Basque food, the Basque language (1).*

Chapter 19 **Culture Shock** – Maggots in the Toy Chest.. 194
The local death toll, genetics.

Chapter 20 **A Family Business** – Hangman and
the Unfortunate Word................................... 200

Chapter 21 **The Basque Language** – Strawberry Ice
Creams and Greedy Pigs 204
*History of the Basque language (2), Basque rhyming
bards (*bertsolariak*), Basque mythology (2).*

Chapter 22 **The Village Calendar** – Wheelbarrow Races and Grumpy Coalmen 211
Basque schools, Basque sports, local traditions.

Chapter 23 **Ituren Church** – Stories from Beyond the Grave.. 222
Murdered bodies in Ituren graveyard, life under Franco (3).

Chapter 24 **House and Home** – Mushrooms and Marshmallows 230
Farming traditions and land rights.

Chapter 25 **Gilbert: An Imposter in my Home** – Music Boxes and Mountain Savages........................ 240
Spanish anti-terrorist squads in the Basque country, cultural prejudices.

Chapter 26 **Après Gilbert** – Two Trees and a Headless Woman.. 269
Intercultural exchanges.

Epilogue One **Heading North Again** 279
Identity and cultural integration.

Epilogue Two **Heading Home** 284
Ownership of the land.

Endnote 287

PROLOGUE

MY LIFE ON A BASQUE MOUNTAIN

The title of this book had many unsuccessful candidates: 'Walking Above the Clouds'... 'From Birmingham to the Basque Country'... 'Hostage to a Dream'... even 'The House at the End of the Road that Doesn't Exist', the house from which I am writing these words. (The road still doesn't exist, satellite navigation systems insisting even today on stranding visitors – some two thousand adventurers from as far afield as Madagascar, Iceland and Indonesia – at an old cheese farm on the wrong side of the mountain.)

It was only due to my explorations of the ancient labyrinth of shepherds' paths, smuggling trails and World War II escape routes across the Pyrenees that I stumbled on this tiny hamlet in the first place. It is, however, without a doubt thanks to the Basque people and the beautiful landscapes that I have stayed. Oh, and a Basque baby too – with a habit of losing her wellington boots in the snow.

This book is the true story of my adventures here, perched on a Basque mountain. How and why I came, the beginning of this story, is undoubtedly the longest and most winding path of them all. It all started in a helicopter heading in totally the opposite direction.

PART I

SCANDINAVIA

HEADING NORTH

THE WHEELCHAIR IN THE SNOW

Some 65km north of the Arctic Circle the helicopter swooped and lurched in screaming winds, rattling my bones and rebooting my soul. Peering through its grimy windows, I drank in these other-worldly landscapes: below us, mountain crevices plunged into darkness while their golden tips glinted like broken glass in the final rays of the sun. A moon of gargantuan proportions scaled the horizon to the east and icebergs the size of five-star hotels swanned southwards across the bay. Never had I felt so humbled by Mother Earth but, of course, having lived in the dreary suburbs of Copenhagen for the past five years, I had had little opportunity to contemplate her more exalted features.

To be fair, it was courtesy of the Danish Ministry of Education that I was in the helicopter in the first place. In an attempt to attract foreign tourism to Denmark's northernmost territories, one December morning in 1995, a teaching colleague and I were dispatched to a small Arctic fishing village on the west coast of Greenland to inaugurate the island's first-ever language school. Here, in Sisimiut, we taught basic English conversation skills to the Inuit hunters and guides, our classrooms ranging from sterile audio labs at the school itself to bloodstained whaling boats in the port, and to husky-drawn sledges – the dogs breaking wind as they sprinted across lakes of ice.

After a couple of weeks of the most bizarre and exhilarating teaching experience in my life, we prepared to leave. That morning, while we huddled over a crackling radio in a shack near the helipad, glacial winds howled like rabid wolves, whipping up hissing, spitting, biting tornados of ice and snow. It seemed that the frenzied ogres of the Arctic had mutinied, and the Norse gods had more important matters on their hands than overseeing the safe passage of our insignificant flying machine. And then, just as we were about to abort the idea, the winds eased, and we were off, hurtling through the storm like some demented dragonfly towards Kangerlussuaq, the Greenland airport hub: our only connection with civilisation, some 130km inland.

As we circled away from the village, the racks of dried fish fading into zip lines in the snow, I began to reflect on the overwhelming sensations of the previous weeks: the shifting green and pink chiffon of the incredible aurora borealis and that comforting cod liver oil smell of husky-pup fur that still emanated from my clothes. Here, my bones wracked and shaken by the storm, at the frozen extremities of the planet (and beyond the wit of any mortal being), rarely had I found such peace.

❖ ❖ ❖ ❖

Like some rite of passage this trip to Greenland changed my life. Had I never gone, I would not have found myself, almost a decade later, on a hospital bed in southern Europe, my skeleton once again shuddering and buckling under the forces of nature. But this was a very different experience. Now, the powers that ransacked me came from within, not from without, and the comforting, musky scent of husky fur was replaced by the sharp tang of disinfectant. But perhaps the most striking difference of them all was the total absence of any inner peace.

At 12.03 on 15 May 2004, Marion was born. At 12.05 she was unceremoniously placed in my arms with no explanation as to what I should do next. Her thin, pale torso contrasted comically with a crash helmet of black hair, and she was so light, so weightless, a thing of such surprisingly little substance that had I not physically experienced her clawing her way out of the inner cavities of my body, I could have been tempted to consider this some tasteless practical joke. She too seemed equally unimpressed. On the rare occasion that her eyes cracked open, I discerned a reluctance to meet my gaze. Whether this was simply due to the exhaustion of her birth, I was not entirely sure – but I suspected it was exasperation, as she contemplated her lot and the Herculean task upon her shoulders of whipping this incompetent mother of hers into shape.

Her father's reaction was unequivocal. He was delighted by her arrival, just as I had expected. '*Txiki, txitxina, txitxina,*' he trilled, delighted, '*torri, torri,*' his tone softening, reminiscent of that used by the shepherds of his clan to call their sheep into the fold. Basque was the third language she had heard since her birth fifteen minutes earlier. The first, undoubtedly, was my own, expressed in a string of Anglo-Saxon expletives as she made her way out along the birthing channel, and the second was the Spanish of the nurses awaiting her debut appearance in the Virgen de Camino maternity ward in Pamplona (Iruña).

Her father lifted her out of my arms and nested her tenderly in the crook of his neck, the pallor of her skin and black hair a clone of his own. Then, bending his legs slightly, he danced off slowly around the ward, past the trolleys of swaddling blankets, gauzes and antiseptics, his hips lunging and flicking – forwards and backwards – *pulunpa… pulunpa… pulunpa* (ding dong… ding dong… ding dong) – under the imaginary weight of the bells.

Wearing the bells was his birthright, just like all the other eight hundred inhabitants of the twin Pyrenean villages of Zubieta and Ituren, where we lived, situated along the banks of the Ezkurra River in northern Navarre. On certain days in the village calendar, the men – and in latter times women too – would pull their lace petticoats over their workman's trousers and strap ten-litre copper bells on to their backs with a thick rope. These carnival figures, or Joaldunak, as they are known, emerge in January to chase away the demons from the village streets, in August, accompanied by fire and flame in the village festivals, and then again in December to usher in Olentzero – a foul-smelling, beer-swilling Basque coalman with a donkey.

'*Pulunpa… pulunpa… pulunpa,*' her father whispered, nuzzling her hair, and the tiny head upon his shoulder trembled in reply, quivering at every thrust of his hips, father and daughter tapping out their own private Morse code. *Pulunpa… pulunpa… pulunpa.*

And then there she was again, startled black eyes staring back at me briefly from over his shoulder as they set off for another circuit of the maternity ward, searching me out – or so I fancied – before fleeing for cover again behind heavy lids. Poor wee thing, she was undoubtedly busy recomputing the increasingly bizarre hand that destiny had served her, and the cultural and linguistic mulch that was her legacy. From the bed, in a faded flowery nightdress, innards still thumping with the pain of birth, I observed these two strange beings. Her father was undeniably the more foreign of the two given all the shipwrecked hopes and painful misunderstandings that had come between us, making the chasm between past expectations and present reality all the more severe. *Pulunpa… pulunpa… pulunpa.*

Half an hour after her birth I still had no more clue about the technicalities of breastfeeding, but this was not to say that I was devoid of maternal instinct altogether. At seven months pregnant, I had decided to build an extension on to the isolated fifteen-square-metre barn, and former sheep shed, that had become my home several years previously. The barn, like all Basque dwellings, had a name, Iaulin Borda, but after I moved in it simply became known as The Borda. A variety of creatures have been lured into The Borda's embraces over the years, from the mice in the understairs cupboard and the toads on the terrace to the spiders lurking in the grouting of its grey sandstone walls. But none has come quite so far as this thirty-something English teacher from Copenhagen. Perched high up in a lonely mountain hamlet, with spectacular views of the Pyrenean foothills, The Borda has become central to my life and identity in so many ways. And so, a couple of months before giving birth, I set about building the first of a lifetime of extensions and converting its outdoor toilet into an indoor bathroom: a birthing present to us both and one that I hoped would make this new mother-and-child partnership a more tenable state of affairs.

Reaching out from my bed awkwardly, I fed Marion back into my arms, cautiously cupping her head in my hands, hands still stained with the paint I had applied to the beams of The Borda the day before. And I remember thinking that her tiny, mottled fists, raw from the struggles of her birth, looked almost as battle-scarred as my own. There it was, a connection, a bond between mother and daughter at last.

❖ ❖ ❖ ❖

Any bonds I felt with Denmark were not so enduring. They had fizzled away almost before the Air Greenland flight from Kangerlussuaq touched the tarmac in Copenhagen, its listless horizons evaporating into a grey haze before simply giving up from lack of interest. With the colours of the northern lights still lingering in my mind, I wrote an article entitled *Teaching Irregular Verbs at Minus 40 Degrees*, but it failed to capture the imagination of local publications and so remained sandwiched between my teaching notes until one day it slipped out of my bag and disappeared.

The reasons for my move from England to Denmark in the first place had been unoriginal. I had moved to Copenhagen for a man. Somewhat appropriately, on Valentine's Day, 1990, I gathered together a bag of possessions which included a jar of Marmite, a book of French poetry by Jacques Prévert, and Harry, a teddy bear with floppy ears. With a language degree under my belt and some bitter memories of working for a marketing agency in London, I drove east and sailed across the North Sea. Yes, I was chasing a romantic dream, and like most foreigners, I had been seduced by cosy, comfortable Danish *hygge* too. But slowly, as the crumbs of cinnamon biscuits gathered on my friends' white linen sofas, and our mugs of hot chocolate grew sticky and cold, my soul sagged with the ingratiating ease of it all. Ironically, had it not been for that trip north to Greenland, its vast landscapes, its deafening silence, its call of the wild – or whatever it was – my journey south to the Pyrenees may never have happened.

My decision to leave Denmark was made at Christmastime, soon after my return from the Arctic. Pitifully disguised as an English lesson, I had just finished a hilarious couple of hours in the company of Bernardo and Carmen, two students from the Spanish embassy, and, thanks to their cheery company and regulation glasses of Rioja, I waited, aglow, at a frozen bus stop in Hans Knudsen's Plads. It was snowing and, at four in the afternoon, already dark. Unlike helicopters in Greenland, Copenhagen city buses benefitted from slightly more amenable weather conditions and the Danish Transport Ministry – having done an admirable job of calculating all the risks likely to befall city buses in rush hour – had executed a service of near-perfect precision. A tad too perfect, or so it transpired.

Observing the busy square from the bus shelter I peered up at the grim, grey façades of the buildings above me, cracked into life by small candle-lit windows and their promise of IKEA homecomings and freshly baked rye bread. And it seemed to me, in a moment of nostalgia, that had it been left to the Danish people, and not to the Danish state, it would have been Christmas – or Yuletide (*juletid*) – every month of the year.

On the other side of the square, a crowd of ashen-faced commuters, collars up and chins down, huddled together at a pedestrian crossing in the snow. In their midst, at waist height, and barely visible amid the rucksacks that swung around his head, was a man in a wheelchair who – like everyone else in the square – was waiting, frozen and patient, for the lights to change.

The moment they did, the crowd scurried across the road and the man in the wheelchair pumped into action. But he was unable to advance. His wheels, caught in the grooves made by the car tyres in the snow, swung him parallel to the pavement and channelled him off down the middle of the road, into the blizzard, on his own solitary course. Only at the last moment did he succeed in spinning the wheelchair around and, jerking it hard over the ruts, he lurched back towards the safety of the kerb once again.

Despite the crowds in Hans Knudsen's Plads that evening, no one took any interest in his predicament, nor noticed the blue rucksack that had shaken itself free from the handlebars of his chair and lay sodden in the slush on the road. It was a scene that I would revisit several years later, on a distant mountaintop, when retrieving a small wellington boot from the snow.

In a snap decision, I bolted across the traffic lights, scooped up his bag and ran after him, turning back just in time to see my bus disappear on the other side of the square with perfect Scandinavian precision. Evidently no contingency plan had been factored into the system for spontaneous acts of human kindness.

And that was my breaking point. This country, with its scratched Tupperware skies and cowardly horizons, its anonymity and statistics, was not for me. The pall of comfortable discontent that had cocooned me for so long had been finally flung to the winds and I was free. Free to go. But how? To do what? And to go where?

And then, a management company commissioned me to write a book. *Freedom to Choose* was written with the aim of encouraging their clients to define their dreams, set goals and make more of their lives (and, of course, sign up for their 'personal effectiveness' training programmes, which were fashionable at the time). Given my increasing disenchantment when I wrote it, this modest self-help book probably inspired few people to forge meaningful changes in their lives, but at least it provided me with some interesting ideas for my own. And so, I decided to put my own untested and inexpert theory into practice. The idea was to find a way to unite my passions for language and landscape – passions which were poorly nourished in suburban Denmark.

Four years after my adventures in Greenland – and almost a decade after I had sailed east from British shores in pursuit of love in Copenhagen – I fled Scandinavia for the very last time. It took me four whole years of failed prison breaks and frustrated returns, of wracking my brains and scrutinising my maps in an attempt to tunnel my way out from beneath the quilted, slumberous covers of my Danish existence.

Finally, 'I'm off,' I told my friends, as I packed my possessions, terrified and thrilled by the adventures ahead of me. 'And this time I'm not – definitely not – in search of a man!' I bade farewell to those *hyggeligt* evenings of confidences and cakes, to my Danish partner and wonderful friends – friends who will be with me long after this tale comes to an end. I was off in search of something that was as yet still a dream. A land of rocks, mountains and limitless horizons where, my instinct told me, among the majesty of Planet Earth, I could finally trust that some greater wisdom would make sense of it all.

On one grey and bitter morning in February 1999, I drove south with Fred, my sole travelling companion and ally. Fred, my blue two-door Ford Escort. Among the chattels in his boot, a set of Danish candleholders, a box of Earl Grey tea and a couple of hand-painted African mugs (souvenirs from one of my unsuccessful jailbreaks) now held company with Prévert's poems, my floppy-eared teddy bear and the inevitable – and utterly indispensable – jar of Marmite.

PART 2

THE BASQUE COUNTRY

HEADING SOUTH

ALICE IN WONDERLAND

Madrid, March 1999

My map of Europe rattled in the breeze on Fred's passenger seat as I drove southwards into the sun. I rearranged my hair clip, digging its prongs deep as my hair thrashed around like a deranged Medusa in the winds whipping through the open windows. It was the only air conditioning Fred could provide, but it was the best.

I was heading for Spain and straight to Madrid to visit Bernardo and Carmen, my former students from the Spanish embassy, who had just returned from their temporary posting in Copenhagen. It transpired that we had all evacuated Denmark at about the same time. Already charmed by their vivacity and laughter during our English classes, I had been easily seduced by their vision of Spain, too.

Feeling a little like a teenager presenting herself for her first-ever newspaper round, I parked in a residential street outside their apartment in Pozuelo, on the outskirts of Madrid, and rang the intercom. Having turned my back on life in Denmark, and driven halfway across Europe for this moment, one would have thought that I had a little more idea of what I was doing. As I waited for their voices to come over the tannoy system, I felt suddenly overwhelmed by the sheer inanity of the one question I had to ask. Where, exactly, did they think I should be going next?

I knew nothing about Spain, and the little Spanish I spoke was a pidgin version of the Italian I had learned during a stint teaching English in Modena, Italy, and at a summer job in Cognac,

France, as an Italian-speaking guide. Even my Italian was little more than a mutation of the French that I had studied before that. Any authentic Spanish vocabulary I possessed had been gleaned, indirectly, during those lessons with Bernardo and Carmen, which had, for me, become the highlight of each week – brief flashes of life, colour and joviality in a damp and monotonous Danish winter.

The first Spanish words I ever learned were *¡cállate Patty!* (shut up Patty!), which greeted me on my arrival at their apartment every Tuesday afternoon, accompanied by the frenzied percussion of scraping claws and heeled shoes on polished floors. Even before they opened the door, the sound itself revealed the foreignness of the occupants, as most Danes slip into thick woollen socks the moment they step over the threshold. Patty, an English sheepdog, would bound out into the stairway with Carmen and Bernardo in hot pursuit, my bag of English books would be prised from my hand, and I would be swept inside amid a frenzy of barks, laughter and kisses (some rather more slobbery than others).

It was a set-up from the start. Every time a verb had to be conjugated or a new word recalled, Bernardo would top up my crystal wine glass with a Rioja Reserva, and Carmen – large green eyes intent on mischief – would sabotage the lesson by corralling my notes with tapas of olives and Manchego cheese.

'I have to go, Bernardo, I just have to… I simply can't live in this country any longer,' I blurted out one gloomy January afternoon while the winds wailed through the Scandinavian streets below the stately sash windows.

Bernardo, in his yellow cashmere sweater, grinned at me while he dabbed at a second wine stain on Carmen's white linen tablecloth. He had the smile of a savant.

'Georgie,' he said, '*tu país es España.*' (Spain is your country.)

❖ ❖ ❖ ❖

And so, having managed to spring ourselves free from Danish soil, we all reconvened in Madrid. Here, united by the complicity of runaway convicts and buoyed by the rapidly depleting stocks of Bernardo's excellent wine cellar, we spent a few happy days reminiscing about our lives in Copenhagen and congratulating each other on our respective escape routes. During their more lucid moments, Bernardo and Carmen sat me down with a large leather-bound atlas and, bickering constantly, endeavoured to give me a potted introduction to Spanish geography from two very different perspectives.

Within a week, Fred and I were on the road again, heading northwards towards the Pyrenees, several bottles of Faustino V Reserva now jostling for space between the Danish candleholders and African coffee mugs in the boot. My aim – so we had decided – was to make for Burgos and Pamplona, and then on to Huesca, which – in a rare moment of consensus – both Carmen and Bernardo assured me was stunning. And so, never having been there before, it seemed as good a place as any for me to start.

But it was to be several years before I actually arrived.

Like liquorice strips, the road unfurled in front of me across the lunar orange flatlands of central Spain, while the hum of Fred's motor tuned into the crackling, stuttering frequencies of my mind. I have always travelled this way; I have never needed a radio.

As I sped towards the Pyrenees, somewhere between a past life and a future one, my mind flitted back to the various elements that had conspired to bring about this moment. Much, of course, had to do with my general despondency with life in Copenhagen, and the writing of *Freedom to Choose* had served its purpose by channelling my energies and focusing my thoughts. However, had it not been for the prophetic words of an elderly lady in a Sydney shopping mall, I may not have plucked up the courage to set out at all.

❖ ❖ ❖ ❖

The Deep South, Sydney, Christmas 1998

The Christmas before I left Copenhagen for the final time, I flew to Sydney to spend time with Barry, an Australian friend and a charming raconteur with a business background. Here we spent long lazy lunches on his veranda, a gaudy Christmas cracker on one side of the plate and my bare-boned activity list on the other. At the top of the page were the words 'Spanish and English Language Exchange and Walking Holidays'.

'Barry, oh Barry, do you really think I can do it? I mean I've never done anything like this before – and, you know, I don't even speak Spanish!'

As we talked, my eyes scoured the nooks and crannies of his apartment, seeking out possible hiding places for spiders, a phobia I have had all my life and which, quite possibly – quite probably – played a pivotal role in the conception of my one and only child several years later.

'Y'know, gal,' Barry said in his thick Australian drawl, picking up his beer as he tenderly watched the drops of condensation skate down the side of his glass, 'ya'can do it, ya'can. Business's just the sum of its parts.'

For one significant moment, he drew his eyes up from his beer glass while I peeled mine down from the shadows on the ceiling and our gaze met halfway. He looked me straight in the eye and grinned.

Just before Barry dropped me off at the airport, we stopped at a local shopping mall. In my pocket was a crumpled sheet of paper with six bullet points, the conclusion of a fortnight's endless conversations.

At the entrance to the shopping centre, I noticed a thin, elderly lady sitting at a small Formica table with a sign saying 'Palm Reading $20'. I didn't normally give such things a second thought but, if ever there were a moment when I needed a little divine guidance, then this was it. Momentarily aware of the stiffness of the folded sheet of paper in my pocket as I settled into the plastic chair opposite her, I mutely offered her my outstretched palm, conscious that my unmistakably British accent would give away clues.

'You have never been really successful in life,' she launched in, bruising my pride, 'but I see you spending time roaming about Europe... exploring... doing research... and if you invest lots of time and energy, then you are sure to find success.'

She paused. I refused to react.

'Now clench your fist for me,' she said, squinting at the creases made between my folded little finger and the palm of my hand, 'I see one... yes one... no, I'm sorry, two children and... and I see a house... a big house, with lots of land around it. Yes, lots of land.'

❖ ❖ ❖ ❖

A short while later, Barry and I sped along the highway towards the airport. In my pocket, the activity list read:

Spanish and English Language Exchange and Walking Holidays
1. _Find house_
2. _Marketing_
3. _Make flyers_
4. _Wait for phone to ring_
5. _Find teacher and cook_
6. _Find walks_

As I waved him goodbye at passport control, he boomed after me, 'Go fr'it, gal! Go fr'it!'

And I did.

❖ ❖ ❖ ❖

Pamplona, March 1999

So, almost three months after my return from Australia, here I was heading north from Madrid in search of a house. By the time we had reached the medieval town of Puente la Reina – an important watering hole along the pilgrimage trail to Santiago de Compostela (the Saint James's Way, universally known as the Camino de Santiago) – Fred and I were running out of steam and I stopped for the night at a hotel on the high street. After dinner, I ended up chatting with the hotel owner, who suggested that I first explore the Pyrenean foothills of Navarre before driving to the higher and steeper-sided valleys of Huesca further east. With no knowledge of the area – and hence little opinion on the matter – this is exactly what I did. The nearest tourist information office was in Pamplona, the capital of Navarre, and it was to be my first stop.

Ernest Hemingway, with his penchant for wine, women and the bovine species, was an easy convert to the Fiestas de San Fermín in Pamplona, immortalising them in his book *The Sun Also Rises*. Like many people, I had only Hemingway's introduction to guide me, with little more than a vague image in my mind of these wild festivals, where crowds, waving red handkerchiefs, ran through cobbled streets chased by raging bulls. So, on seeing a sign for a car park near the *plaza de toros*, I decided to stop and have a look around before exploring the old town and the Plaza del Castillo on foot. On the outside of the square, a narrow staircase led to a dingy tourist office where I tried to explain, in my mongrel French-Italian-Spanish creole, that I was looking to rent a large country house as a base for a series of language and walking holidays. Whether they failed to understand my rudimentary Spanish or were simply uninterested, I never knew, as this clumsy declaration of intentions was met with a rather terse reply. Only years later did I come to realise that for much of Spanish history – and particularly during its bitter Civil War in the 1930s – curiosity has been viewed as a double-edged sword.

Eventually, the woman at the tourist office dispatched me with a map of the northern valleys of Navarre, on which she had circled several villages with bizarre-sounding names. To this, she had added a list of names, addresses and telephone numbers of potential rental properties, none of which sounded particularly Spanish either.

Later that afternoon I charged around the Pamplona ring road (several times) trying to identify the turn-off to France, of which there are many, before finally locating the N121 towards the border and Irun. This infamous road, the most dangerous in Navarre, haunted by the ghosts of all the lives it had claimed, meandered northwards into green, undulating landscapes until we were swallowed up by the mountain tunnels of Belate. Reappearing out of the darkness, some 4km later, the delight I felt as I beheld the scenes on the other side made me feel, or so I imagined, like Alice on her descent into Wonderland.

NAVARRE AND THE BASQUES

HEADING INTO THE BEYOND

Even before we disappeared into the tunnels of Belate, something strange had been happening. The signposts and indications along the side of the road felt different. Suddenly there was an abundance of Zs and Xs (Baztan, Elizondo, Zozia, Etxalar, Dantxarinea) – those letters that you don't want at the end of a game of Scrabble!

Little did I know that I had entered a most mysterious, unique and controversial part of Spain. This area within the province of Navarre had, due to a Spanish aversion to all things 'Basque', fallen under the radar and, although attitudes are changing today, the region still receives surprisingly scant mention in standard travel guides.

This is a complex subject (see page vi), but I had entered an area that forms part of Euskal Herria, a collective, local term for the Basque Country, which embraces all seven Basque-speaking provinces regardless of whether they lie in Spain or France. This is, however, a contentious term and it is not administratively 'correct'. In general, the Spanish (as opposed to the Basques) take the more official line: politically, the Spanish 'Basque Country' or 'Basque Autonomous Community' (Euskadi) limits itself to just the three Spanish provinces of Gipuzkoa, Bizkaia and Araba. Unfortunately for the Basques, it excludes their Basque-speaking neighbours in the province of Navarre, parts of which are – as I was soon to find out – arguably, the most intrinsically Basque of them all.

And so, for the Spanish, I was simply and unequivocally in the Spanish province of Navarra, albeit in its rather dissident mountainous northern territory which, a thousand years ago, in a treaty signed by Navarrese kings, was cryptically described as 'The Mountains Beyond'.

Interestingly, the word 'Navarre' appears to have several possible etymological explanations, none of them particularly helpful. One translates as 'the flat lands before the mountains' and the other as 'tawny, sandy-coloured landscapes'. Yet neither of these seemed to describe the verdant woods and mountain peaks that were coming into view. Quite clearly, we had entered the 'mountains beyond'.

Emerging from the tunnels of Belate, a steep, straight road shot us downwards into an enchanted land of green valleys and tiny whitewashed mountain villages. Fairy-tale turrets peered out from among the treetops while tendrils of mountain mists and corkscrews of woodsmoke entwined to give it an ethereal, other-worldly feel.

None of the fields had straight edges, creating a crumpled, drunkard's tartan of meadows, woods and granite outcrops stitched together by a labyrinth of drystone walls. It was a land of hobbits, hidden dwellings and mythical creatures, of dappled glens and secret rock pools. You could look at it a hundred times and always discover something new.

In contrast to its patchwork of green pastures, the valley slopes were deep and V-shaped, cleaved by stream gullies and fringed with craggy tors. It made me think of some wild animal that had fallen on its back, its soft, vulnerable belly exposed to the elements while its claws thrashed defensively at the skies. This was a landscape that had forged the identity of the people who inhabited it, their culture and their language. And – little did I know then – it was about to shape mine.

One of the Pyrenean villages circled on the map by the woman in the tourist office was Bera, a small frontier town in the northwest of Navarre on the banks of the Bidasoa River. From here, the Bidasoa cuts through a steep-sided ravine and flows northwards out to the Atlantic, its final 10km forming the physical divide – and once violently guarded frontier – between France and Spain.

Escorted by a caravan of Portuguese and Spanish lorries heading for the border, I followed the river past small dams and hydro-electric plants, obsessively checking landmarks against the map spreadeagled on the passenger seat. I had little idea then of the significance of the Bidasoa River to the smugglers, refugees and resistance fighters who had given their lives to crossing its torrent of fast-running waters. What I also did not know was that soon, led by their children and grandchildren, I would be walking in their footsteps, documenting their stories, and mapping their paths.

My first night in these valleys was spent in a modest hotel at a crossroads just out of town. I checked in and headed for the bar, carefully placing my glass of wine to one side as I unfolded my already dog-eared map on the dark wood counter. Finding the village of Bera had been easy enough, but the map from the tourist office was in no way sufficient for me to track down the various rental houses that I had on my list.

Lost within a labyrinth of meandering mountain tracks, Basque farmhouses traditionally offer little more than a two- or three-word address that continues to befuddle foreigners, courier services and online booking processes to this day. There are neither house numbers nor street names, only the all-important house names and the names of the villages or hamlets to which they belong.

❖ ❖ ❖ ❖

In traditional Basque mountain culture, all houses have a name that is far more instrumental in determining a person's identity than any official surname – the latter an honour reserved for the likes of speeding fines and tax inspectors but rarely used between the villagers themselves. No matter how many times someone moves house, they are branded at birth with the name of their natal home, which becomes as intrinsic to their identity as their nationality or the colour of their eyes.

Much more than just bricks, mortar and monetary value, the Basque house is revered as an institution, something more akin to a 'family seat' or even – somewhat like racehorses – the 'stable' to which all descendants are traced. It is a shrine to past generations and both a cradle and refuge for generations to come. Under the ancient Navarrese laws (*fueros*), the Basque house (*etxea*) had the same status as an embassy or a church and was thus above the reach of the law. If a family member was wanted for even a serious crime, the police had no right to enter the house and were obliged to sit out the long wait in the bushes outside until the suspect finally made an appearance.

Due to the small-scale transhumance farming in the area, every village house has its corresponding network of summer barns (*bordas*) in the hills, and here families would live with their sheep during the important periods of haymaking, bracken-stacking and lambing. Over the years these rudimentary *bordas* slowly evolved into more hospitable dwellings where – rather like swallows nesting in the eaves of a house – the shepherds would insulate corners of the hayloft with a limestone sealant, adding fireplaces and hollowed-out sandstone sinks into the near-metre-thick walls.

Windows at that time were a necessary evil and remained true to their etymological origins (the word 'window' is of Germanic origin, meaning 'eye of the wind'). Traditionally, there was no glass, so the openings were protected by layers of ever-more-diminutive wooden shutters, the smallest leaving little more than a tiny funnel of light (and wind) the size of a rabbit hole.

As the local population expanded, many of these makeshift summer dwellings were converted into more permanent lodgings by adding a top floor to the structure, thus creating a *planta noble* (a middle or 'noble' floor). Here, cocooned between the warmth of the animals rising from the stables below, and the insulating, sweeter-smelling hay in the attic above, burgeoning families of 'aristocrats' could live in style all year round.

In more recent years, however, as the locals moved towards bigger towns in search of work, many of these mountain *bordas* have been abandoned. However, more enterprising families have diversified into the world of tourism, converting their cavernous forms into attractive summer rentals, the likes of which I was now in the process of tracking down.

❖ ❖ ❖ ❖

'*¿Por favor, dónde está Casa Etxeberria?*' ('Do you know where the Etxeberria house is, please?') I asked a youth at the bar. The contrast between his ebony hair and ivory skin was softened by the bar's dim lighting, the slight slump of his square shoulders indicative of a certain shyness common among Basque men. I pointed to the name on my photocopy from the tourist office: Casa Etxeberria, Bera de Bidasoa. Tel: 948776651.

The Basques are not famed for their voluble nature and, after politely nodding at his well-meaning and short – but unintelligible – reply, I gently steered him towards a paper napkin so he could draw me a small map of how to get there. Hijacked by a battalion of Italian verbs, my Spanish-language skills were no match for the obscure instructions required to track down farmhouses in the mountains: 'turn left at the washing stones, pass the field of bracken stacks and, after the *borda* in the chestnut grove, turn right.'

The next couple of weeks were spent driving from village to village, unscrupulously dragging barmen and bar-goers alike to the dreaded dial phone and encouraging them to develop their cartography skills on paper serviettes as they deciphered conversations with perplexed house owners.

Over that couple of weeks, I visited some twenty different rental houses. In the process I zigzagged my way 300km along the coast of northern Spain but, inevitably, ended up where I'd started, in these magical Basque valleys of northern Navarre. Nothing I saw anywhere else could compare with the charm of their architecture and the mysterious and seductive lie of the land.

Finally, I narrowed the choice down to a house in the Baztan Valley and decided to rent it for a couple of weeks that coming summer. Casa Tristantenea was a large, renovated farmhouse situated in a grove of walnut trees with sublime views from its wooden balcony. Its eight bedrooms, gym and large open-plan kitchen offered expansive and interesting spaces for my group holidays while its swimming pool offered the perfect retreat from the language classes, be they the caprices of the Spanish subjunctive or the ins and outs of English phrasal verbs.

Standing at the entrance of Casa Tristantenea, I shook hands with Marie Luisa, her eyes looking deep into mine as she accepted a reservation on the house for a fortnight in August from a total stranger. Naturally, I insisted on paying a deposit, feeling slightly disconcerted when I saw her reluctance to accept it and automatically presuming that she really wasn't keen to rent the house to me at all. She had no idea who I was, where I was from, or whether I would ever return. I really couldn't blame her.

Well, that is what I thought then.

Quickly, I would understand the extraordinary importance of the handshake in the Basque culture. Here, in the north of Navarre, in the very cradle of the Basque-speaking lands, a handshake is an act of honour more binding than money, and a formal agreement is often settled with a firm handshake known as the *euskaldun hitza* (the Basque word of honour). In hindsight, I realised that following up our handshake with a bundle of cash may have been interpreted as evidence of a lack of faith in either her word or mine, and Marie Luisa may even have taken it as an insult. As it turned out, this was virtually the last time I paid a deposit for anything in the area.

Basques have been respected for their hard work and honesty for centuries, and way beyond these shores. Following in the wake of the California gold rush of the 1850s, and for years after that, young, impoverished farmers from the Basque Pyrenees emigrated to the isolated sierras of the American Far West. Here, the 'sheepherders', as they were known, roamed the mountains for months on end with little more than their sheepdogs for company, the coyotes and rattlesnakes for distraction and the monthly honk of the supply truck deep in the valley promising fleeting solace in a bag of beans or a packet of bacon. Even if the 'chore girls' (listed on an original order form from the 1960s) offered them the possibility of more companionable diversions, this was a harsh and lonely existence, notorious for breaking spirits. But it was never known to compromise their word of honour. Such became the reputation of the Basque shepherds that, no matter how downtrodden they were when they occasionally hit town, their *euskaldun hitza* alone was usually enough to secure them a loan with no other guarantee but their 'Basqueness' required.

Very quickly, the *euskaldun hitza* became an integral part of my life and work within the Basque community. During the first couple of years, while piecing together the walks and establishing the logistics for my holidays, I based myself at a friendly B&B in Elizondo, the capital of the Baztan Valley. Consequently, Elizondo became the main hub for my operations. It was here that I bought the bread, sourced the wine, shopped for supplies, found my internet cafés and hardware stores, and very soon I was given free run of the town. Having gained a reputation as a person of my word, the local Baztandarrak (people of the Baztan Valley) had esteemed that my promises to pay the bill were as trustworthy as their own and settling my debts became increasingly complicated. Lourdes, the baker, never had the bill made up, waving me away as soon as I put my head around the door. And Roberto, the butcher, gave the distinct impression that squaring up was far more of an irritation than a help as he fumbled through stacks of receipts with sticky fingers, a queue of loyal clients watching on in silence. As for Francisco, my faithful friend and taxi driver, when I knocked on his door, he would dismiss my furtive attempts to reimburse him for his services by jumping on his bike and disappearing over the mountains, abandoning me on the porch of his house, purse in hand, while Donald, his pet duck, flapped around my heels.

It took me a while to realise that this odd behaviour was *not* because the local people were averse to money. Quite the contrary.

There was a long history of smuggling in the area and, allegedly, Elizondo, the capital of the Baztan Valley, once had more banks per capita than any other town in Spain. In fact, by refusing to take my money, the Basques were presenting me with the ultimate token of acceptance. They were offering me their trust, something that would have been less easy to demonstrate had they pocketed my cash from the start.

While this credit extended to me by the Baztandarrak was an honour – and undeniably good for my cash flow – it did little for a peaceful night's sleep. In those first years, as I drove backwards towards the UK at the end of each summer, I agonised over whether I had paid everyone – whether I had, unintentionally, reneged on my *euskaldun hitza* – imagining myself ambushed in the ravines of the Bidasoa River for overlooking a set of photocopies or a round of drinks in a village bar.

It was during a chance encounter with a bandy-legged horse dealer at a livestock fair in Elizondo that I learned that oak trees played their role in the matter too.

'On matters of great importance,' he confided in that slow, laboured Spanish typical of native Basque-speakers (and a godsend to non-native speakers like me), 'then you would do best to shake hands beneath the shade of an oak.'

To the Basque people, the oak tree has always been a symbol of strength and justice. There's no greater example of this than the tree found in the central plaza of the town of Guernica where, since medieval times, Basque lords and presidents have convened beneath its leafy spread to take their oaths of loyalty and allegiance. This famous tree, an iconic symbol of Basque identity, only narrowly survived the 1937 bombing massacre of Guernica at the outset of the Spanish Civil War. The same cannot be said for the more than 1,500 citizens who happened to be in town that day.

❖ ❖ ❖ ❖

The Spanish Civil War, lasting from 1936 to 1939, was set off by a military uprising led by General Francisco Franco against the Second Spanish Republic. Dividing the country in two, pitting ultraconservative nationalists against progressive republicans, neighbour against neighbour, brother against brother, it was the bloodiest conflict western Europe had witnessed since the end of World War I. It offered a breeding ground for mass atrocities, mob violence and torture and, although the death toll is officially set at some 500,000 people, the true numbers are known to be far higher, and unmarked mass graves are being discovered to this day.

With the rising fascist governments in Mussolini's Italy and Hitler's Germany, Franco found the allies he needed and, as the Basques sided against him, he magnanimously offered up the Basque-speaking lands as a training ground for the German Luftwaffe. In 1937 several Basque towns were bombarded from the air, Guernica being the most famous, bombed on a market day and razed to the ground, a tragedy brought to the world's attention through Picasso's famous painting, *Guernica*. Within just a year after the start of the war, Franco had swiftly overrun the Basque provinces, the republican Basque government had been exiled, Spanish Basques had fled over the border to the French Basque lands and the Americas, and 29,000 Basque children, *niños de la guerra*, had been evacuated to Europe, Mexico and Russia. In May 1937 almost four thousand child refugees docked in Southampton,

England, on the SS *Habana*, each wearing an identification number and a hexagonal cardboard disc around their necks with the words '*Expedición a Inglaterra*'.

By the time the Spanish Civil War had come to an end in 1939, Franco had seized power and some half a million republicans, many of them Basques, had fled over the border into France, fifteen thousand of them ending up in the concentration camps of Franco's allies in Nazi Germany.

Over the following thirty-six years, and until his death in 1975, Franco retaliated with a vengeance against the republican 'traitor provinces' with frequent prison sentences and executions. One of the objectives of his many policies to stamp out dissidence within the Spanish population was the eradication of the Basque culture and language, something that he almost achieved. But not quite.

MARKETING

TELEPHONES AND WITCHES

While an understanding of the tumultuous history of the Basque Country would become central to my work as a local guide and writer, the ramifications it later had on my personal life lay beyond the realms of my imagination. The idea that my movements could be of interest to anyone else but myself seemed utterly absurd. Insouciant, I busied myself with my increasingly crumpled, tapas-stained activity list and turned to the next points on the list: Marketing. Make flyers.

A deposit made and photographs of Casa Tristantenea in hand, I headed back to my parents' home in the UK to print a wad of flyers, agonising for days over how best to depict my untested, pie-in-the-sky language exchange and walking holidays. For want of a better name, I christened my company 'Language Adventures' and improvised an amateur logo combining the images of a book, a wine glass and a leaf.

'Mum, am I mad?' I asked her in desperation one morning, warming my hands on the radiator while the printer gave fitful birth to the first run. She looked at me apologetically, her honest nature in conflict with the belief that a mother's role is always to encourage and support her children.

'Oh darling, I don't know,' she replied. Gazing down at the patterned carpet in the living room for inspiration, she shook her head slowly. 'Really darling, I just don't know.'

My first brush with the fickle world of marketing had been just after university – a year or so before I packed my bags and headed east to Copenhagen – when I worked for a London PR company in Chelsea Wharf. Although the position was the envy of my friends, as I approached the office the knot in my stomach would tighten with every step. The day's highlight was the lunchtime arrival of a young Polish sandwich seller, and not for his food nor his chiselled Slavic looks. Screened by packets of cheese and pickle sandwiches, the happiest moments of the week were spent with him in the lobby enjoying fleeting dialogues on the cultural differences between Poland and the UK.

Within three months of starting the job, I had handed in my notice, determined to dedicate my life, henceforth, to the world of languages and cultural exchange. And more than a decade later I was still true to my values. Or so I thought.

Inevitably and ironically, I was to come full circle. For these holidays to flourish, I needed to publicise them, plunging me once again into the capricious and unforgiving world of marketing. With websites not yet common in those days, I filled a plastic bag with homemade flyers and trudged around Birmingham, Manchester and London city centres, calling in at Spanish cultural institutes, universities and adult education centres in an attempt to reach those British people interested in learning Spanish.

It was possibly only the tourism lecturer at Staffordshire University who had any inkling of my true loneliness. Politely averting his gaze, he sat in the students' common room swirling his coffee silently with a plastic spoon while tears trickled irrepressibly down my cheeks. I had paddled myself out into fathomless waters and he seemed as out of his depth with the situation as I was.

Unfairly, perhaps, my academic family background had ingrained in me a certain wariness of the world of commerce, and this was compounded by a personal phobia of telephones. A recurring nightmare from my childhood had me running down dark lanes towards a solitary telephone box with a witch trailing me from behind. Panic-stricken, I would dial for help, misdialling again and again with trembling fingers as the witch's image slowly came into focus through the glass door. I had no idea what this nightmare symbolised but now was not the time to find out. Although witches' tales would make a reappearance in my life later on, irrational phobias had to be banished if I was to get these projects on the road. There was little time for self-analysis, just sheer hard graft.

Having toiled around Britain with bags of homemade flyers, I now needed to apply my efforts to the Spanish market and find a matching cohort of Spanish-speakers interested in learning English.

In Spain, my marketing strategy took a different slant and, identifying a handful of hiking organisations in Madrid, I took out a crumpled map of the metro from my pocket and went knocking on their doors. A sales pitch is challenging at the best of times, especially with nothing tangible to sell, no track record, no references and no common language. But I managed to persuade a couple of dynamic young directors, mountaineers themselves, speaking a little English (and Italian – always a help), to insert a few lines about my holidays in their brochures.

It was only months later that I understood that the greatest drawback in my sales pitch was something entirely different: the Basques!

❖ ❖ ❖ ❖

When I talked to friends back in Denmark and England about the Basques, the first images that came to their minds were of ETA and terrorist attacks. In the Basque region, however, the subject was largely avoided, making an impartial understanding of the subject virtually impossible. There was an official and unofficial narrative to the story, which I gradually came to understand through personal experience. It took me some time to realise that despite the peaceful appearance of my beloved Basque valleys of northern Navarre, strong political currents surged beneath the surface.

Having survived the brutally repressive years of Franco's dictatorship (1939–75), and suffered draconian policies designed to eradicate their culture and language, the Basques gained a considerable degree of autonomy in 1978 with the creation of Euskadi (the Basque Autonomous Community). As the northern Basque-speaking valleys of the Pyrenees were not included within this political structure, they found themselves stranded in the Spanish-speaking, and predominantly Franco-supporting, province of Navarre. In the main, however, their true cultural and linguistic affinity firmly remained – and remains to this day – with the rugged Atlantic coastline and Basque-speaking Euskadi to the west.

It was only when I was asked by the local tourist board to write a press release in English to promote the area that I realised the embarrassment these Basque valleys presented to Navarrese politicians. While my poetic turns of phrase and passion for these bucolic valleys were applauded, I was politely advised not to associate them with anything Basque. Consequently, the word 'Basque' had to be struck from my copy altogether.

After their cruel treatment under Franco, for some Basques, even those living in the official Basque Autonomous Community, partial autonomy was simply not enough. They wanted total independence and, in the last decades of the twentieth century, ETA, *Euskadi Ta Askatasuna* (Freedom for the Basque Country), the military wing of the Basque pro-independence party, brought infamy to the region with its terrorist attacks.

Naïvely trusting when I first arrived in the Baztan Valley, I had only a nebulous understanding of the stormy passions churning within the breast of Basque society. For some, I learned, the violence was seen as a justified bargaining chip in the struggle for self-determination and independence, but the great majority of Basques abhorred the methods. Nevertheless, united by a common language and identity, many simply turned a blind eye.

The statistics state that by the end of the crisis, ETA had claimed some 820 victims while the Spanish *Guardia Civil* (national military police) had 'officially' taken some two hundred Basque lives. Hundreds more were tortured and hauled away to prisons at the other end of the country, a deliberate policy to socially isolate the prisoners and punish their families.

Although the desire for independence lingered, there was no appetite among the general Basque populace to pursue it via car bombs, shootings and kidnappings, and in 2011 ETA announced a permanent cessation of its armed struggle for independence. Even so, the heavy-handed presence of the *Guardia Civil* remained. Some Basques believe that the police used the ever-diminutive threat of an ETA attack to give themselves *carte blanche* to do whatever they liked in the region.

Today, a traveller in the Basque Country finds little sign of these struggles, apart from an insistence, certainly in the smaller towns, on carrying out their daily affairs in Basque and the inevitable graffiti sprayed over the Spanish spellings on road signs and village names. To non-Basque-speaking Spaniards, this may feel deliberately alienating, but as a linguaphile, I sympathise with the need to protect one of the crown jewels of the Basque culture from extinction: their exquisite and unique minority language, Euskara.

Even the least observant traveller in the Basque Country, however, cannot help but notice the ubiquitous presence of two different flags. One is the *Ikurriña*, the red, white and green Basque national flag, an unequivocal symbol of Basque identity. The *Ikurriña* has been adopted by the Basques as the flag for both Euskadi and the broader Basque-speaking area of Euskal Herria, which embraces the seven Basque-speaking provinces in both France and Spain (see page vi).

The second flag is far more curious. It is white with a black ink stain in the middle in the shape of the geographical boundary of Euskal Herria, with red arrows pointing inwards from the margin. Across the flag are the words *Presoak Etxera* (Prisoners Come Home). Protest marches are still held to defend the rights of Basque prisoners to be brought back closer to their families and friends.

Slowly, personal experience revealed various insights into the political environment and soon I realised that these beautiful valleys of mine, which had long offered hiding places for refugees and smugglers, were also sheltering Basque political fugitives, with undercover police hot on their heels.

❖ ❖ ❖ ❖

High-heeled sandals and a crumpled summer dress surfaced from the bowels of my rucksack and – dragging my hair clip through the tangles in my hair – I enjoyed a few self-indulgent moments of dialogue with the hotel mirror before heading into the nightlife of Madrid. The buzz and energy of city life was invigorating. I had missed it.

My agents from the Madrilenian rambling organisations stood up ceremoniously to greet me as I walked into the restaurant, welcoming me with unreserved smiles and bonhomie before settling me down at their table and launching into passionate conversations about their latest hiking excursions in la Cumbre de la Maliciosa or the Sierra de Guadarrama.

Meanwhile, I relished the ease and flow of Spanish business meetings. The first rule of thumb was simply to banish any talk of business until the end of the meal, and only after due reverence had been paid to the quality of the olive oil or the *jamón de bellota*, or the vintage of the Ribera del Duero wines. Mercifully, by the time the last round of coffees and liqueurs came around, and business matters were finally addressed, the wine had loosened my Spanish-Italian tongue and any previous concerns about my Basque connections appeared all but forgotten.

❖ ❖ ❖ ❖

These delightful moments of urbane sophistication induced a sense of nostalgia, but they were always short-lived. Soon I was back in my tatty clothes and walking boots in the Basque Country with an increasingly dog-eared activity list. The next bullet point, the most unnerving of them all, was simply to wait for the phone to ring. But waiting requires patience, a quality I just don't possess, and as time dragged on, my high spirits slowly started to wane. What prevented me from catching the next plane back to Denmark and returning to the *hygge* and cinnamon biscuits of my former existence? The ingratiating ease of my former life looked positively blissful from where I was now.

And yet, this was my brainchild, my firstborn; could I abandon her so easily? When I thought of her, of what she could be, what she could become, I concluded that we were passionately and fatally united. By conjuring up vivid images of my guests laughing over after-dinner conversations in the kitchen of Casa Tristantenea, or exchanging cultural anecdotes as they hovered on the balcony, united by the beauty of the views, my brainchild grew in both form and spirit. Undoubtedly, there would be method in the madness as each day alternated strictly from one language to the other, and there would be lessons too (if only I could find the teachers). Then, after lunch and a brief siesta – which would undoubtedly be imposed by the Spanish contingent – we would slip into our walking boots and step out into the hills, conversing strictly, of course, in the language of the day. Could I honestly give up on all this and traipse back to the comfortable discontent of life in Copenhagen?

And then, one Tuesday in May, while I was trying to track down a path through a misty bracken field in the hills north of Elizondo, my mobile rang in the bottom of my rucksack. Scrabbling through a pile of maps and sweatshirts to locate it, I glanced quickly at the number on the screen to compute the caller's time zone and ascertain which language I should adopt for my reply.

'Hello, good afternoon… good morning, Language Adventures, uh, how can I help you?'

'Hello… ' came a soft and equally hesitant voice at the other end of the phone. I waited as the crackling intensified on the line.

'Um, I was just wondering if you still have spaces on your Spanish-English language holiday this summer? I've seen a flyer on the noticeboard at the Instituto Cervantes.'

The voice was received by stunned silence. As if someone had put a match to a gas fire, my whole body flushed with adrenaline, part fight, part flee, my heart kicking off at a wild and uncontrollable gallop.

Disguising my shock with a few hesitant, guttural sounds until I could finally articulate, I formulated my reply.

'Ah, well, yes, thank you, um, I'll just have a look.' I desperately bought myself a few seconds, shuffling my paper maps to give the impression that I was flicking through some well-worn booking calendar. I could still say no. It wasn't impossible. It wasn't too late. I could still escape from this torment, retreat, turn myself around and build a sane, stable and respectable living somewhere else. There was fear, a feeling of vertigo, a churning in the pit of my stomach. Then, with a knee-jerk reaction that has got me into trouble all my life, I answered:

'Yes. Yes, there is still a space. What is your name please, and – and – yes, your address?'

'Margaret Goff. I'll spell it for you. That's G-O-double F.'

I scribbled down her name and address on the back of a map. 'Well, Margaret, thank you, I'll pop some more information – oh, and booking forms – in the post to you this week. Uhm, yes, I really look forward to meeting you this summer. Thank you so much, thank you,' I repeated a little too effusively. 'Goodbye.'

I waited as she rang off. For some time afterwards, I sat motionless among the bracken, my unfolded map lying on the grass next to me, the paper sagging slowly in the fine mountain drizzle. Shocked, I tried to fathom the vastness of what now needed to be done. And then, imperceptibly at first, a high-pitched scream surfaced from within me. There was a different quality to the anxiety and panic now, a subtle, ever-so-subtle, sense of victory. The show was on.

And so it was that one chilly May morning in 1999, Language Adventures' 'Spanish and English Language Exchange and Walking Holidays' became a reality. The lack of booking forms was the least of my problems. I had no Spanish teacher, no walks, no cook and – apart from Margaret – no participants. And I spoke barely a word of Spanish.

THE BAZTAN VALLEY

NOBLE PEASANTS,
PILGRIMS AND CIDER

In early June, after a couple of months marketing the courses in the UK, I piled Fred high with language books and videos and headed south again to set up the holidays. We boarded the night ferry from Portsmouth to Caen and, after my customary *pain au chocolat* in a café on the French docks, I drove south through France to the Pyrenees. Eleven hours and exactly 1,001km later, I crossed the border into the Baztan Valley near the tiny village of Zugarramurdi, famous for its smugglers and witches. Unlike that first drive northwards from Madrid and Pamplona through the tunnels of Belate, which keep Spain and the Spanish at bay, this time I was driving south over the French Pyrenees directly into the Baztan Valley. There were no tunnels, just a steep, winding road that led up through dense forest to the mountain pass at Otxondo.

Despite the fatigue from driving so long, I felt exhilarated on clearing the top of the pass. As the green and bucolic folds of the Baztan came into view, I pulled over to the side of the road and, stepping out of the car and stretching stiff legs, breathed her in. My heart swelled with a fierce sense of possession. She was mine, all mine.

❖ ❖ ❖ ❖

At the top of the Otxondo mountain pass a yellow arrow painted on a rock indicates that the pilgrims' path to Santiago also passes this way. The Camino de Santiago curls up to the pass through oak and beech trees, taking a slightly alternative route off the road after leaving the shelter of the eleventh-century monastery of Urdax on the valley floor. For more than one thousand years, pilgrims have toiled over this mountain pass on their way to Santiago de Compostela in search of penance or spiritual enlightenment, and I wondered whether their hearts – like mine – would have leapt for joy when they first beheld these views.

Most probably not. In the twelfth century, the Baztan Valley would have been a very different place. The pilgrim, wiping his brow at the top of the pass and gazing at the valley below, would have discovered dense oak and chestnut woods, with hazelnut and blackthorn bushes on the lower lands, and bracken and broom on the higher mountain slopes. Thin spirals of woodsmoke would have mingled with the hovering mountain mists to indicate the presence of tiny hamlets of wooden houses where women in long skirts and high crooked hats cooked rabbit and broad-bean stews. The ancestors of today's shepherds were mainly swineherds and hunters, spending their days sharpening knives, laying traps and preparing brews from the apples and berries that grow abundantly in the area.

Cider was their main drink. It was far safer than water, which could carry disease, and pagan rituals were – and still are – performed in local villages to bless and protect the apple crop. (In the sixteenth and seventeenth centuries, when Basque fishermen were following the whaling and cod routes as far as Newfoundland, the apples proved their worth once again. 'Rationed' to three pints of cider a day, the sailors were not only kept merry but were also offered a life-saving ingredient to keep scurvy at bay. Unlike rum or whisky, cider turned out to be an excellent source of vitamin C.)

There is little doubt that in the twelfth century, the intrepid pilgrim would have found the Baztan Valley a frightening place. And, even had he not feared the bears and wolves roaming the hills, he most certainly would have dreaded his encounters with the Basques.

As early as 1140, Aymeric Picaud wrote the Codex Calixtinus, the first 'tourist guide' to the Camino de Santiago. This gave the Basques of Navarre a rather bad reputation. In the guide, Picaud describes them as 'fierce-faced men who terrorise people with their barbarian tongues,' going on to describe the Basque people as 'full of evil, dark in complexion, of aberrant appearance, wicked, treacherous, disloyal and false'. (He went on to say that their food was awful too.) Unfairly, in some Spanish circles, certain aspects of this reputation – or echoes of it – still persist today.

Although it seems that his writings were founded on little more than rumour, it is easy to understand how pilgrims, crossing the Pyrenees for the first time from France, would have been filled with fear when they met these rugged, distinctive-looking people of alien culture with their indecipherable language. No matter how erroneous Picaud's image of the Basques may have been, it would linger on throughout the centuries, fanning the flames of the witch hunts of the Spanish Inquisition (more on that later).

Despite centuries of prejudice, in the thirteenth century, after fighting valiantly for the King of Navarre, the Basques of the Baztan Valley were accorded 'noble' status and declared lords and owners of their own land. However, it wasn't until several hundred years later that their right to self-rule was recognised after a legendary court case in which the Baztan people took a subsequent king to court for grazing *his* pigs on *their* land. And they won! Even so, this formal recognition of their rights did them little good. Apart from an honorary title and a Baztan coat of arms – visible in the form of a chessboard motif on most Baztan houses to this day – the Baztan 'nobles' were still no better off, continuing to eke out a miserable existence as impoverished swineherds and pedlars.

But their fortune was to change during the golden age of the Spanish Conquista. When the Baztandarrak (Baztan people) found their way to the Americas in the sixteenth and seventeenth centuries, their tatty dog-eared titles gave them the right to foreign lands and wealth. On their return, palm saplings in hand as souvenirs, they spent their money building palatial manor houses and grandiose village churches which, even today, make an incongruous skyline against their traditional rural landscapes. The work ethic of the Basques – combined with the strong commercial instinct of most border people and a land rich in minerals and natural resources – served them well. Extremely well. Today, the Basque provinces are some of the wealthiest regions of the Iberian Peninsula.

❖ ❖ ❖ ❖

Yes. I was back. Back over the smugglers' passes into the Baztan Valley. With my heart leaping for joy, Fred and I rolled over the mountain pass of Otxondo and down the winding road towards Elizondo. We passed the ruins of Amaiur castle, a symbol of Basque identity after a heroic but doomed battle in 1522 to save the area from the united forces of Castile and Aragon. Gaily, beneath blue skies, we freewheeled down the valley road, passing bright green fields strewn with wobbly lambs and knock-kneed foals – a children's painting waiting for the watercolours to dry.

Finally, I drew up at the B&B in Elizondo and, turning to my activity list once again, got started on the rest of my life.

Find teacher and cook.

Staring down at a ponytail of magnificent thick black curly hair, I launched into a conversation with the shop assistant bent over my feet in a shoe shop in Irun. Koldo, a tall, sallow-faced youth, told me that he was working there part-time to help pay for his university studies in San Sebastián (Donostia), where he was studying to be a Basque teacher. The word 'teacher' was all the encouragement I needed and, ignorant then of the cosmic differences between the two languages, I presumed that if he could teach Basque then he would be equally capable of teaching Spanish. By the time I reached the checkout counter with my new walking boots, I had a Spanish teacher on the books too. I did not mention that the sum total of his future students, to date, was just one. Margaret Goff.

Later that week, it was spiky green and pink hair that won my attention in a campsite bar as Nagore dexterously slid a slice of Spanish *tortilla* (potato omelette) out of the microwave and on to my plate. Once more I believed I had struck gold and, by the time the bill was settled, my future cook had been enlisted. It turned out that neither of my staff were to last very long.

FINDING THE WALKS

CHOCOLATE CROISSANTS, MAPS AND COLD CUPS OF TEA

My love of languages and my fascination for paths have been constants for as long as I can remember. In retrospect, they both have much in common, manifesting my passion for systems and strategies of communication. Just as the smugglers' paths duck and weave through the woods to connect the villages on both sides of the French-Spanish border, so my halting sentences in a foreign language seek to bridge the divide between one person and the next. They also provide an unavoidable source of amusement.

Yet, for me, speaking a foreign language also serves a higher purpose. No matter how rudimentary the phrase one cobbles together, making the effort to communicate in the language of the people around you is an important symbol of humility and respect. It is like being invited into somebody's home for the first time proffering a rather insignificant slice of homemade cake, wrapped in a slightly stained and sticky serviette. The cake is a little too crumbly perhaps, and undoubtedly insufficient to feed the family, but, at the very least, it is a personal token of appreciation. Learning just a smattering of words in any language is a little like saying, 'I know this is not enough but thank you for having me.'

Now, finally, with the house rented and staff enlisted, I had a valid and incontestable excuse to indulge myself in my passion for the walks, the paths of the Basque Pyrenees quickly seducing my heart with their stories of hardship and secrecy, smuggling and resistance.

My mornings would start with dropping by Lourdes's *okindegia* (bakery) on the high street in Elizondo to buy my daily *napolitana* (a poor cousin of my French *pain au chocolat* at the dockside in Caen but the best the valley could offer). I then popped into the small roadside café next door, croissant in hand, for freshly squeezed orange juice and a cup of tea, spreading my notes out over a table on the terrace while waiting for my tea to cool. Here map after map would disintegrate delectably between buttery fingers as I pored over the unique blueprint of these valleys, tracing the intricate swirls of the contours like a love-stricken teenager, seduced by the odd-sounding toponyms of every mountain pass. And inevitably, my tea was cold by the time I looked up.

Maps and hot cups of tea have always made an ill-fitting couple and I am incapable of enjoying them both simultaneously. It seems that the time required for tea to stew is just the amount of time it takes to become distracted by another activity, but not enough time to complete it. Consequently, to my perpetual disappointment, cold cups of tea have plagued me most of my life and during map-reading sessions in particular.

Those sunny mornings on the terrace of the café in Elizondo were no different as I scrutinised the details of my maps. Gentle mountain spurs were represented by a series of U-shaped curves, while a cluster of sharp V-shaped contours revealed fast-running streams and the exciting possibility of discovering a waterfall, or the ruins of a watermill tucked away in a leafy glen. Long ovals would announce broad saddlebacks and ridgetops, while smaller circles indicated the 1,000m or so mountain summits of Auza, Saioa, Eskiz or Mendaur, their names replicated on the façades of village bars, garages and computer stores. Despite the entrepreneurial efforts to monetise the local mountain names in company logos, it would be the sheer presence of these ancient giants in our midst that would truly brand their names on our souls.

When I finally headed out to the hills to track down the walks and experience the landscapes for myself, I was able to add a third dimension to the maps. Bronze Age dolmens faced east on the mountain passes; a wooden bridge with missing planks straddled a narrowing in the river; herds of *pottoks* (stocky Basque ponies) grazed on the ridge. Small black dots on the map would come to life as I discovered a tiny *borda* with a grey slab roof or a ramshackle farmhouse with an old limekiln in the yard, locally known as a *sorgin zulo* or a 'witches' hole'. It seemed that every tiny change in the relief of the land, every cliff, glade or mountain spur, had been given a name, indicating the importance of each crevice, nook and cranny to the men and women who had lived here since Stone Age times. This was something so foreign to someone born in suburban England where only shopping malls, roads and industrial estates are deemed worthy of appellation. Each name and toponym on the map revealed curious insights into the history and legends of the area, adding depth and intrigue to every step.

❖ ❖ ❖ ❖

On the French border, to the north of the Baztan Valley, a series of dramatic limestone cliffs, dissected by mountain streams and waterfalls, bids walkers a dubious welcome. This area, home to some spectacular vulture breeding grounds, is known as Peñas de Itxusi, which translates into English as 'the ugly cliffs' – an incongruous denomination for such a magnificent place. This name was given to the area by local shepherds worried about their livestock falling down its steep ravines and ignorant of the effects its outstanding beauty inspires in walkers of a more poetic disposition.

Likewise, on old floodplains, riverbanks and bridges, I discovered many places called Lamieta or Lamiarrita, their names deriving from the *lamia*, a mythological Basque figure. The *lamia* is often compared to a Greco-Roman nymph or the mermaid and siren of European legend. Many individual family coats of arms – which differ from the ubiquitous Baztan coat of arms, which has a chessboard-like motif – portray a *lamia* with either ducks' feet or a fish's tail, holding a golden comb in one hand and a mirror in the other. Renowned for her guile and beauty, the *lamia* can often be found on the banks of rivers and rock pools, combing her golden locks seductively in the dappled light and causing mischief for those who cross her.

According to Basque mythology, the *lamia* often brought the locals good luck and, if a farmer left her a present, he was likely to wake the following morning to find his fields ploughed or his wood cut. She was also thanked for her help in building bridges, although if a stone was suddenly found missing it was a sign that she had abandoned the river and the farmer's luck was about to turn. However, it was the wandering shepherd who had to be most on his guard. Whether it was for her golden comb or her golden tresses, I am not sure, but the *lamia* is often blamed for luring lonely, overambitious shepherds into the woods and spiriting them away. Perhaps if the shepherds had investigated the origins of the word *lamia* they may have thought twice about their romantic aspirations. Lamia was the daughter of Poseidon; a child-eating sea monster and demon of the night.

❖ ❖ ❖ ❖

Gradually, I built an intricate labyrinth of walks, alive with their own individual stories and anecdotes. In time, I could fold away my mutilated, croissant-stained maps and stride out on instinct, reading the landscapes and interpreting the signs at a glance.

Admittedly, a few trails had already been marked for me, such as the well-known red-and-white GR 10 and 11 long-distance walks which zigzag their way across the Pyrenees from the Atlantic to the Mediterranean. I, however, was more interested in the smaller, circular walks around the valley and the opportunities they presented to come into contact with the Baztan culture and people. Several shorter paths marked supposedly with yellow and white stripes by the local tourist board, were of dubious help. Moss and bracken soon mask signs on trees, horses love to scratch their backs on signposts, eventually knocking them over, and tractors are notorious for upturning stones on their way to the fields. Often a vital waymark goes missing and the walk almost invariably has a prickly end. The lack of signposting on the Camino Baztanés – the oldest stretch of the pilgrims' path to Santiago – makes walking it a double act of faith. Although much of the signposting has been improved in recent years, modern pilgrims usually opt to do penance amid the greater luxuries of the Camino Francés, the so-called 'French Route', which passes through the bistros and restaurants of Saint-Jean-Pied-de-Port further to the east.

And so, in short, there was really nothing else I could do other than rely on my deepening instinct for the lie of the land, learning to read the signs and piecing together the walks for myself. The simple discovery of a dilapidated *borda* (barn) in the hills often revealed a network of trails, a consequence of the transhumance farming which moved sheep between winter pastures on the valley floor and summer pastures on the ridge. Naturally, there was always a path linking the mountain *borda* to a farmhouse, and the farmhouse to a village, and I became an expert at hunting down the *bordas* and unravelling the thread. Reading the trees helped. Over the years, many of the *bordas* have fallen into ruin and now lie hidden beneath the gorse and bracken, but telltale signs, such as a line of cherry trees or a copse of ash trees, often give the game away. While fruit trees were planted near the larger *bordas* for human consumption, the shepherds planted the ash trees for the sheep, feeding them the dried younger shoots and leaves during the winter months.

Chestnut trees were also a comforting sign. Seeing these immense, other-worldly titans lining a path, twisted and blackened with age, indicated that these were the oldest paths in the area. Before the arrival of maize from South America, chestnuts were one of the main staples of the local diet, and villagers planted chestnut trees for food and shade along the principal pathways from one village to the next. Pine forests rarely offered interesting paths, and I soon learned not to be fooled by their heady menthol smell and wide, inviting trails. Planted as a source of cheap wood during Franco's years, pine is not indigenous to this area and the dry, scratchy tracks through sterile pinewoods invariably end in turnaround points for logging trucks and bulldozers.

There was, however, little doubt as to which were my favourite trails. These were the ones laid with large, worn flagstones, which have an altogether different purpose. Usually running between drystone walls, they are often wider tracks, designed to support the weight of ox-driven carts or sledges, leading travellers to churches, watermills and market towns. But my ultimate passion was for the flagstone paths with less urban destinations in mind, deliberately turning their back on civilisation and making a bolt for the hills. These bore the greatest secrets of all. Winding up through obscure wooded gullies to the French border, these smugglers' trails witnessed, up until recently, the clandestine activities of *gaulan* (night work). Here, preferably on moonless nights, mules lumbered through the woods laden with panniers full of cognac and coffee, stealing their way back to the farms before the first light of dawn.

❖ ❖ ❖ ❖

After years of secrecy, the escapades of the Basque smugglers are slowly being revealed. These colourful stories, full of tricks and ruses, have more in common with the adventures of Robin Hood than with the sordid dealings of international traffickers, or the white-collar, billion-dollar corporate tax dodgers of today. I soon realised that almost every household in the area had a smuggler's tale to tell and I added their stories to my own repertoire, digging them out mischievously to hijack staid and predictable after-dinner conversations.

During Franco's regime, and until Spain entered the EU in 1986, Basque smugglers moved all sorts of goods back and forth over the French border, thus avoiding the hefty tariffs and taxes imposed by the Spanish state. Apart from such basics as shoes, radio parts, copper and penicillin, silk tights, French liqueurs and condoms also offered clandestine 'pick-me-ups' for an impoverished population. And, as always, the Basques' intimate knowledge of their land did them proud.

The intricate network of paths and *bordas*, combined with the densely wooded ridgetops and misty mornings, all played to the smugglers' advantage, as did the cultural affinity shared by Basques on either side of the border. United in their loathing of fascist regimes, loyal to their word and loyal to each other, the French and Spanish Basques also shared one of their greatest assets, Euskara. Unlike any other on the planet, this inscrutable and unique language also served as an uncrackable code, converting them into smugglers par excellence.

Understandably, Franco's *Guardia Civil* were at a disadvantage from the start. They were usually inexperienced soldiers from the southern Spanish regions who clung to the main roads and border crossing points in trepidation of the shadows in the woods. Although they were armed, rarely did they shoot to kill, and they were usually far more interested in the loot or bribes they could extract from the smugglers to supplement their own meagre wages and frugal diets.

And so, the adventures commenced, and the stories began.

Shepherds hid transistor radios and alarm clocks in caves and bracken stacks, lumberjacks stuffed hollowed-out logs with silk tights and lace underwear, and butchers filled animal carcasses with French cognac and eau de cologne before driving it all into town in the meat van. Even petrol tanks had secret cavities. Ostensibly to visit patients, an infamous doctor from the village of Etxalar would drive past the border guards on an especially adapted moped with just enough petrol to make the journey over the mountain border to the French village of Sare. After attending to his patients, he would then head to the village square for a game of *pelota*. (With similarities to squash, *pelota* is the quintessential

Basque sport. Virtually every village square in the Basque Country has a high wall running along one side, converting it into a *pelota* court known as a *frontón*.) Here, while he enjoyed a match with his French neighbours, the smugglers topped up his tank for the return journey. One half was filled with petrol while the other half was crammed with penicillin for use back in Spain. Another famous anecdote, with a less altruistic moral, tells of a priest who was known for his daily cycle rides backwards and forwards over the border. His constant comings and goings did raise suspicions but, although he was frequently stopped by the *Guardia Civil*, they found nothing – never realising that his frugal Catholic stipend was blessed and multiplied by the regular sale of bicycles.

Another priest, of less healthy countenance, was once raced over the mountains towards the hospital in Pamplona, uttering his final Hail Mary's while sweating profusely beneath a pile of blankets on the back seat of the car. Once safely past the guards, the blankets were drawn back and the priest took his cut from the packets of coffee hidden under his robes, and now safely smuggled into the city.

One favourite tale is of a lorry arriving at the border from France loaded with left-footed shoes supposedly intended for amputees from the Civil War. Of little value and therefore little interest, the lorry was waved on. Meanwhile, a fishing boat, its hidden cavities crammed full of matching right-footed shoes, would steal quietly into a rocky bay further down the Basque coast.

Women dressed in figure-hugging jeans distracted the attention of the guards on the borders. Hairdressers smuggled French perfumes and lipsticks from one household to the next. Even children were involved. In exchange for a *bocadillo de txistorra* (a sausage sandwich) they were encouraged to perfect their stone-throwing techniques at the village street lamps, putting them out of action so that the smugglers, on their return, could carry their loot undetected into town.

As a couple of nights' work smuggling over the border could earn the equivalent of a month's wages in a factory, *gaulan* became an intrinsic part of life for virtually every mountain farm in the area. The naturally frugal Basque lifestyle belied the wealth hidden beneath their lumpy mattresses, and even to this day, few mountain farms can be found without a decent bottle of French brandy hidden away in an old cupboard under the stairs. (More on smuggling ruses later.)

❖ ❖ ❖ ❖

After an enchanted spring exploring the area, I had now mapped out several interesting walks which I hoped to include in my itineraries that summer. However, each walk had to conform to a couple of limiting criteria. The first limitation was Fred's inability to be in two places at once; consequently all my walks had to be circular. The only exception to this rule was when a walk ended near a main road and I could leave my guests chatting in a bar, the importance of speaking the language of the day now secondary to the need for securing a cold beer and a couple of *pintxos* (tapas). I could then thumb a lift back along the valley road to pick up Fred. Hitching, with all the fun it entails, would become an indispensable element in my logistic toolkit.

The second limitation was Fred's inability to cram more than five people inside at any one time, and all this meant that the greater number of circular walks I found starting and finishing at the farmhouse door the better. However, I decided that the problem of Fred's capacity was still only theoretical, to be tackled at a later date when, or if, the situation arose. At this point in time, I still had just the one solitary participant: Margaret Goff.

In order to appeal to the largest number of guests possible, the walks had to be relatively gentle and, if possible, access a variety of short cuts in case the weather changed, or a client ran into difficulties. I was fully aware that had my holidays required applicants to have both mountaineering skills and in-depth knowledge of the Spanish subjunctive, I would be dramatically reducing my market. And one look at the solitary name in my bookings register told me that I needed all the marketing help I could muster!

❖ ❖ ❖ ❖

Until recently, the Baztan and Bidasoa valleys had seen little foreign tourism and I had the impression that the locals saw me as a vaguely amusing but innocuous novelty. They appeared flattered by my interest in their land and culture, and, once they had understood my questions, were happy to help and tell me their stories. There was no hiding my whereabouts either, as Fred's right-hand-drive immediately alerted the locals that there was a foreigner in their midst and in some parts of the valley his fame lingers on to this day.

The Basques love their mountains, and many were keen to share their favourite walks with me. Fernando, the brother of the baker in Elizondo, took me on several, as did Francisco, my taxi driver. Even the bank manager joined in. I have forgotten his name, which is just as well, as his intentions were not always as noble as those of the other inhabitants of the Baztan Valley. If I started off along a path alone, I would inevitably meet people along the way. A tractor driver would rescue me from the brambles, a barman would show me the wash house on the edge of town and a farmer with blackened nails would offer me slivers of peach on an outstretched blade. And with these small interactions and acts of kindness came the stories, tiny peepholes into their lives.

A shepherd with a toothless grin and a well-worn tale told me how he met his wife at a trading post while he was smuggling sugar and lace over the border from France. A miller showed me a hole in the mill floor which allowed him to fish for trout for his supper while simultaneously grinding the villagers' corn. And an elderly cowherd with a crumpled gaze pointed out a small medieval bridge from which his younger brother had stumbled into the river and drowned.

While piecing together a new walk near the village of Amaiur, I ended up in the courtyard of an old farm while trying to locate a path towards an interesting mountain pass that I had had in my sights for some time. There was a natural gully here, and it made sense that there would have been some sort of track linking the farm to the summer grazing lands on the ridge, but I seemed to have lost its trail – unlike the farmyard sheepdogs, who had picked up mine.

As they barked news of my arrival, a lady in her late seventies appeared at the doorway drying her hands on a blue and white dishcloth as she contemplated my presence. She listened to my questions in silence – not out of suspicion, but in bemusement. It was the biological time needed for any human brain to comprehend the sudden appearance of a 'blonde' foreigner on their doorstep, asking never-asked-before questions in a never-heard-before accent. I showed her my map, which she batted away as if it were a piece of propaganda before popping back into the house for some ankle-high wellington boots.

Leaving her husband to watch the beans on the stove, she led me over a stream and up a small path on the other side of the gully, zigzagging uphill between gnarled chestnut trees.

'Do you know that in the old days almost all the paths were lined with chestnut trees?' she said, striding on ahead of me, her boots flapping and sucking like gasping fish. 'My mother always used to grind the chestnuts into flour to make bread. And, do you know what?'

'What?' I asked breathlessly as she steamed on up the path and I struggled through drifts of leaves to keep up.

'I'm sure people these days get all these silly modern ailments just because nobody eats chestnuts any more.'

Although I didn't end up including this walk up to the ridge in my holiday programme, and I never met the woman again, I did stumble upon her farmhouse more than a decade later while documenting the paths of the World War II Comet Line resistance network (*Le Réseau Comète*) with the help of a friend. Juanbi was the proud grandson of Xan Mihurra, a farmer and smuggler from a remote farmhouse near the French border. Xan had been a key player in the resistance movement between 1942 and 1944, hiding pilots and Jewish refugees in his hayloft while Nazi guards boozed on his home-brewed cider in the kitchen below. When the coast was clear, he and his sons would guide the pilots through the night to other safe houses on their escape route towards San Sebastián. How lovely it was to toy with the idea that perhaps this farmhouse, just a few kilometres to the south, had played its role in the resistance too. The locals had certainly all been involved in smuggling in one way or another. Was it possible that the occasional pilot had even hidden here? And I couldn't help wondering whether perhaps – just perhaps – a young girl in ankle-high wellington boots had offered him a chunk of chestnut bread before he continued his journey into the night.

THE GUESTS ARRIVE

MUTINY IN THE KITCHEN

The Baztan Valley, August 1999

My hair streamed out behind me as I bolted down the hill to the village bar in my white welcome dress, heeled sandals clattering, splashing and skidding through the muddy puddles of a recent downpour. This is the first image I retain of Language Adventures' premier language and walking holiday, not that of a calm and collected director of studies, but rather a panic-stricken and exaggerated character from a children's cartoon.

Over the previous month, I had acquired three paying guests: two from the UK, and Ann, a retired actress from the USA (who offered invaluable advice about getting old in bright-coloured dresses). A handful of friends had also allowed themselves to be bullied into coming – but these were all English-speakers.

Marketing in Spain had proved less fruitful, and the reputation of the Basques undoubtedly had much to do with it. No matter how inaccurate and unjust, there was no avoiding a certain stereotype of the Basques as little more than simple, lawless peasants who jollied up their dour lives by prancing around village squares in gaily coloured costumes. A stereotype that may be changing but, unfortunately, hasn't completely disappeared.

Consequently, my attempts at recruiting Spaniards for the week were far less successful and I had failed to rally more than one paying guest. María, a native of Barcelona, was probably slightly more sympathetic to the Basques as Catalunya also harbours dissident tendencies.

Confronting my aversion to telephones, I called the Spanish Tourist Board and, in painful, faltering Spanish, cajoled them into sending a couple of their employees along for free to brush up their English. There was now a vague balance between the Spanish- and English-speaking participants, without which no self-respecting language exchange programme could ever take place. It was not a matter of making money at this stage – I had long given up on such delusions – and neither was it a respectable education experiment into new teaching methods. No, by the time the curtains rose on my first-ever language holiday it was purely a matter of survival. 'What on earth,' I asked myself, 'have I got myself into now?'

Francisco had driven off in his taxi over Otxondo pass into France to pick up my English-speaking guests from Biarritz airport while Koldo, my Spanish teacher from the shoe shop, was scheduled to head off to Pamplona to collect the Spanish participants from the train. But his call, two minutes earlier, had delivered blood-curdling news. His boss had been unable to give him time off work from the shop in Irun and, not only was he unable to go to Pamplona, but it also looked increasingly difficult for him to do any of the Spanish teaching either. Glancing at my watch, I noted that the train was due to arrive in ten minutes and Pamplona was almost an hour away.

Koldo's call had totally floored me. Every way one looked, my intrepid Spanish clients, braving an untried and untested English course in rebel Basque-speaking territory, were ten minutes away from being stranded, unattended on a platform at Pamplona train station. And I was acutely aware that one never gets a second chance to make a first impression.

During my panicked preparations for the day, I had temporarily misplaced Fred's key somewhere in the cavernous interior of Casa

Tristantenea, so I had to sprint down to the village bar to find the number for a local taxi. But no taxis were available – none that could have done the one-hour journey in ten minutes – and so I called Alberto, my only tentative contact in Pamplona. Alberto was the director of a language school and, up until then, had formed part of a friendly network of professionals within the sector, humouring my ideas and providing me with contacts. Having spent years giving intercultural sensitivity courses in Copenhagen, I knew that Sunday business calls in Spain were a serious cultural faux pas (worse even than calling during the two-to-four-o'clock siesta), but I was desperate. So, on that sunny Sunday morning, while Alberto was undoubtedly enjoying aperitifs with his wife and children in a rare moment of domestic bliss, he picked up my garbled call, begging him to ditch all family commitments and dash to the station to greet my guests and call them a taxi.

That lunchtime, two taxis converged on the gravel drive at Casa Tristantenea, seat of Language Adventures. One taxi came from Biarritz over the Otxondo pass from the north and the other had driven here through the gloomy tunnels of Belate from Pamplona and the south. One taxi transported the weary but excited English-speaking contingent, while the other bore some shaken – and understandably sceptical – Spaniards. Waiting in the doorway to welcome them to this wonderful multilingual, multicultural experience was none other than myself, Georgina Howard, Director of Language Adventures, with sweaty armpits, wild, unclipped strawberry-blonde hair and splashes of mud over her white cotton dress.

Casa Tristantenea lies about a kilometre outside the tiny village of Arraioz in the Baztan Valley, and is accessed by a steep lane from the main valley road. It is a beautiful example of the many eighteenth-century Basque farmhouses in the area, with the corners, doors and windows framed by impressive slabs of pink sandstone characteristic of Baztan Valley architecture. Behind the house, a small orchard of kiwi fruit offered scant shade for the rickety deckchairs strewn around the pool.

The main entrance was through a cavernous flagstone hallway on the ground floor, cool and dank even in the height of summer. From here a wide wooden staircase spiralled up to the *planta noble* above. The 'noble floor', as it was known, had been the original living quarters but, despite Maria Luisa's contemporary interior design in other parts of the house, the first floor still offered its 'nobles' a rather sombre existence. A dimly lit lounge with an open fire and a pervading smell of stale smoke doubled up as the teaching room. Further down the corridor were three old-fashioned bedrooms with dark wooden bed frames and towering footboards. Incongruously, a modern bathroom at the end of the corridor, with an enormous circular bath and Jacuzzi, promised the 'nobles' slightly more refined diversions at the end of the day.

Fortunately, the attic, the building's crowning architectural glory, compensated grandly for any shortcomings found in other parts of the house. Here, higher-ranking 'nobles' could enjoy brighter and loftier bedrooms and gaze at the stars through large – if slightly leaky – skylights. An en-suite master bedroom led into a spacious bathroom with black-and-white floor tiles and a rather neglected pot plant which scattered its leaves in the bidet. But the best room by far was the wonderful open-plan kitchen-living room with its high beams and semicircular lilac-and-lime sofa.

This room would soon become the heart and soul of the house. At its centre, an upturned wooden threshing board, studded with grey flint chips and covered with glass, served as an inspired coffee table. Once the hayloft, where legs of ham and strings of sausages would have swung from the rafters, the kitchen-living room now vibrated to the sounds of my international house parties, where guests gathered and enjoyed the to and fro of international dialogue.

At the far end of the room, a corner had been sectioned off to form a pantry. Home to our stock of wines and beers, it would come to be known affectionately as the 'medicine chest' and become especially popular with some of the more elderly linguists who would disappear and reappear from behind the partition with increasingly glowing cheeks. My favourite place, however, was a tiny balcony leading off the main room. The view from here embraced the whole sweep of the Baztan Valley from the rounded crests of Saioa to the rugged purple crags of Auza on the French border. Their pull was magnetic. Once a landing platform for bales of hay, it was now my podium for reflection and inspiration. It was my place to find sanity away from the overwhelming responsibility of it all.

After a nervous and garrulous welcome, I showed everyone to their bedrooms, making an on-the-spot psychological assessment as to whom I should lodge where. The more easy-going people were shown to the rooms on the dingier 'noble' floor and the fussier guests were ushered into the more sophisticated bedrooms on the floor above. As for me, my bed was simply a sleeping bag on a yoga mat in the former animal quarters on the ground floor.

In the brief interlude that followed, while my guests made themselves comfortable in their bedrooms, I darted into a downstairs toilet, yanked a comb through my hair and scrubbed feverishly at some of the larger mud stains on my dress. I then bolted up the stairs to the kitchen to feign composure and wait, anxiously, for them to join me for lunch.

While the paella simmered on the stove, I twittered nervously through an introduction to the week ahead of us, alternating between English and my Spanish-Italian mix. I was banking on the deficiencies in my Spanish being overlooked when the wine was uncorked and the paella served.

Innocently, I had asked Nagore, my Basque cook, to make paella for the welcome lunch and, cooking never having been my strong point, I had no idea that it was not a local dish at all. Had she been asked to make a Basque dish, black bean stew for example, with its *sacramentos* (literally 'sacraments', an interesting word for pork cuts), the outcome may have been different. The anglophone contingent entered the spirit of the occasion immediately, cooing characteristically over the food, smiling politely at the after-dinner conversations and, after knocking back a third or fourth glass of wine, heading off for a siesta with all the cultural adaptation one could have wished for.

The Spanish, however, didn't move from their seats and waited in ominous silence for the British guests to exit the room. There was mutiny among the ranks, I could smell it. They all bore identically stony expressions, making me think that, unbeknown to me, they had conferred, and were just about to let me know their collective verdict.

'Georgina, can we talk to you for a moment?' asked one of the guys on a freebie from the local tourist board. His eyes flickered towards the door to make sure that there were no other witnesses to the scene about to unfold around the kitchen table, now covered by the red-and-white-check tablecloth proudly bought for the occasion.

'Fine, yes, what is it?' I asked, fabricating a smile to hide the second wave of panic.

He looked around at the other Spanish guests, eliciting their tacit approval before he continued. 'That meal was awful,' he stated coldly, in that direct, no-frills style that has spelt the end of many Anglo-Hispanic romances. 'The paella was lumpy, blotchy... probably frozen... and the *natillas* (custard puddings) were so thin and... and watery, they probably came out of a packet.'

I was horrified, but also surprised by a vague feeling of resentment. I had been so absorbed in the dynamics between my guests, in sniffing out alliances and potential adversaries, and frogmarching Italian words into Spanish sentences, that I – not known for my cooking skills – hadn't given the food a second thought.

'I'm awfully sorry,' I replied, mortified, while the vestiges of my pride bristled within me, *but don't forget that you are lucky to be here in the first place and that you haven't even paid*. But, of course, these thoughts were never expressed, vanquished immediately by a feeling of inadequacy that gnawed at my stomach as I battled back the tears.

'Thank you, thank you for telling me... I'll do something about it... I really am so, so sorry,' I apologised as they scraped back their chairs and made their way to their rooms. Just a couple of hours after my guests had walked in the door, I found myself alone once again, wiping wine stains and rice crumbs from the red-and-white tablecloth, chin down, shoulders hunched, nursing the child inside me.

And so it was that after so much preparation for what was, until then, one of the most important weeks of my life, I now found myself with neither a Spanish teacher nor a Spanish cook. I was filled with terror, sickened and shaken to the core as I watched my dream fall apart and crash around my feet.

Luckily, the next day – the first of the official programme – was an English-speaking day, which gave me a few extra hours to hunt down a new Spanish teacher. Also, my dear friends Mary and Barry had just arrived the previous evening from the UK, offering desperately needed moral support. At least I had reinforcements and a twenty-four-hour respite before the lack of a Spanish teacher the following day would surely condemn me to purgatory.

Barry had happened to be travelling in Europe that summer and had offered to give English lessons to my Spanish guests, witnessing for himself the fruits of our conversations on his terrace in Sydney the previous Christmas. With a cold beer in hand, his relaxed humour and roguish Australian charm enthralled both Spanish and English guests alike. Mary, gracious to a fault, rustled up an undeniably British steak and kidney pie for lunch, a lunch that on second thoughts – and in view of the consternation it caused at the butchers and the carnage in the kitchen – was perhaps not one of our brightest ideas. But it was at least an improvement on the paella the previous day and provided an element of cultural integrity, even if the Spanish, notoriously fussy eaters, didn't appreciate the offal.

After lunch we pulled on our boots and stepped out on our first walk together and, while the Spanish and English cuisine had failed to hit the spot, the delights of the Baztan Valley soon wrought their magic over our small and disparate group. The enchanting Basque village architecture, coupled with the fresh mountain breezes and rich, metallic smell of the soft earth beneath our feet, lightened everyone's spirits and assuaged the memories of the earlier disasters. The group began to relax in each other's company, and with strong participation on the English-speaking front conversation began to flow. A ramshackle farm building or a kitten on a wall, or even a difficult latch on a gate, all triggered funny, impromptu exchanges between my guests, whose personalities slowly began to bubble forth. The English-speaking cohort assumed their responsibilities to the full and, in the politest possible way, made sure that the Spanish spoke English too.

Yet I was living in a parallel universe. I was on countdown to disaster. The Spanish-speaking day (tomorrow) was fast approaching and there was still no Spanish teacher in sight. Whenever the path was straightforward, I would hold back, crouching behind a tree to make frantic phone calls to any contacts I had, bribing Spanish acquaintances to improvise the role of Spanish teacher, or at least help me locate somebody who would. Given my track record for untimely calls, it was quite possibly siesta time when I called Alberto in Pamplona to ask for his help once again. But, while he had been happy to jump into the impromptu role of taxi co-ordinator on a Sunday lunchtime, he assured me that he did have a job of his own to go to and preferred to focus on his own language school during the week.

When a fork in the path appeared up ahead, I would abruptly truncate the conversation and chase after my merry band, taking the lead to indicate the correct turning before, once again, dashing off behind some gorse bushes to make another panicked call. I felt a little like Yogi Bear stalking a group of American students on a field trip.

The situation was absurd and the odds of finding a Spanish teacher in these remote Basque mountain villages were stacked against me. My lasting memory of that first walk, which should have been that of relaxed camaraderie, tinged with an element of self-congratulation, was actually a silent scream of panic welling up within me as the Spanish-speaking day approached.

Divine intervention occurred late that evening when Koldo called me once again. He had managed to convince his boss to give him more time off work and, although he couldn't make it for the walks, he would at least do his best to come to the house and give Spanish classes to my guests. And true to his word, he did. Over the years I have learned that when a Basque person says that they will 'do their best' then they, almost invariably, never let you down.

For the moment, my honour had been saved, and the relief – commensurate with the panic of the past forty-eight hours – was almost equally debilitating as my muscles relaxed and my bones stopped shaking. Thanks to the diligence and application of my British guests (most probably because they had paid to come, flown in from so far away, and liked the wine) and the easy camaraderie of the Spanish (most probably because most of them were on a freebie and had nothing to lose) we all pulled through the week.

Our Spanish catering dilemmas were resolved by a family restaurant in the village which prepared delicious take-away food, and one of my lasting memories of the week was the image in Fred's rear-view mirror as we drove up the lane towards Casa Tristantenea with lunch. Crammed into the back seat of the car my guests laughed hysterically as they desperately tried to keep the Tupperware containers and pans of stew horizontal while Fred lurched in fits and starts up the vertical track to the house.

Ann, the elderly American actress, had been entrusted with a number of small terracotta pots of *mamia* (a traditional sheep's milk yoghurt) which were skating dizzily around on a tray. 'My babies, my babies,' she cried in a shrill theatrical voice as the car lurched violently around the final bend and they all landed on her lap. Naturally, we all collapsed into laughter.

By the end of the week, news of my holidays and the eccentric group of visitors that they had united had spread beyond the mountains of the Baztan Valley. A TV station called to ask if they could make a short news clip about my work, and a regional Basque newspaper was asking for an interview. Ann kitted me out in my most colourful clothes and, on a sunny afternoon during farewell cocktails by the swimming pool, my guests coaxed me out in front of the cameras.

A few days later I found myself sitting in a lively Baztan bar watching a broadcast on national Spanish TV. Gesticulating wildly on the screen was a young woman in a gaudy orange-and-gold dress talking about the methods of her Spanish-English language exchange holidays. I strained closer to pick up what she was saying but it was a little difficult to understand, not due to the background noise in the bar – everyone, by that time, had stopped talking to listen – but because she seemed to be speaking in a strange, but not completely unfamiliar, dialect of Italian.

Amid laughs and promises to keep in touch, I waved my guests off at the front door of Casa Tristantenea, listening to the taxis crunch down the gravel drive to the track as they headed back to Biarritz or Pamplona. Some of my guests went north, others went south. All of them had made friends and acquired a few more language skills in the bargain, and their initially pristine walking boots were now caked in mud, stained to an identical hue. But I was numb. Totally, utterly, numb. Crushed between the bedrock of experiences I had just been through and the solid weight of a million thoughts and emotions yet to be processed.

I felt wafer thin as I turned towards the house and climbed the stairs. One step. Two steps. Three steps. Vaguely registering the silky touch of the worn chestnut bannisters on the palm of my hand, I realised that I must still be alive. Somehow. Somewhere. Ever so slowly, I pushed open the door to the attic, where the sunlight, streaming in from a skylight above the table, spotlit a peach stone on a plate. Van Gogh, I thought. Or not, I thought. A Spanish phrasebook lay open on the sofa and a sticky jar of Marmite sat on the kitchen counter by the kettle. Robotically, I adjusted the clip in my hair and dabbed at a coffee stain on the red-and-white tablecloth before stepping outside on to the balcony. There, surrounded by these mysterious, silently breathing Basque mountains – at the altar of whatever it was that had brought me here and now held me hostage – I crumpled on to the floor and wept. Never, I vowed, never would I put myself through such needless torture again. Never.

PEOPLE

SHEIKS AND SILVER ROBOTS

But, of course, one should never say never. Perhaps it was the fact that I had dreamed so long and so hard of this project, of Language Adventures, that it had taken on a life force of its own. Letting her go, letting her down, would have felt a little like turning my back on my child. Perhaps it was this, or simply – far more mundanely – that in burning all my bridges with my former life I had absolutely no idea where else to go or what else to do. And so, at the end of my first year in the Baztan Valley, I found myself shaking hands once again on renting Casa Tristantenea for the following summer. Gradually the holidays took off, and within a couple of years the first four paying guests – and various stooges – had multiplied to eleven guests and then to twenty-four as I expanded the number of holidays on offer. I now rented Casa Tristantenea for a month at a time and, as the years progressed, experimented with other farmhouses in different Baztan villages – each one offering a fresh landscape, and new paths, to explore. Inevitably, it was these enigmatic mountain paths, winding their way from one Basque village to the next, along smugglers' tracks and over humpback bridges, that seduced us all. They were the vital, magical ingredient in everything we did. And so, keeping the walks as the staple ingredient, I experimented with different combinations. In addition to walking and language holidays, I tried out walking and Basque carnival weeks, walking and painting weeks, singles' walking weeks and even yoga and walking weeks – although that was not the most spiritual of combinations; the yoga teacher complained that everyone ate and drank too much and then spent her classes complaining of indigestion.

As the range of holidays on offer expanded, I decided to change the name of my company to encompass this new diversity. Thus the embryonic 'Language Adventures' toddled into the future as 'Pyrenean Experience Ltd'.

We had some amazing farewell parties at Casa Tristantenea, but one of them will stand out forever. It was a fancy-dress party, instigated by a large and lively group of Spanish- and English-speaking guests, who had also organised a communal meal for the final evening. I cannot remember the ingredients, but they will undoubtedly have included the inevitable and irreproachable Spanish *tortilla*. The last couple of days had been characterised by whispers and furtive laughter behind closed bedroom doors as my guests improvised fancy costumes from the few objects in the house with a little help from the hardware store in Elizondo. For my British guests at least, obtaining the extra props from the shop had been a Spanish vocabulary lesson in its own right.

There was a true babble of languages that evening as everyone gave up on the strictly enforced 'language of the day' and launched into a free-for-all with whatever words first came to mind. There was excitement in the air as we all helped to prepare dinner, keeping the secrets of our fancy-dress costumes to ourselves. Bob, a builder from North Yorkshire, in fluffy slippers with rabbit-head toes – which were actually a feature of his daily attire – waltzed around the table counting out the cutlery while Ramón and Isabel argued over the use of onions in the *tortilla* sizzling on the stove. Enjoying an animated couple of hours around the kitchen table, we cleaned the dishes and then scampered off to change.

Ángel, a lawyer from Madrid, arrived as a chubby Arabian sheik thanks to an old bed-cover and a cushion from the sofa, and Joan, a retired Glasgow GP, out of her depth with the frivolity of the moment, slipped sheepishly into the room as a spring lamb with a white walking sock pinned to her bottom for a tail. But the first prize went to Wally. Wally had silver-sprayed a series of cardboard boxes which he had taped around his arms and legs and placed over his head, cutting small square holes for his eyes and nose, before entering the room in a series of slow, jerky steps. His robot outfit was outlandish, and the prize he took away that evening more than compensated him for his efforts. Pilar, that year's Spanish teacher, wooed by his artistic vigour, moved to live with him in London the following year, leaving me without a language teacher once again.

Our euphoria raised the roof and, accompanied by the smell of fried garlic and onions (finally admitted into the *tortilla*), our laughter floated out of the balcony door to mingle with the sounds of the sheep's bells and the hoots of the occasional night owl. We were the world. We were eternal. And yet, as far as the world was concerned, we were but a pinprick of light on a dark mountain on a summer's night. It was all a matter of perspective.

❖ ❖ ❖ ❖

Over the next few years, the gradient of the learning curve that faced me as I built my business into a more economically viable venture was steeper than any mountain slope I had climbed. But finally, fuelled by passion and bloody-mindedness, the formula worked. Improbable families were forged from disparate individuals, united by the moment's folly of signing up for an obscure walking holiday in the equally ambiguous borderlands of the Basque Pyrenees. Those truly enchanting occasions were impossible to contrive, springing from the unpredictable qualities of human nature, and the magic – at times mayhem – that arrives from isolating incongruent personalities in a topsy-turvy farmhouse at the end of a mountain track. The caprices of the weather with its rain bursts and leaky skylights, electric storms and power cuts, combined with the generosity of the Basque farmers and the beauty of their landscapes, offered up a recipe to shake, inspire and humble us all. Private detectives, belly dancers, spider experts, tax inspectors, gynaecologists, stand-up comedians, submarine captains, priests, magicians and spies all fell under the spell. Some of them a little more so than others.

Alone on the balcony of Tristantenea, contemplating the amphitheatre of hills that encircled the house, I recalled that Australian shopping mall and the words of that frail, silver-haired fortune teller. 'I see a house,' she had said as she retraced the lines on my hand, 'surrounded by land, lots of land.'

Living in close company with such different people offered me intriguing insights into the paradoxes of human nature as well as a powerful challenge to my preconceptions. Surprisingly, what puzzled me most was not how frequently our stereotypes were proven wrong, but how impossible it was not to default to them in the first place. Despite the theories on cultural awareness that had formed the basis of the communication courses I had given in Copenhagen, despite my years of working with people from all over the world, I couldn't help but fall victim to certain innate biases. They would kick in from some primitive fight-or-flee mechanism within me but were almost inevitably proven wrong in the end.

A Texan, in an unguarded moment of lucidity at a local fiesta, hinted at a lifetime of brutal underworld dealings before welling up with tears at the sight of children folk dancing in the village square. A vegan from Papua New Guinea stole off for *foie gras* tapas in San Sebastián while others remained at the house, dutifully finishing their Spanish homework and secretly hoarding bottles of gin or bunches of bananas beneath their beds. A guest from Surrey blatantly refused to lift a finger to help all week until the farewell party on the final evening. As the festivities drew to a close, and we eyed the tower of greasy pots and pans in the kitchen with increasingly heavy hearts, he headed towards the sink, loosened his tie, slipped on an apron, and dispatched the rest of us off to our beds. And the examples continue ad infinitum, teaching me – knee-jerk reactions aside – that if we are going to pigeonhole people, then each one of them deserves a brand-new well-appointed pigeonhole of their own.

And then there are the hundreds of fascinating individuals who, by the sheer uniqueness which is their right of birth, offer us singular insights and inspirations by their example alone. I remember Harry, an octogenarian from Guernsey with a whimsical smile and bushy eyebrows, who would deliberately stride out ahead of us towards the end of a walk, beating us home so that he could greet us at the farmhouse door minutes later in his tartan slippers with a freshly brewed pot of tea. Never will I forget Mary, who joined our Spanish courses years after her husband's death so that she could learn his native language, always choosing his favourite dish, *calamares en su tinta* (squid in black ink), from the menu whenever she had the chance. Carol was a paralympic coach who taught people in wheelchairs how to ski; Pony and Rich, surgeons working in simulated lunar environments in the Arizona desert, advised NASA on how to mend broken limbs on the moon; and how could we forget Bill and Barbara? Bill, a butcher, hobbled out of the taxi on crutches and Barbara, a teacher for the blind, felt her way down the steps to the terrace with severely impaired sight. Unlike Gillian, a ninety-year-old language student from Glasgow, who tersely refused any help whatsoever, they both clung resolutely to our hands as we guided them step by step, stone by stone over hill and dale.

And then there was Cecil.

Cecil booked on to an advanced Spanish course and wrote to me months before he arrived, attaching a photo of himself in the exact clothes he intended to wear at the airport so that I could recognise him easily. True to the photo, a replica awaited me in the Biarritz arrivals hall, glancing nervously at his watch, a small rucksack on his back and a creased leather satchel in his hand.

'*Hola*, you must be Cecil.' I bounded over to him in a flowing marigold-yellow dress, tucking my Pyrenean Experience sign under my arm and hastily combing my hair clip through my hair to give a slightly less dishevelled corporate image. Effusively, and with embarrassingly little thought to cultural sensitivity, I went to kiss him on both cheeks, as is the habit in Spain. He recoiled stiffly.

'I'm going to be the most difficult client you've ever had,' were his first words, glancing over my shoulder to see if anyone else was watching.

'I'm sure you won't,' I said, already suspecting that there might be some truth in his words.

'I have Asperger's,' he said, clutching his satchel to his chest, 'but I've been trying to beat it all of my life.' What he never realised was that sharing a week with him turned out to be one of the most rewarding experiences I have had with any of my guests. And not for the most obvious reasons.

Cecil was a fascinating person, with a fathomless and inexhaustible knowledge of Spanish, Russian and Italian, but he struggled to relax into the emotional ebb and flow of the dynamics of conversation. His presence that week bore heavily on the group as he continually corralled the conversation and led it off on endless technically brilliant tangents in enviably perfect Spanish. That week we were all instructed in the complexities of nuclear physics, thermodynamics, entropy, and the history of the Chevalier camera lens. During our walks, every guest took turns to talk to him individually, allowing the conversations between the rest of the group to relax into a more natural rhythm – and to embrace slightly less highbrow topics – but, as both he and I suspected, he never managed to integrate on anything more than a perfunctory level. That is not until the final evening.

For the farewell ceremony, Edorta, a talented local guitarist, arrived at the house to sing an eclectic mix of Spanish, Basque and international songs. As the sun set over the valley, all eight of us squeezed on to the sofa in my living room, singing along to any songs we knew and suggesting a few of our favourites for him to play at the end of his performance. Cecil suggested a song too and, cheek by jowl, we all sang along in a discordant but happy choir. Although, unfortunately, I can't remember the words, Cecil spoke out and said something amusing which made us all laugh. He was visibly stunned. Looking around the room at the rest of the group, he slowly comprehended the nature of our laughter. We were all laughing *with* him, not at him, nor without him, nor in spite of him, and his joke had briefly united us all. Uncomfortably sandwiched between the other guests, he looked over at me stiffly from the other side of the sofa and our gaze met. He smiled and I am sure that I detected a tear in his eye.

A BASQUE FIESTA

AS GOOD AS IT GETS

Madrid, May 2001

Early one Sunday morning a bus ferried a group of hikers off for a
day in the Sierra to the north of Madrid. A video played on a small
monitor suspended from the ceiling but few people were watching.
Lulled by the drone of the bus engine and the inconsiderately
early hour of the departure, most of the passengers were catching
up on their weekend beauty sleep. Yet the woman on the screen
continued regardless, gesticulating wildly in her bright orange
dress, struggling to compensate for the rather strange Spanish-
Italian blend in which her message was delivered. I cringed.

A couple of years had passed since that first meeting with
Carmen and Bernardo in Madrid, and I had been back to visit the
Spanish capital several times. This time I had seized the opportunity
to join a hiking excursion organised by one of my agents who had
made a copy of the old TV interview, and still played it on the bus
to promote my holidays to his clients.

Later that day, on an uncomfortably rocky outcrop in the Sierra,
as I tried unobtrusively to extract a string of *jamón serrano* from
my teeth, I met Alfredo. I remember him standing out among the
gregarious band of walkers, perhaps for his reserve or his composure,
maybe simply for his great legs. He had intense, intelligent eyes
the colour of burnt sienna, and was interested in practising his
English – and he seemed to have no problem with the ham.

The physical differences between the people from central
and southern Spain and the Basques of the north never ceased

to surprise me. Alfredo's smaller build and swarthy, satin skin contrasted starkly with the stubbly white complexions of the sturdy Basque men of the Pyrenees. Just as the landscapes changed, so did the regional flora and fauna, so I suppose it would have been unusual had there been no differences at all between the people of the north and south. I could clearly understand the Basques for saying that they went to Spain for holidays, an attitude not dissimilar to the British people's take on Europe.

Alfredo was a gentle guy with an easy smile. He was tireless and resourceful, and we struck up a friendship surprisingly quickly. I invited him to join me in the Baztan Valley and to give me a hand exploring new routes and taxiing my guests around.

Whatever his job was it certainly offered him flexible working hours, and he drove up to the Baztan Valley to visit me on several occasions that summer. Within a week of our meeting, he had driven up from Madrid and was ready to pitch himself at any task I tossed his way, inseparable from a small notebook that he used to scribble down new English words and expressions.

I enjoyed his presence and the luxury of having a strong and seemingly inexhaustible companion at my side. As he swung my rucksack up on to powerful shoulders, I surprised myself at the ease with which I let him take the lead, trotting docilely behind him, proffering him my tatty but treasured maps at every new intersection in the path. Where I would normally battle bullishly through the brambles and hurl myself over gates, I found myself taking his hand to step over the puddles, hovering demurely while he beat back thorn bushes, slayed dragons and deflected thunderbolts in my name.

Looking back, I suppose it was inevitable; I was out of my depth and alone here in the Baztan Valley and he offered a kind and reassuring presence that I thought I needed. And so, with the arrival of new, toned contours to explore, Alfredo and I slipped into a brief and uncomplicated romance that summer which lacked a certain intensity but worked well for us both. Surprisingly well.

On the one and only weekend that I spent with Alfredo at his apartment in Madrid, he received a phone call in the middle of the night and left immediately. It didn't come as a surprise. He had told me it could happen and had warned me not to ask. Several hours later I woke to the grid lines of sunshine burning through the blinds, promising another golden day in the Spanish capital, and padded over the cool floor tiles to the wardrobe in search of a towel. Sliding open the door, I stopped in my tracks. Hanging inside the wardrobe were ten – perhaps fifteen – identical, white, perfectly ironed T-shirts hanging from identical hangers, all evenly spaced along the rail.

Back in the Baztan, Alfredo was an immense help with the logistics, driving my guests around in his car when Fred's minimal capacity was stretched beyond the limit, and running emergency errands when we ran out of milk or wine. His outdoor survival skills also brought me great peace of mind as my guests naïvely tripped along behind me, a girl from the concrete suburbs of Birmingham with little formal mountain training leading the way along the smugglers' paths into the heart of the Basque Pyrenees.

That Alfredo was a gentleman, there was no doubt. Deeply protective of me, his concern was at times unsettling and led to some disconcerting conversations. One day, on our way home from a walk, he mentioned the dangers of running a company in the Basque Country, warning me that if my company became any bigger it could attract the attention of the Basque independence movement and that, in all likelihood, I would be blackmailed into paying them protection money. I laughed this off as just another Spanish prejudice against the Basques. Although I had heard of the recent bombing of a discotheque nearby, purportedly due to the owner having refused to pay up, the idea of my tiny company attracting such attention seemed utterly ridiculous. And I was right: although the number of clients expanded in the following years, I was never once approached.

In exchange for his help, Alfredo improved his English and gleaned much interesting information about the people and culture of the area. It never occurred to me to question his motives. After all, I had fallen under the spell of the valley and, in my innocence, I believed that his delight in the area was for similar reasons to my own. The last time he joined me, he assisted with the logistics of a particularly lively group whose fame will go down in history thanks to a voluptuous blonde called Sherry and her performance in the fiestas of the historic Basque village of Amaiur.

I had found the fiesta programme pinned up in the village bar. Rarely do they publish local information in Spanish in these staunchly Basque strongholds, so I went to clarify the Basque text with the bar owner, asking her whether the villagers would mind our joining in. It wasn't as if they hadn't seen me before. For the past couple of years, I had been leading walks through the village along the Camino Baztanés and the bar had become one of our regular watering holes. '*Sí, sin problema,*' came the reply the following week, so I bought a fistful of tickets for the Saturday lunchtime banquet in the village hall.

In Spanish circles there is a commonly held opinion that Basques are reserved and surly folk, but I have not found that to be the case. Admittedly, they are not as gregarious as the southerners, but their welcome is invariably genuine and the people of Amaiur were no exception.

In hindsight, everybody had measured us up long before we met them. No movement in this valley went unnoticed in these turbulent political times, when ETA's armed struggle gave little reprieve and the *Guardia Civil* were equally virulent in tracking them down. The locals, however, seemed to have got the measure of me and the handful of walkers and language enthusiasts that followed in my wake. Although they probably thought that we were barking mad, they appeared to see us as relatively innocuous.

If Alfredo were still alive today, he would corroborate the story that follows, and the sheer brilliance and madness of the moments that we shared in Amaiur on that crazy, beautiful September afternoon. No doubt Sherry had walked over the hills from our rental house to the fiesta in her golden trainers, her party gear in her rucksack, but the first image I have of her was dancing in the village square in high heels, a skintight grey pencil skirt and a low-cut pink angora top. We were all excited and slightly nervous, clutching our tickets to prove a *bona fide* reason for our presence, and we were acutely aware that an invitation to participate in Basque culture at this level was an honour indeed.

The clock struck one when we arrived in Amaiur, just in time to see groups of Basque youths in traditional dress file into the square, the boys in berets and waistcoats, the girls in headscarves and colourful pinafores. They performed intricate – if somewhat tame – dances, more reminiscent of Scottish folk dancing than searing, passionate flamenco with its Arabic undercurrents, and illustrating, yet again, the vivid contrasts between the northern and southern Iberian cultures.

At three o'clock we followed the crowds up the stairs to the attic in the town hall, circumventing men with large stomachs and even larger knives who were keeping vigil over a row of lambs roasting tantalisingly on a spit. Beneath a vault of high rafters and oak beams, rows of tables were kitted out with cider tumblers, red serviettes and toothpicks. Nervously, we awaited our cue at the entrance to the hall and, sure enough, anticipating our uncertainty, a couple of village elders came up to exchange a few awkward pleasantries, disconcerted by the fact that some of us spoke even more laboured Spanish than they did. When we had all filed along our benches, a vast banquet unfolded: girls with thick ankles and polka-dot aprons slapped bottles of cider in front of us on rickety trestle tables that trembled in anticipation of the spread to come. *Jamón serrano* and duck liver pâtés were followed by plates of langoustines and mayonnaise and a crisp salad of gloriously green lettuce with shavings of spring onion.

Our table companions showed us how to 'break' the cider by pouring it into our glasses from a height, encouraging us to down it in one while the froth still fizzed and sparkled in the glass. With their knives, they fashioned strangely shaped stoppers from the corks, topping up our glasses with the devotion of religious zealots. And then came the *pièce de résistance*. To a bawdy fanfare of cheers and a drum roll of hands on tables, one heaped platter after the next of tender roast lamb, cooked to perfection, appeared from the kitchen. Our fellow diners, proud as kings, leant towards us with forks clasped in heavy fists, fat glistening on cracked knuckles. Screaming above the din, they would ask '*¿Más? ¿Más carne? ¿Más?*' ('More? More meat? More?') until even the most ravenous of Basque lumberjacks – of which there were many – had had their fill.

Overwhelmed by their generosity, we joined in, gnawing at the meat with our bare hands, knocking back the cider and slurping and sloshing our way through desserts, coffees, champagnes and liqueurs.

If ever there was a day when vegetarians turned into carnivores, teetotallers became alcoholics and non-smokers sat angelically in halos of smoke, then this was it. We were excited and humbled by this extraordinary welcome from the tiny mountain village of Amaiur, and punch-drunk with the sheer honour of it all.

While we leant back to rest our bloated stomachs and pick the last of the meat from our teeth, the table was cleared and a *trikitixa* (button accordion) started playing. A group of adolescent girls rattled tambourines while a straight-backed youth in a large Basque beret played Celtic melodies on the *txistu* (one-handed recorder) in a minor key. Later, a couple of *bertsolariak* (rhyming bards) improvised rap-style songs to popular tunes while the crowd sang along, whooping and cheering. Our table companions threw their arms around us as we all swayed to the music like drunken sailors – of which there may also have been a few. Yet, to everyone's surprise – and ours in particular – the final act was on us.

At a break in the music, Sherry stood up. Her long golden locks hugged the enviable curves in her pink top as she slunk up on to the table as if she were a mermaid, hoisting herself out of the sea and on to a rock. Carefully, she pushed the plates and glasses to one side, replacing them with one high-heeled sandal after the next and, drawing herself to her full height, began to gyrate, swaying her wide hips in her tight skirt to the pulse of the music.

Shimmering and shaking, she snaked round and round on her makeshift stage charming, teasing and hypnotising the room. Most of the locals had never heard of a belly dancer, let alone witnessed one in full flight, and the spectacle of this beautiful blonde temptress, the perfect incarnation of a *lamia* – object of Basque legends and male desire – momentarily paralysed the audience. Men, women, children – even the dogs – were suspended in bewilderment. And then came the cheers, the unconditional raucous joy of surprise and amazement as the crowd banged on the table, shouting, whistling and willing her on.

After a while, a couple of rotund middle-aged men hauled themselves up on to our table and, with notably less elegance, Basque bellies bouncing, joined Sherry for a dance and the party continued.

We laughed, we drank, we cheered and took photo after photo in an attempt to capture this moment for the rest of our lives. Our hearts swelled with pride, overjoyed that – in the strangest of ways – we were able to reciprocate the generous welcome offered us by our hosts. We were high on a sense of oneness with the world.

I remember exchanging confidential looks with Alfredo at the other side of the room who, like us, was snapping photos of Sherry and her Basque dancing partners, cheering them on.

'This is as good as it gets,' I beamed.

This was the first really significant cultural exchange between my merry bands of guests and the local people, and the first of many heart-warming moments to come. Although none of us would ever have included 'belly dancing' as part of our own cultural heritage, that actually wasn't the point.

In the fading light of day, we staggered home along the flagstone paths of the eleventh-century Camino Baztanés. Over the past centuries, the path had guided hundreds of thousands of pilgrims across the Pyrenees to Santiago de Compostela, but this was surely the first time it had seen a belly dancer in a tight skirt and high heels. Or maybe not? We were so proud of Sherry, our mermaid, our *lamia*, and her act of heroism remains a legend in Amaiur to this day.

Later that week, Alfredo drove back to Madrid. By the end of that summer, our brief relationship was over and within a couple of years, his life came to an abrupt end.

Many years later, a friend, helping me with research for this book, sent me a link to an article which led me to believe that this enigmatic man was not all that he had seemed. Although I like to believe that he was genuinely fond of me, I now deeply suspect that other characters in the Baztan Valley had also caught his eye, and that his interest in joining me was not only to do with my walking itineraries and the acquisition of a few English irregular verbs. I have my suspicions, but here, in the pages of this book, it would be difficult – even unwise – for me to say any more.

A NEW VALLEY

THE GRANDMOTHER, THE MILLER AND THE OSTRICH

One summer's day, just a year after I had first set eyes on the Baztan Valley and the year before I met Alfredo, I chanced upon a completely new river valley to the west. On the map it seemed to be virtually a continuation of the same geographical valley formation as the Baztan, but in reality it was just a minor tributary; the main Baztan-Bidasoa River taking a sudden turn northwards at this point and making a dash for the Atlantic. Home to charming villages and farms luxuriating along the banks of the Ezkurra River, this smaller valley lay almost completely off the radar – another example of the constant surprises thrown up by these intricate, magical landscapes. I had been informed that there was an interesting watermill and ethnographic museum upstream and that, if I could piece together a circular walk in the area, this could provide an interesting activity for my guests.

As I entered the valley the sunbeams streamed in from the south, filtering through the alders and willows along the river, refracting on the water to burst into meteorites of golden stars. It was a glorious, blessed day, a day of the gods, whoever they were.

Within a few kilometres the valley opened out and soon I entered an area of meadows and farms built on the floodplains of the river, a village looming in the distance. I parked outside the porticoes of a bar in the plaza. A ragtag group of children ran about playing *pelota* while I wrestled with my tattered map, spreading it out on the bonnet of the car. I was in the main square of a small village called Ituren, known, as I would soon find out, for some rather unusual local characters.

Earlier that morning, over my *napolitana* in the roadside café in Elizondo, I had identified a circular walk starting from this square which, according to the map, was possibly – but probably not – signposted. In theory, the trail headed off westwards from the square over a bridge towards a cluster of houses and then zigzagged up the mountain to an altitude of some 350m where the spaces between the contour lines indicated a gentler saddle on the ridge. Here, a series of black dots revealed the presence of a mountain hamlet called Ameztia, scattered with farmsteads and barns, that I had yet to see. On entering the hamlet, the route appeared to lead up the ridge, climbing a further 300m before dipping northwards towards the village of Zubieta back on the valley floor. I smiled, noting that the mountain was peppered with strange toponyms which implied that it was well loved and had been frequented for a very long time.

Folding away my map, I clipped back my hair and headed west, drinking from a small fountain along the way, where someone had been thoughtful enough to leave a pink water glass for thirsty passers-by. From the fountain, I headed up into the woods and towards the ridge where a sheep dip and a metal crucifix offered the first signs of habitation.

A little further on, I noticed the small, hunched silhouette of a person lumbering up the track ahead of me. As I approached, I saw that the figure belonged to an elderly lady, bent double, swaying painfully from side to side on two crutches as she edged her way step by step up the hill. Evidently unaccustomed to finding strangers on the track, she was surprised to see me, and we struck up a conversation. A gentle, charming soul with bright eyes, she spoke surprisingly good Spanish for the Basque farmers of the area as she explained to me that she lived at the farm at the end of the path and was just recovering from a hip operation. In turn, I told her that I was an English guide, trying to locate the path which climbed up over the back of the ridge. I resisted the temptation to reach for my map as I knew it would be futile; a map being as meaningless to her mountain life as a cookery book in her kitchen.

We climbed up the track together towards the hamlet of Ameztia and as we reached the saddle a hidden paradise of immaculate green fields and farms stole my breath away. How could anyone have suspected these infinite mysteries simply from a change in the contours and a scattering of dots on a map?

Hilaria's farmstead, for that was her name, included a collection of barns and an impressive vegetable patch. The large traditional farmhouse was surrounded by a flower garden which was evidently her pride and joy, and on the oak lintel above the door the name 'Zubialdeko Borda' was carved in naïve, childlike letters. Here she lived with her son, his wife and her two grandchildren. She offered me a glass of water from an outside tap and then took me over to the corner of a field where she pointed out a faded yellow-and-white mark on a stone wall.

'That's the way to Zubieta,' she said, indicating a wide track that ran along the ridge. 'And watch out for the right turn before the antenna.'

I admired her flowers for a while and then kissed her farewell before heading on my way, savouring the brief exchanges of this serendipitous encounter. Smiling to myself, I romanticised about visiting her again one day with my guests and pausing to talk and appreciate her flowers. Simple encounters with the local people added charm to every walk. If my entrance to the hamlet had not been blessed by the crucifix on the wall, it certainly had been by my meeting with Hilaria.

But this was just one of several surprises in store for me that day. As I climbed the ridge road, I was astonished by the sudden view of a whole new valley to the south, another valley that I never knew existed. I wrenched the map from my bag to have a better look. *How could this be? How could I have overlooked this valley too?* The view was breathtaking. Unfolding in front of me was an immense open valley, far wider than the valley of the Ezkurra River that I had driven through earlier that morning. This valley was formed by a cascade of rippling hills and verdant pastures, which slowly gained in height and culminated in undulating wooded crest tops, reminding me of a waterfall over soft limestone rocks or the flowing drapes of a Roman toga. And there, just off-centre, in the eye of the golden ratio – creating a composition of scientifically proven perfection – sat a tiny nut-cluster of medieval houses. The sudden apparition of this spectacular new valley with its one picture-perfect village nestling at its heart seared its imprint on my soul so profoundly that days afterwards I could still recall the view in the greatest detail.

Unfortunately, distracted by the views, I had forgotten Hilaria's advice and turned off the ridge too early. Ending up back by the river in Ituren, not far from the car, I decided to drive to Zubieta instead of walking. As I travelled further upstream, the mountain slopes narrowed in, quick to cast their shadows over the valley floor and then, just before the impressive double-arched bridge from which the village of Zubieta takes its name, I found the watermill.

Parking Fred up against the mill chase, I skipped down the stone steps that led to the door, noting that one of them was formed from an old sandstone mill wheel, evidence that recycling was a simple fact of life in the seventeenth century. A damp, fusty smell with a hint of vanilla greeted me as I poked my head around the door, noting the immediate temperature drop in the mill's dark and cavernous interior. Seeing no one, I pushed the top of the stable door which, creaking open on old rusty hinges, tugged on a rope that rang a sheep's bell shrilly into the void. And thus my entrance into this new world was announced.

A tall man appeared out of the twilight of the mill's gloomy interior. He wore a white T-shirt with ivory-coloured jeans and his pale, bluish-white skin gave the impression that he rarely emerged into the sunlight. This picture of whiteness was broken only by a head of coarse black hair which bore streaks of creamy-coloured cornflour, bringing the image of a badger to mind. It occurred to me that I had never seen so many shades of white on the same person at the same time. Like a spectre, he moved towards me out of the darkness, as if he had long awaited my arrival, immediately launching into a tirade of nervous banter and gesticulating to various parts of the mill before leading me outside and introducing me to his kiwi trees and Bibi, the resident ostrich.

In later years, I came to realise that he had, quite possibly, been expecting my arrival. Almost a year before, when my first language course had been featured on Spanish TV, a print journalist had also taken up my story, publishing an article – and photos – in a local Basque newspaper. For reasons that I will never fully understand, the miller had torn out the article, fastening my picture into the frame of his bedroom mirror. Whether it was destiny calling, or the prophecies of the newspaper horoscope columns that he pored over every morning, I had the feeling that he had predicted my arrival at the mill that very day.

Despite the interesting characters and spectacular scenery that I had encountered during my walk, the fact that I hadn't been able to nail down a good circular route for my clients meant that I had little reason to return to that pretty mountain hamlet of Ameztia, or the villages of Ituren and Zubieta in the valley. But life had it otherwise. Little did I know that that day had offered me an uncanny preview of the rest of my life.

Within a few years my daughter's Paddington Bear T-shirts were fluttering in the breeze from the washing line in Hilaria's flower garden and the fabulous views of the southern valley, with the bijou village of Urrotz, provided the backdrop to dozens of dinner parties. What is more, in a certain light and at a certain angle, the miller's ivory-white skin and long nose could be discerned on my daughter's face. That walk had linked the family that was to adopt me, the hamlet of Ameztia in Ituren where I was to build my home, and the man who was to father my child.

PART 3

MY BASQUE MOUNTAIN

A HOUSE WITH A VIEW

THE TURTLE ON THE TAP

The Malerreka Valley, 2001

The real estate agent from Elizondo called almost a year after I had first stumbled upon the hamlet of Ameztia. Having scraped together just enough money for the smallest deposit on the cheapest apartment the Baztan Valley could offer, I hadn't given him an easy task, and his efforts were never going to be highly rewarded. I felt vaguely guilty; just when he thought that he had found me the ideal apartment and was looking admiringly at a new kitchen counter or some expensive light fittings, he would spy my disappointed expression gazing out of a window.

It wasn't as if the views weren't good. Compared to the monotonous, listless horizons of Denmark or Birmingham, everywhere in the Baztan area was a scenic delight, but something always seemed to mar its perfection: an electricity pylon, an industrial sawmill or simply the side wall of a neighbouring apartment block. Of course, I had been spoiled for choice. Having spent the past couple of years renting beautiful mountain farmhouses like Casa Tristantenea, perched high above the villages with their sublime and unadulterated views, these modern rabbit hutches simply couldn't compare.

He remained patient and unfazed.

'*Hola*,' I answered after the five-second delay that my brain always needed to register the nationality of the call and calculate the language of the reply.

'*Kaixo Jorjina. Zer moduz?*' ('Hello Georgina. How are you?') 'I have something new that I think you might be interested in.'

'Great, where is it then?'

'Well, firstly, it's not exactly in the Baztan Valley, but… ' His words faded into the distance as my heart sank and my inner voice took over. Surely if I were about to invest all my savings in a base in the area, it simply had to be in my beloved Baztan Valley? That was the whole idea.

'But,' he persevered, 'it isn't far. It's just twenty minutes down the road from Elizondo.'

I waited on his words.

'And the price is right… only twelve million pesetas.'

That still didn't help.

'Oh, and there is one other thing, it's not really an apartment, it's a renovated *borda*… just for weekends really… or summer holidays… and, well, it doesn't exactly have a bathroom. Well, it does, but it's not in the house, it's… it's outside.'

Things weren't getting any better, but I was beginning to feel a little sorry for him. This wasn't the usual slick patter of a salesman trying to palm off a dud, and I started to wonder if he made any money out of his business at all. (It was only later that I found out that he was one of the wealthier men in town.)

'But there is one thing,' he persisted.

'Uhuh?'

'The views.' And with that, I heard a shuffling of papers before he continued. 'Look, it states on the form… yes, here, that the views are "*inmejorable*". That's the word, *inmejorable* (unbeatable).'

Three hours later I sat in the passenger seat of his 4WD Toyota as we sped south along the banks of the Baztan River and out of the valley. On my lap was the information about Iaulin Borda and a photo of a square, stone building with the small poky windows characteristic of all mountain barns in the area. But halfway down the page on the right-hand side was a box entitled *vistas* and next to it the assessor had written just one word: '*inmejorable*'. It wasn't one of those usual, generic terms such as 'bad', 'average', 'good' or even 'excellent', and I fancied that there had been something personal in the choice of words, as if the clerk had been briefly shaken from his run-of-the-mill tasks and had become truly inspired.

Within twenty minutes I recognised the barcodes of light through the willow trees by the stream and recalled the walk I had made that previous year from Ituren when I had met the elderly grandmother on crutches and the eccentric miller from Zubieta. This time, instead of parking by the *pelota* court in Ituren plaza, as I had done then, we turned left and continued over a bridge and up an extraordinarily winding and rough mountain road into the wilds. Although I had been heartened by this one-word description of the views and was possibly prepared to make some concession for the distance of the *borda* from Elizondo, by the time we had swung around the eighth or ninth hairpin bend without any sign of civilisation, I had given up on the idea of buying a home in such an isolated area. So I simply decided to sit back and enjoy the ride.

Eventually, reaching the ridge where the road flattened slightly, a cluster of recycling bins announced human activity before the primary colours of the hamlet came into view. Here, bathed in lemony sunlight, lime-green fields soft as cats' ears saddled the ridge and red geraniums drooped from balconies beneath a powder-blue sky. If ever there were a candidate for a painting by numbers template, then this was it.

As we sped past the first farmstead, its miscellany of flowers in terracotta pots and recycled tubs caught my eye. Within metres, I recognised the path of the crucifix that joined the ridge road from the valley and the stone wall which bore the faded markings of that elusive walk a year earlier from Ituren to the mill in Zubieta. I swung round to scour the farmyard for signs of the grandmother, Hilaria, but the only signs of life were a row of tea towels on the clothes line, flapping in the breeze like a gaggle of geese.

Turning around to take another look at the road, the memories of my first visit to the hamlet flooded back with each detail of the ridge. At a sudden break in the trees, I was shaken once again by the view of that sublime southern valley with its tiny bijou village of Urrotz pinned centre stage on to the landscape.

As the daughter of a mechanical engineer, the scientist in me resisted such ideas, but I couldn't ignore the feeling that somehow destiny had intended this spot for me. Later that week, as I bent over the sales contract and signed my name above the notary's seal, I realised that my fate had also been sealed, already a full year before, on that serendipitous walk from Ituren to Ameztia. But exactly what my destiny had in store for me now, I had no idea, nor could I ever have imagined what was to come next.

❖ ❖ ❖ ❖

For the first time in my life I had a place that I could call my own and, as I changed gears on the steep mountain bends towards my new home, I was acutely aware of the heavy old house key in my pocket. The gear changes paralleled those of my own emotions as I swerved from fear to ecstasy and back, the bends jackknifing up the mountain, alternating between sublime views of the mountains and sheer drops to the valley floor. I was to soon learn that each of these bends had a name: the Woodpile Bend, the Holy Mary Bend, Maribi's Bend and the Goat Bend – previously known as *Ziñakolekukoerrekako Kurba* (literally 'The-Stream-That-Passes-The-Place-Where-We-Cross-Ourselves' Bend), referring to the crucifix on the path further upstream where I had first encountered Hilaria. Later, this name dropped out of use when a family of goats took up residence there and – even for the Basques – *Ahuntzaren Kurba* (Goat Bend) was easier to say.

As we passed Hilaria's house, Zubialdeko Borda (which everyone in Ameztia simply abbreviates to Zubialdea), I automatically sought her out in her flower garden but, unlike on countless days to come, she was not there and we did not stop, continuing on up the rise towards a small crossroads. Ameztia, with its roughly twenty inhabitants, is divided into the Ameztia 'before' the crossroads and the Ameztia 'beyond' the crossroads and I – once again – found myself heading into the 'beyond'.

Rumours had undoubtedly circulated that an English woman had bought Iaulin Borda, so although I was a curiosity, I was not a total surprise. But Fred was. Although few people in the area had ever met a British person, even fewer had seen a right-hand-drive car and Fred's movements soon provided a conspicuous marker of my whereabouts in the valley. Several years later he would be replaced by a left-hand-drive VW van which, for a while, with its Spanish number plates, would offer me a little more anonymity. Until, that is, my neighbours improvised its broken bumper with a conspicuous jerrycan and rivets and – once again – my trusted steed would become a topic of local curiosity.

After the crossroads we turned off the main Ameztia ridge road – which in later years would be known as 'the lovers' escape route' – and sidled off along a smaller road to the south of the mountain. Just beyond a line of walnut trees, we came to another smaller crossroads where a stocky man in a blue-and-white-check shirt was sharpening pickets with an axe. As I passed him, he swung round, pausing with undisguised curiosity, his axe in mid-swing, while Fred and I veered off along an even smaller, pot-holed track.

This was my first introduction to Luis, my closest neighbour, a bachelor shepherd living on the farm to the east of Iaulin Borda. His cries of '*tox, tox*' to the sheep echoing through the hills would become a constant of my life, together with the church bells from the village of Urrotz across the valley sounding the hour and the braying of the donkey in the fields below.

For the following twenty years, this junction would cause confusion. The natural inclination is to follow the wider track to the left, swinging down the back of a protruding spur towards Luis's family farmstead, Sunbilleneko Borda, where he lives with his brother Ignacio and sister-in-law, Sagrario. Taking a wrong turn at this point would be an error repeated by visitors, tradesmen and anti-terrorist squads alike, but one that none of us would seem particularly interested in correcting.

As far as most visitors are concerned, turning briefly down the wrong driveway offers them an immediate vignette of mountain life. Here they are greeted by a cacophony of farmyard activity, men tinkering with tractors, children playing football and barking dogs christening the wheel hubs of every new vehicle that passes by. This infrequent arrival of newcomers is generally well received, offering the Ameztiarrak (the people of Ameztia) an amusing distraction from their tasks and a glimpse of all my curious visitors, some of them – if my neighbours are lucky – arriving in sensational right-hand-drive cars.

However, the correct route to my home, Iaulin Borda, is counter-intuitive and ignores this wider turning down the spur to Sunbilleneko Borda (known simply as Sunbillenea to everyone in the hamlet). Struggling up to the right, the road to my house trundles along an unlikely, narrower lane and passes an old stone barn whose juxtaposition of windows and doors conjures up – or so I fancy – the image of an Australian marsupial. The Koala Bear Barn, as I call it, would soon become a landmark feature for family and friends, and a reference in driving directions and walking instructions alike. Of course, my Basque neighbours have absolutely no idea what we are talking about.

The road continues hugging the mountain on its right for about 200m, allowing only tantalising glimpses through a line of chestnut trees of the views to the south until, suddenly, the trees clear and a rough gravel farm track drops abruptly away to the left. Only a metre or so of the track is visible from the junction as it rises slightly, forming a lip, before dipping sharply downhill and bobbing quickly out of sight behind the hazel bushes. As a result of the track's duck-and-weave nature, it is only visitors with suicidal tendencies who dare pitch southwards down my drive as – ostensibly – the track cuts off in mid-air like a ski jump over the valley floor. This provides the perfect deterrent for unwanted guests – or most of them, at least. Even if today a carved wooden sign points to Iaulin Borda, it is a fickle friend, as it is a favourite scratching post for wild horses and often ends up pointing in totally the wrong direction. Therefore, all options considered, taking the wrong turn to my neighbour's farm is actually no bad thing at all. Here, visitors are greeted and vetted and – if approved – dispatched on their way with reassuring directions as to how to navigate the final 800m to my door.

But I had no idea what fate had in store for me and this tiny mountain barn, nor the answers to the myriad questions percolating through my mind. Between the exhilaration of buying my first home and the incredulity of having landed myself on an isolated mountaintop so far from civilisation, one familiar enemy stalked me. Fear. How could I, a person who so enjoyed the affection and company of others, learn to live in such isolation with just these famously insular Basque shepherds as company? Would they ever really accept me as one of their own? And even then, could I ever really belong?

As I pondered my future, I followed the gravel track down towards Iaulin Borda, flanked by a row of cherry trees to the south. After 100m, the track arrived at a small brook scored into the mountain, a running stitch of froth and sparkle as it hurried down a limestone gully towards the river below. Here the track turned ninety degrees to head southwards along a spur into an oak grove from where the red roofs of Luis's farm, Sunbillenea, could now be viewed across the valley on the eastern spur. Like two armrests of a high-backed mountain throne, the landscape offered the perfect setting for its Lilliputian queen, Iaulin Borda. Perched high above the morning mists, she reigns supreme over the southern valleys at her feet, protected from both the easterly and westerly winds by the spurs, and from the bitter north winds by the mountain slopes at her back.

I parked on the bend and, leaving the track, took a small, muddy path downhill, above the stream, to a squat shoebox-shaped barn of some fifteen square metres, with new terracotta roof tiles and a recently varnished stable door with an ornate iron lock. Just a few metres to its left lay the blackened metre-high outer walls of the former farmhouse which had crumbled into ruins decades before. Between these two structures lay a rusty swing gate that led down a couple of steps to a small patio where a miniature hibiscus tree took centre stage.

As I walked down the steps, overwhelmed by the spectacular view that unfolded, I gave little thought to the barn door on my right. I was far more interested in what lay outside my home than inside and for the next couple of years – especially at night – I would find myself taking a deep breath to gain the courage to push open the door and walk inside between its shadowy and spidery walls.

Thus, I hurried past the entrance to the southern terrace which extended out above the void like a small landing platform. Once again, my breath caught, my soul sighed and my heart leapt for joy as I beheld the amazing, other-worldly landscapes beyond. This priceless tableau was mine, all mine. It was the first time I had ever lived in the countryside, and as I contemplated the vast horizons surrounding me, the words of that elderly fortune teller from the Sydney shopping mall came back to haunt me once again: '… and I see a house… a big house, with lots of land around it. Yes, lots of land.'

Indisputably, the jewel in the crown of this tiny property was this terrace and its glorious views. It was the perfect launching pad for olive stones, hang-gliders, and dreams and – if a little care is taken in calculating the wind direction – one day my ashes will be joining them too.

Iaulin Borda lies on ten thousand square metres of land which extends below the barn rather like a bib. A wide swathe of immaculate green fields drops steeply below the house, bordered by a raggedy fringe of mixed woodlands and an overgrown orchard of apple trees. It would be years later that I would discover the remains of the moss-covered walls by the stream, hidden beneath banks of leaves and fallen trees, which would have once proudly defined the limits of the Iaulin Borda 'estate'.

At a corner of the terrace was a tap with a miniature bronze turtle perched on top. During my first few years here, my friends would refer to Iaulin Borda as *La Casa de la Tortuga* (The House of The Turtle, or Turtle House), attributing to this tiny reptile an importance that was entirely justified, given the activities she would preside over every night. But finally, Iaulin Borda would simply be known to everyone as 'The Borda'.

Snuggled up against the west wall of this small, rectangular building were a couple of two-square-metre outbuildings and a small porch with purple passion flowers climbing up the beams. One outbuilding was a storeroom, while the other was a bathroom with an impossibly small shower. This was a pretty room with a window looking out over the stream, and the decorative blue-and-gold tiles framing the mirror gave it a gay and bohemian air, unbefitting of the role it would play in my kidnapping charges several years later. The bathroom's one drawback was the sprinkling of fly carcasses that greeted me most mornings on the toilet roll, evidence that the *maître de cérémonie* (a large black spider hidden in the beams above) had feasted well the night before.

This was not an en suite, and any trip to the bathroom entailed leaving the barn and walking the entire length of the terrace to the outhouse on the far side. On summer evenings, these nightly forays to the water closet would take on an added dimension as one would be likely to trip over a coven of toads communing with the turtle on the tap.

The Borda had been lovingly converted into a summer cottage by a couple from Bilbao, the 60cm-thick stone walls having been carefully rendered and the original oak roof beams restored. Two small ventilation slots in the south-facing walls, testimony to The Borda's humble stable origins, were the only source of light into the downstairs room, the weak light barely illuminating the features within. There was a small camp kitchen in one corner where a white embroidered curtain lent a more frivolous touch to the austere interior. Drawn back, it revealed a pair of plates, a scattering of cutlery and a ceramic pan with a wobbly handle, left behind by the previous owners. Next to the wood burner, at the opposite end of the barn, was a bony bamboo sofa beside a handmade table cobbled together out of wooden slats where, over time, drifts of breadcrumbs had accumulated in its deep and irregular grooves.

In front of the door a steep, narrow staircase climbed from the kitchen up to the former hayloft, which had been converted into an open mezzanine bedroom, partitioned off for safety from the stairwell with wooden railings. Thanks to a couple of more modern windows, the attic space was brighter than the room below, offering perfectly framed views of the village of Urrotz on the other side of the valley, and it was here, beneath one of the windows, that Pyrenean Experience would establish its first headquarters. A large futon bed lay beneath the vault of eleven oak rafters which would be closely scrutinised for unwanted inhabitants and, on sleepless nights, counted and recounted by the light of the moon.

Into The Borda I brought my few eclectic chattels, scant testimony to my previous life and uncertain of their role in things to come. Along with Harry, my teddy bear, I unpacked the essential Earl Grey teabags and jar of Marmite, the Danish candleholders and the African mugs, and a turquoise hand-dyed bed-cover from Indonesia.

I carried these things with me to bring me comfort, of course. They were the miscellaneous vestiges of identities that I once had. But now – how, I could not say – I had wrenched myself free from my British and Scandinavian bonds to find myself a home on foreign soil. Such *foreign* soil. Delaying my entrance into my dark and shadowy home, on that very first day as a house owner, I absent-mindedly fingered the rusty iron letters nailed to the gate: IAULIN BORDA. How strange. This name would now be associated with me for the rest of my life and become almost synonymous with my own. This was it. This was my home. A fifteen-square-metre mountain barn in a shepherding hamlet of the Basque Pyrenees. What on earth had I got myself into now?

❖ ❖ ❖ ❖

Soon I learned that one of the most important features of any Basque house was its name, often derived from local landmarks or toponyms; consequently, most villages have their fair share of 'Next To The Church' or 'At The Top Of The Hill' or 'At The Bottom Of The Hill' houses. These names are then systematically applied to all the mountain farms and *bordas* owned by the village mother house. Given their very different settings, this gives rise to some charming incongruities. It is not unknown for the 'At The Bottom Of The Hill' barn to be found at the *top* of a hill, or the 'By The Side Of The Bridge' farmhouse (Zubialdea, for example) to be located

4km from the village bridge from which the mother house derives its name.

And yet my new home, Iaulin Borda, didn't fit the mould at all, its name deriving from the profession of its former owner rather than any toponymic characteristic. The name is thought to have come from 'Ehuleen Borda', meaning Weaver's Cottage, and refers to the weavers who had once lived in the house. Hilaria – universally referred to as Amatxi (simply meaning 'grandmother' in Basque) – still recalls the quality of the socks and blankets they once produced. But Iaulin Borda was now in the hands of someone with barely the skill to sew a button on a shirt and its once flourishing vegetable garden – reputedly the best in the hamlet – had also fallen from grace. My well-intentioned but novice attempts to restore it to fame have been continually thwarted by the slugs lying in wait in the fields below the house. And the cats.

According to Basque tradition, the corresponding 'mother house' in the village should have been called Iaulinenea (Weaver's House). But when I brought this up one day with Miguel, whose sisters had been the weavers, and who was in the process of purging a nest of grass snakes from the mother house in Ituren, I was told that it had a very different name altogether. Atypically, the name Iaulin Borda had simply started as a nickname that had stuck. Many years later, while I would be talking about this book with a friend in the shade of the trees by the stream, we would realise that although the mother house in the village and its mountain barn did not bear the same names, they did at least share the characteristic of the two-metre-long reptiles lurking within their garden walls.

❖ ❖ ❖ ❖

But on that very first day in Ameztia, as the light faded over the valley, it was not the subject of snakes that came first to mind. Turning my back on the terrace and its sublime views, I reluctantly pushed open the barn door and stepped into the dark, spartan space inside. Utterly despondent – and at a complete loss as to what to do – I clung to the habit of a lifetime, filling up the kettle with the spring water running from the taps. Making myself a cup of Earl Grey tea in my African mug, I sat down on the hard, rickety bench and stared at the grey stone walls. In a desperate attempt to introduce an element of Scandinavian *hygge* into this dismal situation, I lit a Danish candle on the table. But where once this candle would have offered cosy, intimate lighting to a group of friends, it now cast ugly shadows upon the walls where centipedes and spiders shuffled and stirred.

So, this was it. Home Sweet Home. The enormous scale of what I had done bore down on me and I was shocked by the extremities to which I had gone in order to wrench myself free from all that was comfortable and familiar. Was this really what I had been dreaming of: a dark stone barn in the anonymous hamlet of Ameztia on the outskirts of the equally anonymous Basque village of Ituren at the end of a road that doesn't even exist?

MY BASQUE VILLAGE

THE HELLO KITTY FOUNTAIN

Thanks to the imperfections of satellite navigation systems and internet mapping services, Ameztia really does lie – quite literally – at the end of a road that doesn't exist. Despite (or perhaps because of) its tiny population and obscure location, this is a hamlet with a huge heart, full of community spirit, presenting a unique insight into farming life in the Basque Pyrenees. Soon I would come to know its landscapes, its derelict barns, secret springs and smuggling trails better than any other place on the planet.

Ituren, the village on whose jurisdiction we all depend – in theory, if not in practice – lies 4km and ten hairpin bends below us on the valley floor. With its five hundred or so inhabitants, it is a traditional Basque village, crouching in the shadows of Mendaur, a 1,100m mountain in the Basque Pyrenees. Situated just half an hour's drive from the French-Spanish border, this is perfect hideaway territory. When the locals desire more urbane entertainment, they spruce up, polish their shoes and drive off through river valleys and tunnels to the more sophisticated towns of Pamplona or San Sebastián, accessible within the hour.

Downtown Ituren refers to a kernel of large stone houses straddling the valley road. Just like the neighbouring village of Zubieta, with whom its relationship is somewhat strained at times, the village is a perfect example of Basque architecture and town planning. One of the main characteristics of Basque houses, differentiating them from the Alpine chalets to which they are often likened, is the distinctive sandstone features that frame the doors and windows. Because most façades are whitewashed these days, the striking markings around the windows stand out, giving the houses a rather startled panda-like appearance which is utterly endearing. Basque houses (like the people themselves) are also renowned for their independent streak. Houses rarely share a common wall, even though these immense buildings may lie a mere 50cm apart, creating a series of narrow, dark and virtually useless chasms between one house and the next. These jealously guarded and independent properties extend their terrain to the very tip of the eaves, keeping local lawyers busy solving petty wrangles between residents whenever modern balconies are extended too far, or cars parked beneath neighbouring gutters.

The obsession for fiercely protecting even the outermost centimetres of a property may, however, have its origins in something more spiritual. In the olden days, the unbaptised bodies of deceased newborns – refused access to hallowed church grounds during the first weeks of life – were buried underneath the eaves of the family house. Even for healthy babies, the church imposed all sorts of restrictions on mother and child. Not only was the infant banned from entering the church during its first forty days of life – which may be why many baptismal fonts are found on the outside walls – but the mother was subject to 'quarantine' too. For those first six weeks after her child was born, whether pigs had to be fed or black beans planted, the church forbade the mother from straying out from beneath 'the roof of her house'. Naturally, the Basques' pragmatic instinct for survival found ways of getting around this and, taking the saying literally, young mothers would be spied in their vegetable gardens with a terracotta roof tile firmly tied to the top of their heads.

As in most Basque villages, Ituren's main square is the centre of village life, offering a stage for everything from village fiestas to the itinerant vehicle inspection units which set up shop once a month to service the tractors from neighbouring farms. During sunny afternoons, it fills with children playing *pelota* while mothers wave Nutella sandwiches at runaway infants on tiny bikes. On the east side of the square three impressive stone arches announce the entrance to a large eighteenth-century building. The ground floor of this one-size-fits-all construction houses the *ostatu* (village bar), while two floors above lies the *Pulunpa Eskola* (literally the 'Ding Dong School'). Between the bawdiness of the adults below and the shrill excitement of the children above, the mayor of Ituren tries to keep a sober eye on village affairs from the town hall on the first floor. The attic, on the fourth floor, is a large open space with high ceilings and huge oak rafters. It doubles as the school gym and village party hall, and during festivities rings with the sound of the bells that give the school its name.

The municipality of Ituren also incorporates three smaller satellite hamlets, Latsaga, Aurtitz and Ameztia, each one equally proud of its separate identity but bullied – on occasion – into conformity by the routines of the Ding Dong School, the uproar of the winter carnival and *auzolan*. *Auzolan* is an ancient system of community work organised by Ituren town hall, offering locals the chance to pay their village taxes through several days of hard graft on the land. After a frozen morning of pruning hazel bushes, clearing ditches and plugging pot-holes, residents from all Ituren neighbourhoods gather around the back of a trailer. And it is here, knocking back the cider and tearing ravenously into greasy bacon baguettes, that a true sense of communal identity can be found.

Nevertheless, insurgent influences lie in wait. The largest and westernmost of Ituren's hamlets, Aurtitz, lies furthest upstream between Ituren centre and the reputedly lawless, so-termed 'gypsy' village of Zubieta. It appears that Zubieta's rebellious spirit has drifted downstream with the waters of the Ezkurra River, as Aurtitz is now rooting for all-out independence – not an unfamiliar theme in the Basque Country. Latsaga is the closest of Ituren's satellite hamlets, lying just 500m upstream from the square on the other side of the river and the infamous Ituren bridge. In recent years, the exact measurements of this bridge have been threatened by civil engineers from Pamplona and, given that these dimensions are a life-or-death issue for the farmers' trucks that cross it daily, the heated stir that it caused among the inhabitants of Latsaga and Ameztia was entirely justified. Evidently, this did little to improve relations between the Basque villages in the north of Navarre and their capital over the mountains to the south.

The cluster of houses in Latsaga congregate around a small square and the 'Hello Kitty' fountain – or so I call it, because the glass that once lay at its side was stamped with the 'Hello Kitty' logo and a picture of a kitten in her trademark pink bow. Due to the presence among them of three important Ituren personalities, the people from Latsaga are well respected: José Mari, one of the leaders of the Joaldunak, the infamous protagonists of the pagan village carnivals; Juanito, a logger with the biggest tractor in town; and our beloved Maika, the Basque female champion anvil-lifter and wood chopper. I suspect that the girly Hello Kitty glass was originally hers.

And then there is our tiny mountain hamlet of Ameztia, with a total of twenty or so shepherds and their children, where I have now finally made my home. Darling, beautiful Ameztia. Ameztia is the smallest and most distant hamlet from the centre of Ituren, completely hidden from view. It was first populated after the arrival of maize from Latin America in the seventeenth and eighteenth centuries when corn replaced wheat, its less productive cousin, in the local diet. As a consequence, the population expanded and superfluous siblings, on reaching adulthood, were packed off to fend for themselves. Some emigrated overseas, others joined the clergy, while the least adventurous simply sidestepped up the mountain slopes to inhabit the small shepherds' *bordas* that satellite the villages. By the nineteenth century, Ameztia had come to life, and many of the *bordas*, owned individually by the various households in the village, changed from highland summer barns into bustling year-round farms.

Due to both its history and geography the inhabitants of Ameztia are regarded as Ituren's country bumpkins and are often the last to be consulted on village affairs. Most of the time they like it this way, as it also means that they can keep their secrets to themselves, but heaven help anybody who messes with their bridge or their road. This road – *our* road, with its ten hairpin bends – is sacred. It is our umbilical cord to the outside world and any changes made to it are treated with utmost solemnity. Yes, it is *our* road now and, as a sense of possession wells within me, I realise that I have become just another Ameztiarra (a person from Ameztia). Well almost, but not quite.

I have been called many names over the years: *Gina, Jorjina, Iaulin bordakoa, Jordi, La Hippie Inglesa, La Rubia* and more. I have been regarded as an object of amusement, affection and suspicion – and sometimes worse. Luckily, only years after I first moved here would I learn that a few of the more obtuse characters in the valley – observing the slow dribble of cash going into my home extensions – had spread the word that I was a 'woman of ill repute'. I suppose some people's limited imaginations never stretched to the idea that a 'blonde' English 'hippy' and single mother could earn her income by more innovative means.

A BASQUE BABY

A FAIRY GODMOTHER WITH AN AXE

Despite presumptions and aspersions, my real private life came into the public eye within a year of arriving in Ameztia after a group of British mathematicians and astronomers asked me to find them a Basque language teacher. Only then did I remember the idiosyncratic miller from Zubieta and recall his mentioning that he was a Basque teacher too. The language course we improvised for my clients was a success, and Fermin proved to be a lively and inspiring teacher with an infectious passion for his culture, entertaining us with theatrical caricatures of Basque mountain life with all the colour and verve of a Gauguin painting.

Arachnophobia and a fear of being alone were not the best reasons for turning a professional relationship into a romantic one but, sugar-coated by donkey rides into the sunset and enchanting stories of runaway ostriches and seductive *lamiak* – those golden-haired nymphs of rock pools and rivers – they proved good enough. Fermin's wonderfully burlesque storytelling and detailed knowledge of Basque mountain life had far-reaching influences on my work and can undoubtedly be found in certain anecdotes in this book.

In the autumn of 2002, we started an unhappy and tumultuous relationship. His upbringing in an insular Basque mountain village, coupled with a religious education in a seminary in Pamplona, clashed inevitably with my international background and independent nature. At first, I attributed many of our misunderstandings to my inadequate grasp of the Spanish language, hoping that as it improved, we would find easier tools with which to resolve our differences. Sadly, the opposite proved to be the case. As my Spanish slowly gained ground, it simply served to illuminate the unavoidable chasms between our vastly different lives.

Spoken by a native speaker, Spanish is a lively, rambunctious language full of pithy expressions highlighting the idiosyncrasies of the human condition. Unlike the British escape to euphemism, the Spanish language goes to the crux of the matter with all too frequent references to the testicle (*cojón*). A person who is said to have two balls (*tiene dos cojones*) is understood to have great valour and courage. Even possessing just a single, solitary *cojón* seems little handicap, as in the expression 'to be worth a *cojón*' (*vale un cojón*) which is still used to denote something of inordinate value. Illogically, however, it is with the arrival of the third testicle that the plight of the poor *cojón* takes a turn for the worse. Rather like the rotten apple in the barrel, it seems that the moment there are three balls, they are all worryingly devalued as in the expression '*me importa tres cojones*' (it means three balls to me) which literally means 'I simply couldn't care less'.

All my life, my love affair with languages had been a vital motivating force but while Spanish was a fun companion, it was never a natural fit. This was the first time that my romance with a foreign language had started to wane. Compelled to straitjacket the full repertoire of my emotions into a few childish adjectives or squeeze my unorthodox thoughts into a matchbox of ill-chosen words, I missed more than ever the opportunities to express myself in my native tongue. How short-sighted had I been to think that the only way to truly embrace new and exotic worlds was by wrenching myself free from my own British roots? Had I simply set myself adrift into a shoreless seascape? Anchorless, would I ever be able to express myself fully in a foreign vernacular or blend seamlessly into a different culture and way of life? How much of my own personality – and identity – lay exclusively within the grasp of my mother tongue?

❖ ❖ ❖ ❖

Despite such existential dilemmas and linguistic shortcomings, I slowly began to make my own circle of local friends and mix with an eclectic group made up mostly of artists and teachers. Many of these new friends originated from the bigger Basque cities and had moved to my area for a more peaceful and sustainable lifestyle. Like myself, they too had fallen in love with these Basque homelands and had moved into the pretty mountain *bordas*, spending their lives – and livelihoods – doing them up. Among these characters is Aitor, one of the most charming men I have ever met, combining – like many people here – a disarming array of disparate qualities. His number is my emergency number and, regardless of whether I call him during Saturday morning *aperitivos* or Sunday afternoon siestas, his calm reply is unwavering.

'*Egunon, Gina, ¿qué pasa?*' ('Morning, Gina, what's the matter?') he asks in an amused tone, with more than a touch of *and what scrape have you got yourself into this time?* And then he jumps gallantly into his van and is on his way. At the sound of his wheels on the gravel drive, I skip off to clip my hair up high and go in search of long industrial rubber gloves and a pair of wellington boots.

Aitor is a plumber with a degree in Basque linguistics, born in Oiartzun, a small town on the outskirts of San Sebastián.

Apart from facilitating the smooth flow of The Borda's drainage systems, he also facilitated a meeting with Paco, the elderly owner of Sarobe (code name *Xagu* [mouse]), a large farmhouse hidden high in the hills to the east of the town of Oiartzun and just 11km from the Spanish-French border. This is an important fact, given the farm's history as a safe house during World War II and Paco's role as an eight-year-old child helping his family to shelter Allied pilots, soldiers and members of the Comet Line who had escaped from Nazi-occupied France. There is more of this story later. Serendipitously, Aitor bought and renovated a *borda* in Ameztia – his drystone walls the envy of every passer-by – and he now spends much of his time with his girlfriend just 1km from my house. He is a benchmark of all that is honourable about the Basques and our friendship has become an important constant in my life, accompanied by delightful forays into Basque etymology and the incongruously malodorous smells of septic tanks. We share many interests, not only a love of linguistics but also an interest in maths and science and – thanks to his patient instruction and diagrams drawn with sticks in the mud – I now share his interest in plumbing.

Such friends formed the bedrock of my new life together with my delightful neighbours, the Ameztiarrak, hailing from the two principal farms of Zubialdea and Sunbillenea. The Zubialdea farmstead consisted of Amatxi (Hilaria, the grandmother of Ameztia) and her husband, Atautxi (grandfather), Isidro (their son) and his wife, Lourdes, while hailing from the Sunbillenea farmstead on the spur were Sagrario, her husband, Ignacio, and his younger brother, Luis. And, of course, my dear friend Maika, the Basque female lumberjack champion who has become my fairy godmother over the years – perhaps one of the only fairy godmothers in history to lay down her wand and wield an axe.

❖ ❖ ❖ ❖

No magic wand (or axe) could have conjured up anything more earth-shattering than the revelation, in 2003, that I was pregnant, which came as a total shock to both Fermin and me. At what should ideally have been a moment of shared joy and unity, I had never felt so lonely and wretched in my life. I was thirty-eight years old, living in a foreign country in an isolated mountain barn without even an indoor toilet to my name. Yes, I had struck out for my dreams and had gone some way towards achieving them, it was a great story to tell – perhaps even to write down one day – but the reality was not half so glamorous. Dependent solely on the paltry and unpredictable income of my fledgling company, I was also floundering in a deeply unhappy relationship. The thought of bringing a fragile being into such an insecure existence and whisking it away in my own racing chariot of emotions – the reins biting ever deeper into my flesh – seemed nothing short of insanity. Maybe, just maybe, this baby inside me was simply not meant to be. My mind, so accustomed to the pursuit of alternative solutions, of ducking under barriers and sidestepping obstacles, careened ahead in panic. Maybe there was still time? How many weeks was it now? Six? Perhaps more? Or… I counted again… perhaps less?

But this other being had crawled into my womb and was clawing at my blood and tissue with equal tenacity. This little creature, not yet born, combined my tempestuous genes with those of her deeply rooted Basque forefathers, and she wasn't giving up without a fight. Whatever doubts I may have entertained about my ability to adapt to this strange new culture, I now had no choice. My blood – my life – was, from this moment on, inextricably and eternally linked with theirs.

Predictably, my waters broke in a toilet cubicle in a large builders' merchants in Pamplona, where my traineeship in maternal practices was running alongside a rapid education in construction. In honour of this daunting new dimension to family life, I had decided to rebuild, opening a doorway in the southern wall of The Borda and encasing the terrace in a large glass conservatory to give inside access to the bathroom. My first years of motherhood were characterised by frequent visits to the building supplies store, and my Spanish vocabulary for items such as 'skirting boards', 'drainpipes' and 'grouting' expanded in tandem with the words for 'teething problems', 'high chairs' and 'nappy rash'.

It was on 15 May 2004 that Marion finally clawed her way out into daylight. I looked down at her in sheer incredulity. With her translucent, almost blueish-white skin and tight cap of matt black hair she looked utterly and completely Basque. I was in shock. She looked so foreign, so alien, just like her father and absolutely nothing at all like me. Where was that incredible bond that everyone talked about? It was only when the light caught her hair at a particular angle that I detected a possible hint of red; the sole evidence that I may have been part of the equation at all. As I gingerly cupped her head in my hands, flecked in paint and varnish from the latest renovations to The Borda, I gazed at the thin, wrinkled face in disbelief. I was terrified. Terrified by the unfathomable responsibility of being a mother, which further complicated the unfathomable responsibility of being me.

Two days later I waddled out of the Virgen del Camino hospital in Pamplona and Fermin drove us back to Ituren through the tunnels of Belate, retracing the first journey I had taken alone with Fred some five years previously. Marion arrived home to inhale the fumes of the freshly painted *borda* and to baptise the first of what would one day be several *indoor* toilets. During those summer months, our unhappy threesome staggered on, our conflicts cowering behind the new routines Marion dictated. But inexorably, as the shadows grew longer on the ground, my relationship with Fermin ground to a halt.

The moment is still clear in my mind. Marion was about five months old and we were having breakfast in the kitchen of The Borda when I looked over in her direction to see her wrestling with one of her strange, lopsided smiles. She looked me straight in the eye as if to say *'come on, Mummy, give me a hand here, do your bit, Mummy,'* in her characteristically bossy manner, and I desperately tried to smile back. But it was in vain. We sat there, both of us transfixed, waiting for something to happen but nothing did. My face incapable of smiling, my mouth as contorted as her own. Overwhelmed, I came to the only conclusion possible. Drowning in the quagmire of my own unhappiness, I did not have the life force to smile at my child.

So, there and then, I took the decision that I had long been contemplating. As her father made his way up the drive and back to his home in Zubieta for the last time that year, I swept Marion into my arms and climbed the attic stairs. Crawling under the bedclothes I clasped her to my breasts and nuzzled her fragile form, chanting again and again, 'We can do it, baby, we can, we can, we can do it,' as I sobbed into her silky hair, breathing in the subtle notes of woodsmoke and milk as if they were magic talismans against the spiders in the walls, fairy-tale potions able to spirit away my fear of being alone.

MY NEIGHBOURS

THE WELLINGTON BOOT IN THE SNOW

Despite my worries about being a single mum with an infant in a foreign land, I soon realised that living in Ameztia without a partner actually played to my advantage, my neighbours rallying round me far more when there was no male in sight. As the years went by it became clear that on the occasions when there happened to be a man in my orbit my neighbours would stand back out of respect, allowing him to take charge of his so-called – and utterly contestable – 'man of the house' duties. As a consequence – and somewhat ironically – in those periods where I had a partner, tasks such as wood-stacking, roofing or carpentry rarely got done, and I had no option but to challenge my clichéd gender stereotypes and incorporate these jobs into my 'woman of the house' repertoire.

Romance and practical men rarely seemed to go hand in hand in my life, with the possible exception of an electronics engineer from Lesaka whose identity was blown when a cherry tree fell across my drive early one Sunday morning, blocking his easily recognisable corporate vehicle from escape.

My normal routine was to dispatch him off over the rough ridge road to the antenna – known from then on as 'the lovers' escape route' – in an attempt to keep his identity concealed, something I have come to realise is nigh on impossible in Ameztia. However, finally – and inevitably – we had been caught out. Within an hour my neighbours, Isidro from the Zubialdea farmstead and Ignacio from Sunbillenea, had found out about the fallen tree and could be seen grinning between its branches, chainsaws in hand. Undoubtedly, they were both wondering exactly the same thing: *What electronic emergency had happened to Jordi La Inglesa that warranted calling out the repairman before dawn on a Sunday morning?*

Although the Ameztiarrak had accepted my separation from Marion's father just months after she was born, I had no idea how they would react to my having boyfriends in later years. Amatxi was a particular concern. She has become a true soulmate over time, but she is also extremely religious, praying for our welfare regularly, and ensuring us a safe return from our travels to the UK by leaving a candle burning on the kitchen counter. So, naturally, it was Amatxi I was most worried about offending.

I needn't have worried.

The cherry tree toppled by the previous night's storm had sealed my fate and everyone in Ameztia now knew that I was having a relationship with a man from Lesaka. And how they laugh about the episode to this day! Even Amatxi's eyes sparkle with the naughtiness of it all, discreetly giggling behind an arthritic hand. The Basque mountain shepherds – perhaps more than most – understand the need for human warmth on a cold and stormy night.

❖ ❖ ❖ ❖

On a night equally intemperate as that which toppled the cherry tree and dented my reputation, I was presented with an example of the all-seeing, all-knowing benevolence of the Ameztia community.

It was the middle of winter and Marion was just eighteen months old. During a brief lull in a snowstorm, we decided to head down the road to visit Amatxi and Atautxi at Zubialdea, ploughing fresh tracks through the virgin snow as the last rays of sunlight played hide-and-seek behind racing clouds. Marion was an awkward bundle in my arms, trussed up in her padded snowsuit with a large hood that flopped over her eyes, giving her the air of a miniature medieval monk – an image that was short-lived after one glance at her feet. From her right foot dangled one, just one, yellow wellington boot while her left foot swung limply, clad only in a sock.

We continued down the road between log piles and hazel bushes in the direction of Zubialdea, heading instinctively towards the smell of woodsmoke while Txiki barked our arrival to the family inside. Having stamped off the snow on the mat, I pushed open the front door, noting the silver thistle on the beam above. We glided through the entrance hall, past photos of men wearing lace petticoats and bells, and into the warmth of the kitchen beyond.

Several hours later, replete, we hugged our farewells and trudged back up the rise through the snow, accompanied by the lingering smells of *txistorra* (a local sausage). Arriving home always had the same effect on me; every time the dramatic views of the southern valleys came into view, my heart leapt in exhilaration and wonder. It was an instinctive, jack-in-the-box reaction that would play out every time I arrived at the top of my drive.

But that night, something different caught my eye. A strange object had been hung upside down on the sign to Iaulin Borda and, as I got closer, I realised that it was Marion's other yellow wellington boot. Suddenly, I had a flashback to another snowy day, years ago, at that busy pedestrian crossing in Hans Knudsen's Plads in Copenhagen. Despite the crowds of commuters, no one had stopped to help the man in the wheelchair cross the road, nor thought to retrieve his fallen rucksack from the ruts in the snow.

What a starkly different world I lived in now. On this immense wild mountaintop with its few scattered farms, this tiny community never failed to watch over me. Some passing shepherd had found Marion's boot in a snowdrift on his way back from the fields and left it at the top of my drive, considerately turning it upside down so that it wouldn't fill with snow. In years to follow, the shepherds of Ameztia would retrieve hair clasps and pencils from the bracken and gorse and return them to Iaulin Borda – but they never found that miniature bottle of perfume in the oak grove on the spur. More later about that.

❖ ❖ ❖ ❖

Amatxi – Hilaria – is the cherished matriarch of this sparse but surprisingly close-knit community. One of nine brothers and sisters, she was born in 1927 on the Day of the Virgin Mary, 15 August. As a child, during the winter months, she lived in the family town house, named Sotillenea, which stands on the high street of Ituren next door to the pharmacy. In late spring, the family would herd their sheep up the mountain to Ameztia, coming to live at the family mountain farm which lies upstream from my house and just above the oak wood on the spur. The call of the cuckoo from these woods would become one of Amatxi's most enduring childhood memories and although, at the age of twenty-three, she had moved down the ridge to live with Atautxi in Zubialdea, to this day we wheel her back up the rise into the oak woods to hear the cuckoo's call. Well into her nineties, she still has a sparkle of childish glee in her eyes at the sound of the cuckoo, just as she does when we arrive back from the fiestas in the valley and she spies a packet of deep-fried *churros* lashed in icing sugar in our hands. As in other places in Europe, popular belief has it that turning the money in your pocket at the sound of the cuckoo is a harbinger of good fortune, but Amatxi's private economy had little need to rely on superstition. Her role as Cupid in the Zubialdea pig stalls – for the farm was known just as much for its pigs as its sheep – was a much more reliable source of income.

Once the swineherds from the surrounding villages had herded their sows up the mountain to the Zubialdea farmstead, Amatxi would relieve them from their duties and take over as a sort of 'pre-coital midwife'. Ensuring that the sow was reclined comfortably, and the boar mentally prepared for the task ahead of him, she would help guide them both through the act. On their return, the swineherds would slip her a peseta or two in gratitude for her services and in anticipation of the litter of piglets that would keep the family in *txistorrak* (sausages) for winters to come.

When the Spanish Civil War broke out in 1936, Amatxi was just nine years old, and she still recalls uniformed soldiers passing through Ameztia crying '*¡Hola muchachas!*' (Hi girls!) as they passed by. Most likely, these were some of the first Spanish phrases she ever heard.

Amatxi shared a bed with three sisters and remembers how they woke up every morning with blackened faces, stained by soot from the paraffin lamps that had accompanied them up the stairs to bed the night before. After a quick wash, their mother prepared them milky 'coffee', made of chicory, into which they crumbled the dried remains of the previous night's corn *talos* (a flat chapati-style corn bread which formed a staple part of the farmers' diet). For their school lunches, their mother filled a glass jar with black bean or lentil stew and the occasional wedge of sheep's cheese. Meat was only ever eaten on special occasions.

Gazing at me with great solemnity and purpose, Amatxi would inform me that during her childhood in Sotillenea there was just one pig to feed the entire family for a year. She would hold my gaze that little bit longer as if to say: *Now think about that… and don't ever forget how lucky you are.*

Between the ages of nine and fourteen, Amatxi attended the village school in Ituren. For all the children in Ameztia, school attendance was an erratic affair, only occurring when the weather – and farm work – allowed. So, on many days, much like the majority of children in Ameztia, she stayed at home to milk the sheep or help her mother with the household tasks. In her few moments of free time, she and her siblings played a game of 'sheep's knuckles', akin to the modern game of jacks. This involved throwing a stone in the air and seeing how many knuckles could be turned over before it landed. I recall the spark in her eyes as she suddenly remembered that she had painted her own personal set of 'knuckles' red – a memory she had probably not revisited for almost eighty years.

When she did go to school, she was a bright and conscientious student and her teacher took her under her wing, giving her private lessons in writing, history and sewing. Even in her nineties, she still enjoys sewing, and can often be found on a bench in the yard patching up her great-grandchildren's clothes with a fancy sewing box at her side. This frilly sewing box was one of several gifts I brought Amatxi back from England and blends surprisingly well into the Zubialdea décor. It sits daintily on the kitchen windowsill, delicately framed by Amatxi's lace curtains, and makes an appearance every time the drapes twitch (which is usually every time a car passes up the road). However, another of my gifts, a stylish apron with a modern flower print – the type usually destined for suburban cupcake-making mothers (a skill that I envy greatly) – has not stood the test of time. I only ever witnessed Amatxi use it once, during the family *matanza* (pig-killing), splattering it with pig's blood as she made a local version of black pudding. Perhaps the apron was considered too frivolous for such a macabre and murderous moment – or simply too posh – but neither the apron (nor, of course, the pig) has been seen since.

❖ ❖ ❖ ❖

The *matanza* is one of the most important events in the rural calendar and it can take place any time after Saint Martin's Day (which falls on 11 November). According to Amatxi, it is vital that this ceremonial ritual be carried out on bright, cold winter's days and during a waning moon to ensure that the fatty bacon cuts release all their grease when fried. Families and friends gather round the courtyard as her son, Isidro – revered throughout the valley for his precision with a knife – slices through the pig's jugular. Farmyard flagstones and kitchen surfaces are awash with blood as the women prepare hams, pork cuts and blood puddings, saving the pig's feet and ears for winter stews. One of the most loved products of the *matanza* is the ubiquitous spicy Basque sausage, *txistorra*. Made by mincing the meat and mixing it with lard, salt, garlic and paprika, it is then stuffed into lambs' intestines with the help of a peculiar contraption with an impressively long snout.

Traditionally, at around 11 o'clock, in the heat of the battle, Amatxi would turn her attention to the liver. First, she would sweat a thick bed of finely chopped onions in olive oil before frying the liver quickly on high heat and serving it up for her husband, Atautxi. Customarily, liver is saved for the head of the household but when Atautxi died, as no one else in the family shared his penchant for liver, the honour was bestowed on me. Ever since, if I happen to pass the farm during the days of the *matanza*, I am steered into the kitchen and sat down between buckets of blood and mounds of gristle. Here, Amatxi proudly serves me a plate of slightly crisp, freshly fried liver and onions, indulging me in one of my all-time favourite dishes – one of several things I had in common with Atautxi.

❖ ❖ ❖ ❖

Manuel, the grandfather, affectionately known as Atautxi, was a larger-than-life (and at times controversial) character, born in Zubialdea in 1927. Apart from a passion for fried pig's liver, he loved people, dancing and airplane trails in the sky. At the age of eighteen he and Amatxi were betrothed, their engagement sealed with their first kiss, most probably during one of their Sunday afternoon walks along the shepherding paths of Ameztia. Five years later they were married.

On their wedding day, Atautxi, jingling thirteen pieces of silver in his hands, led a procession of guests towards the Sotillenea town house where Amatxi stood waiting in a black dress, her veil swept back off her face and a flower in her hand. While sounds of the accordion reverberated through the streets of Ituren, Amatxi followed the procession up the hill towards Ituren church where she and Atautxi were married. The following day, Atautxi whisked her off by train on a two-day honeymoon. They passed their first night together in Irun and the next in Pamplona before heading back to Ameztia where Amatxi moved in to live with him in Zubialdea. Although they were away for just two nights, in those days such a honeymoon would have been quite an extravagant undertaking for a Basque farmer, and a sure sign that Atautxi's inquisitive mind and love of adventure were already evident in his younger years.

When I moved to Ameztia, Atautxi and I would spend lazy summer afternoons sitting together on a bench in the yard, squeezed in between a pot of Amatxi's geraniums and a tattered box of tomatoes or courgettes – or whatever the vegetable patch had to offer that day. Here we would rattle on for hours, swatting flies and talking about the ways of his world and the uncertainties of mine. Atautxi's immediate and unconditional acceptance of me during my first years in Ameztia – and his love for Marion later on – offered a seal of approval that not only facilitated my integration among the Ameztiarrak of our hamlet but also among the five hundred or so more suburban Iturendarrak from the village of Ituren.

When the postwoman slipped on my driveway during my first year in Ameztia, Zubialdea became my postal depot. So whenever Atautxi saw my car climbing the hill, he would hurry into the house to fetch my letters, intrigued by the airmail stickers and foreign stamps.

Sadly, Atautxi died in 2012, but even today it is hard to pass by Zubialdea's front gate without thinking of him. He will be remembered with his dog Txiki at his side, a large Basque beret shading his eyes, and his imposing frame resting heavily on a hazel stick as he kept vigil over 'The Road That Doesn't Exist', greeting every passer-by.

Isidro combines his father Atautxi's innate curiosity with Amatxi's saintly patience. Had his hands not been too full of other tasks, he would have been the natural choice for village mayor – just as Atautxi had been years before I arrived. Together with his generous, hard-working wife, Lourdes, they spend virtually every waking hour labouring on the farm making hay, mending roofs and walls or tending to the sheep, cows, pigs, cats, dogs and chickens on their land.

Luckily, I cannot remember the exact number of animals on their farm as – according to Maika – I should never have been so rude as to ask them in the first place.

Maika, my axe-wielding, anvil-lifting, lumberjack-champion fairy godmother has always taken my cultural education to heart. Recently she was responsible for enlightening me as to yet another of my cultural faux pas, albeit several years too late. The conversation arose one cold October morning as I headed up to the ridgetops of Ameztia with a few guests who had joined me for a 'Basque Mountain Experience Walking Week'. Climbing out of the mist we came across a motorbike propped against a bracken stack and, sure enough, Maika was not far away, lunging at the ferns with a wooden scythe.

'*Kaixo Maika!*'

'*Kaixo. Ongi?*' She put down the scythe and nodded towards the snow-capped mountain of Mendaur to the north which appeared fleetingly between the clouds. 'With weather like this I suppose we will soon have to bring the sheep down,' she lamented.

'Yes, I know,' I agreed, changing from Basque into Spanish. 'The snows have started early this year,' I added, an old hand now on the subject of weather in Ameztia. And then, in an attempt to involve my guests in the thrills of conversation with a champion log-cutting, scythe-bearing shepherdess with a motorbike, I continued inanely, 'Maika, how many sheep do you have?'

'You mustn't ask people how many sheep they have – it's rude,' she retorted.

'Really?' I replied, taken aback, my reputation as a guide and 'Expert of All Things Basque' hitting a new low. 'Why ever not?'

'It's like asking someone how much money they have in the bank, you don't do that, do you?'

'Well no, but I'm sure that I've asked lots of people about their sheep – I've asked Isidro, Ignacio…'

'And what did they say?' she asked. And then, in an act of solidarity towards her fellow shepherds of Ameztia, she added quickly, before I could answer, 'Well they must have thought you were very rude, and they probably lied!'

I was momentarily taken aback – the Basques are notoriously more direct than the British – but our friendship had solid roots, harking back to the days when our daughters went together to the Pulunpa School in Ituren. I love Maika. We have had real fun together, playing truant during the Parents' Association meetings, bolting for the door at the first opportunity and scampering down the school stairs to the square like our own naughty children.

'So,' I ventured playfully, 'how many litres of milk do you get from your sheep?' She fixed me with her dark eyes and grinned before picking up the scythe to take another swipe at the ferns. Maika's mind is as sharp as the Australian steel on her prize axes.

Isidro – however many sheep he may or may not have – fulfils an intriguing assortment of roles in our community. Not only has his unwavering hand earned him the role of local butcher during the autumn *matanzas*, but he is also Ituren's Justice of the Peace, thanks to his equitable nature and innate sense of fairness. It is, however, his role as local gravedigger that provides the greatest source of anecdotes for after-dinner conversations.

His clean-shaven, handsome face breaks into an easy smile as he wipes his hands on his blue overalls and muses on how these various jobs allow him to supervise the entire sweep of life's natural processes; from the signing of birth certificates in Ituren's village hall to the shovelling of the final spadefuls of earth on people's graves.

His gravedigging talents benefit the populations of both Ituren and Zubieta, where his role is not only to bury the dead but also to free up space inside the tombs for any new arrivals, and he has advised me to suppress any sudden urges I may have to forage in the wheelie bins at the back of the church. Lowering his voice, Isidro confides to me that the bodies in Zubieta's graveyard actually smell worse than those in Ituren, a hint of the age-old Ituren-Zubieta rivalry twinkling in his eyes. Even so, despite the apparently sweeter-smelling corpses in the Ituren graveyard, I was later to learn that the stories behind their deaths were the more unsavoury of the two.

LOCAL HISTORY

TIN COWS AND TADPOLES

The church of San Martín, on the outskirts of Ituren, is located on a small hilltop amid a grove of old oak trees. While undoubtedly the most macabre events have taken place within its graveyard walls, the woods surrounding the church have hosted some rather colourful dramas too.

Although Atautxi and Amatxi showed many progressive traits for their age, they both strongly believed in witches. One of Amatxi's favourite stories was about the witches who lived in a limekiln near the church in Ituren. At that time limekilns were known popularly in Basque as *sorgin zuloak* (or 'witch holes') and, apparently, the one near the church was the witches' preferred birthing chamber. According to Amatxi, one day a pregnant witch hobbled down the hill to the village to ask the midwife for help, offering her two pieces of gold as thanks for her services on the condition that the midwife did not look over her shoulder on her way back home. Apparently, the witches made such a din, shouting and rattling pots and pans, that the temptation was too great for the poor midwife who – just before stepping over the threshold of her house – cast a quick glance behind her to see what was going on. As she turned back to enter her house – so the story goes – she noticed that one of the gold coins in her hand had miraculously disappeared.

I have heard Amatxi recount this story several times, new details surfacing with every rendition. Nevertheless, I have never failed to be impressed by the witches' generosity. While I am sure that they had the skills to spirit away both of the gold coins, it seems that they only ever stole back one, leaving the midwife compensated – albeit to a lesser degree – for her troubles. It appears that the fundamental Basque trait of fairness may apply to Basque witches too.

One of Atautxi's favourite witch stories also took place near the church. This time the tale was about a farmer from the hamlet of Latsaga who grazed his cows in a field on the other side of the river just beyond the graveyard. One night he woke up to the sound of cowbells below his window and, as each herd has its own set of bells with its distinctive ring, he immediately recognised the cows to be his own. Dressing hurriedly, he headed out towards the sound of the bells which led him over the bridge, across the river, and up into the woods beyond the church. Although he never quite caught sight of the cows in the darkness, he threw a stone in their direction in an attempt to shoo them back towards their fields. According to Atautxi, it was at this moment that the farmer heard a cry in the distance, '*tírame otra, tírame otra*' ('throw me another one, throw me another one'). For some reason that I have yet to understand – as the cry plainly came from a human and not a cow – he did exactly that, hurling a second stone into the darkness in the direction of the voice.

The following morning, a woman from a nearby village was found dead on the very same path near the church. Proof enough – according to Atautxi – that the sound of the cows was, in reality, the sound of a witch and confirming the truth of a popular saying that if you throw two stones at a witch, then someone will die. And I presume this not to mean the witch. Please excuse the rather hazy way I relate this tale; and understand that in addition to being slightly sceptical of its veracity, I am also vaguely perplexed by its logic. Nonetheless, true or not, it has entered into the folklore of our hamlet through its frequent and animated renditions in the Zubialdea household.

Although many such stories of witchcraft survive in local folklore, the witch hunts of the Spanish Inquisition have been far more formally documented and have played a considerably more significant role in local history. Oddly enough, it was a tiny, bucolic mountain village to the north of the Baztan Valley which became the epicentre of one of the more brutal witch hunts of them all.

Zugarramurdi seems a most unlikely setting for such dramatic events and in more recent years its location on the border with France has earned it a reputation for smuggling too. One bar snuggles up so closely to the border that while its front door glides open into France its back door simultaneously creaks open into Spain and, naturally, during Franco's era, this became a favourite watering hole for the smuggling fraternity. However, the name of the village will not go down in history for its smugglers – nor for 'the hill of elm trees' from which it derives its name – but for the blood-curdling witch hunts of the seventeenth century.

On 7 November 1610, the famous witch trials of Logroño took place. After fifteen months of torture, fifty-three people from Zugarramurdi were publicly tried for witchcraft, the trials being witnessed by some thirty thousand onlookers. The penitents were dragged through the streets, some with ropes already dangling from their necks, and led off to be flogged. Bringing up the rear, other prisoners were forced to carry effigies of those who had died in prison, their remains borne alongside in coffins destined for the fire. The four women and two men who had denied the accusations to the bitter end were, as one would expect, led off to be burnt at the stake.

From what I have read, a cumulation of events conspired against the Basques which condemned them to persecution. For a start, Picaud's eleventh-century tourist guide to the Camino de Santiago did little to enhance the image of the Basques to the outside world, and their reputation was in no way improved by their peculiar traditions and alien tongue. However, an unusual combination of other elements also contributed to their fate. Firstly, they had always made medicinal creams and remedies from the plants and fungi found in the area and this old pagan science, or 'magic', naturally found itself at loggerheads with the Church's exclusive faith in divine intervention. Secondly, there was the problem of women.

In the seventeenth century, many men went away for months at a time to work on the whaling boats based along the Basque coast. This meant that their villages were run predominantly by women, making them perfect scapegoats for misogynous zealots. If this wasn't enough, another more tenuous element – and one of the defining characteristics of the Basque people – was the very nature of their blood. Although it wasn't known then, the Basque Country has a very high proportion of people with rhesus negative blood, and this, until the advent of modern medicine, was responsible for a high level of infant mortality.

If the former reasons hadn't sealed the Basques' fate, this last morbid detail hammered the final nail into their coffin. For those who wanted to believe it, God had obviously cursed these people. Suffice to say that only a little leap of the imagination was necessary to presume that Basque Country villages were plagued by witches, and the Spanish Inquisition – hungry to set an example and root out infidels – needed very little encouragement.

With such a dramatic and painful history, it is little surprise that tales of witches still linger in current folklore. However, I have rarely heard of witches taking up residence in Ameztia. Almost all the stories – Amatxi's and Atautxi's included – seem to take place in the darker, damper villages along the valley floor. Ameztia seems blessed. It is on Ameztia that the sun first rises and it is here that it is last to set, and the inhabitants of both Zubialdea and Sunbillenea farmsteads seem positively saintly at times.

❖ ❖ ❖ ❖

The Sunbillenea farmhouse is located on the eastern spur just a five-minute walk from my home. It juts out into the full majesty of the mountains and, with the help of heavy stones along the roof ridge, braves the unfettered forces of the southern winds, welcomed with glee during the autumn hunting season.

Luis, his brother Ignacio and his brother's wife, Sagrario, are as warm-hearted and hard-working as their neighbours in Zubialdea and do me the service of grazing their sheep on my field for the rent of one lamb a year. Well, they did. When they proudly presented me with the whole freshly slaughtered lamb, pink and muscle-toned, eyes bulging, stripped just of its fleece and hooves, I waived the fee immediately. At that time, I had just a tiny camp kitchen and I made the excuse that I had neither a freezer to store it in, nor an oven to cook it in – concealing the underlying fact that I had never roasted a lamb in my life! A fact that, like most things in Ameztia, I could not conceal for long.

The Sunbillenea farmhouse still maintains its original design, with stairs leading up from the cowshed below to the living quarters above. The living area consists of an open-plan kitchen with a fireplace, four small bedrooms, and a bathroom with amazing – and strategically significant – views towards the western valleys (in general) and my house (in particular).

After the welcome from barking dogs and ruminating cows, guests arriving at the front door of Sunbillenea – accompanied by the inevitable stable smells – then climb the stairs to Sagrario's kitchen. Here rabbit stews bubble on the hearth and packets of my Earl Grey tea and coconut Bounty Bars – one of Ignacio's weaknesses – jostle for space in the pantry. A chipped Moroccan table mat that I also bought them years ago still holds its own on the kitchen table.

By necessity, the people of Ameztia are used to multitasking and the Monday morning hairdressing salon in Sunbillenea is a classic example. Several years ago, Sagrario and Ignacio's daughter, Amaia, who has the same luminous green eyes as her father, converted the old milking shed into a hair and beauty parlour where she works on her days off from her normal job in the nearby town of Elizondo. Every Monday morning (and especially during the waning moon) her tiny salon behind the cowshed fills with a stream of locals, and the farm becomes the social hub of Ameztia. Neighbours and relatives congregate to have their hair done and catch up on local gossip, tripping up to the kitchen to pay their regards to Sagrario before they leave.

As they head back down the stairs, unavoidably passing with freshly coiffed hair through pungent stables, Sagrario laughs at the farm's unfailing contribution to her daughter's business: the final faint whiff of '*kolonia euskaldun*' (Basque farmyard eau de cologne).

❖ ❖ ❖ ❖

Although today our lives share many common characteristics – all of us having cars, televisions and even English teabags – it is when I hear the stories of my neighbours' childhoods that I realise the true abyss of experience between us. Amatxi is about forty years older than I am, so it is easier to accept the radical differences in our lives, but Sagrario, Ignacio and Luis, give or take a few years, are of my generation.

Sagrario was born during the time of Franco's dictatorship and is Amatxi's niece – which explains her saintly genes. Just like Amatxi, she grew up in the same Sotillenea household, moving between Ituren and the family's mountain farm in Ameztia, just above the oak woods on the spur where the cuckoo lives. Only when she married Ignacio did she move to live in Ameztia permanently.

Her working life, however, started when she was just four years old and was given the responsibility of looking after her grandmother, keeping vigil by the old lady's chair at the fireside for hours on end while the family were out working in the fields. Reading between the lines, I think it possible that her grandmother may have had a form of Parkinson's disease because she would gradually tip forward in her wicker chair, needing to be righted quickly before toppling over into the fire. The job of keeping her grandmother upright, together with the task of putting more logs on the fire, were among Sagrario's first responsibilities and the beginnings of a lifetime of multitasking. She remembers that she had no toys and would pass hours with just a pair of scissors and a piece of paper, cutting it into tinier and tinier shapes until her parents returned.

During her parents' siesta, she and her sister would scamper off outdoors. In the spring, one of their favourite pastimes was to gather up the tadpoles from the streams and redistribute them between all the streams of the hamlet. As her family farm, Sotillenea, lies just upstream from Iaulin Borda, the rock pools in my stream became their favourite tadpoling haunt.

At other times, she and her sister would play make-believe cooking games in which chamomile flower heads represented miniature 'fried eggs' and dried brown leaves from the hazel bush were 'steaks'. Sometimes, when her parents were working in more distant fields in the hamlet, the two sisters would secretly open the trunk of 'best' clothes, strictly reserved for visits to the church or the doctor, and dress up their younger brothers. At the sound of voices in the yard, they would hurriedly undress the boys, slam the lid back down on the trunk and scurry back to the kitchen.

When Sagrario was seven she was sent away to work at her aunt's house in the nearby village of Oitz. For the next seven years, apart from special occasions such as Ituren village fiestas and carnival – unequivocally the most important annual event of our village – she would return home to her family only once a month. In the meantime, while her uncle worked as a driver of one of the few tractors in the area and her aunt served at a local inn, she took care of her younger cousins and looked after the cows. Only when there was time did she go to the village school, where she was reprimanded for speaking Basque, the only language she knew. Today, Sagrario, Ignacio and Luis all agree that virtually the only good that came from their school days was a basic understanding of *Castellano*, the national Spanish language.

Ignacio and Luis were born in Sunbillenea and, just like Sagrario, their lack of toys meant they had to improvise games with the various objects on the farm. Empty cans of tomato sauce were of prime value. Once they had been opened, by puncturing the top with a knife and rolling back the lid into a couple of metallic strips, the tin vaguely resembled a cow with horns. Then, left outside to rust in the rain, it increased in value as it slowly took on the reddish hue of a local breed of cattle. Using a twig as a yoke, the brothers would couple together two tin cows and drag them as quickly as they could along a tiny track carved out with the tip of a hoe. The winner was the 'cowherd' who succeeded in moving his tin-can cows furthest and fastest along the track without toppling them over.

Particularly harsh were the brothers' recollection of their school days and, although – in theory – school was compulsory between the ages of nine and fourteen, with so much work on the farm they could rarely attend more than five or six days a month. When they did go to school, their mornings started early. Extremely early. By the time they arrived at school, they had already milked the cows, led the donkey with the milk churns down the 4km path to the village, returned home to change clothes and walked back down to school where – tired and hungry – they were routinely beaten and humiliated for speaking Basque.

These were the Franco years and one of the General's main policies in this area was to eradicate the Basque culture and language, Euskara. If the schoolmaster in Ituren heard any of the children utter a word in Euskara, he would deal out a range of imaginative punishments. Ignacio recalls a particularly painful chastisement he received when he was caught whispering to his brother in Basque. He was called to the front of the class and made to kneel on grains of dried corn that bit deeply into his flesh. Outstretched arms, weighed down by a heavy Bible in each hand, added the final touch to one of the teacher's favourite retributions. If he was in a particularly vindictive mood, the teacher would prolong the torture so much that some children had no option other than to relieve themselves on the spot.

Nevertheless, it was a different Bible that Ignacio had in mind one frozen January morning, some twenty years later, as he found himself skidding through the streets of Ituren on his way to the Sotillenea town house. Here, in the same doorway where Amatxi had waited for Atautxi in her black wedding dress some forty years previously, Sagrario now stood trembling in a white dress, waiting for the car to arrive. But, unlike Amatxi's and Atautxi's wedding, this one was not destined to be celebrated in Ituren church. The snow and ice made the climb up the hill so treacherous that they had to make an improvised dash for a lower-lying church in a neighbouring village. Here, shivering at the cold stone altar, hand on the Bible, Sagrario made her vows to Ignacio, the designated heir to the Sunbillenea farm. Just like Amatxi and Atautxi, this was another marriage between the children of Ameztia and – as my home lies directly between Sagrario's and Ignacio's childhood farms – I fancy that a sneaky kiss or two may have been stolen inside the stable walls of the original Iaulin Borda. Although neither of them have ever confirmed my suspicions, by the love and mischief still evident in their eyes some thirty years later, I wouldn't be surprised.

❖ ❖ ❖ ❖

After several years of felling trees in the Alps with his brother Luis, Ignacio stepped into his father's shoes and took over full ownership of the Sunbillenea farmstead. Had he lived in France, Napoleonic laws would have obliged his parents to distribute the family inheritance equally between all the siblings. Navarre, however, has traditionally practised the rule of primogeniture, which means that Ignacio – just like Isidro in Zubialdea – has inherited the whole farm and all of its responsibilities.

In former times, children would fight for the opportunity to inherit the farm, an honour often, but not always, reserved for the eldest child. However, in recent years, values have changed, and the privilege of being named sole heir to the family farm might nowadays be considered a mixed blessing: not only does the house come with all the farm work and the draining expenses of upkeep and repair, but it entails a long list of social responsibilities towards the family. The couple who inherits the house are not only duty-bound to look after their ageing parents, but also to provide food and lodging for all unmarried siblings as well.

Due to the high number of single men in rural Basque areas – an interesting anthropological reality worthy of further debate – a wife can find herself run ragged cooking, washing and caring for not only her parents-in-law but also a cohort of her husband's uncles and brothers. Today's younger generation often prefer to build their own houses in the village and sign up for a forty-hour week in a local factory rather than taking on the illustrious but work-intensive institution of the Basque *etxea* (house).

But this has not been the case for the farms in Ameztia. The beauty and freedom of life on our mountaintop seem to have outweighed the disadvantages and hard graft of farming life, until now at least. When Sagrario married Ignacio and moved into Sunbillenea, she became the life and soul of their farm, offering an open house and a constant supply of homemade stews to all the waifs and strays in Ameztia, among which I am undoubtedly included – and often the first.

The farm's exposed location on the spur to the east of my house affords it the very best vistas in the hamlet. It also offers strategic views of all the comings and goings along The Road That Doesn't Exist – including, of course, the sudden, nocturnal appearance of tradesmen's vehicles and the occasional fallen cherry tree in my drive.

THE SEASONS

BRITISH UNPUNCTUALITY

This 4km, single-lane road between Ituren and Ameztia has become part of the DNA of our existence, a spiralling helix connecting the hamlet to the valley floor. By the time I arrived in Ameztia in 2001, the mountain path that had once led the hamlet's children down to school in Ituren had ceded seniority to a one-lane road carved into the northern flank of the mountain, making the hamlet accessible to cars, tractors and trucks. We are now all dependent on this one precarious road, a daily constant, channelling us between the mortal world of the valley floor and our cherished private paradise above the clouds. The drive itself is almost a rite of passage.

Before I better understood village culture, if I passed my neighbours in their cars in Ituren I would draw up alongside them, wind down my window, and briefly exchange the time of day. In hindsight, I am sure that they sighed in frustration when they saw me, resigned to my suburban inability to understand village life and to comprehend that if everyone stopped to say hello to everyone they knew, every time they bumped into them, nothing would ever get done.

'*¿Vas pa' arriba?*' ('Are you going up?') they would ask as we crossed each other on Ituren Bridge. And I would smile and nod as my eyes flickered up to the ridges high above the village where Ameztia still bathed in the afternoon sun, long after the shadows had staked their claim on the valley floor.

'*¡Sí, sí voy pa' arriba!*'

There was complicity, even a touch of smugness in our smile, like rebels stealing off through the woods towards a secret den when the leader's back was turned. Only those who live in Ameztia know just how sweet life can be. Sometimes.

No matter how often I drive up and down this road no journey is ever the same. Every quirk in the weather, every change of season, adds its own dimensions of colour and texture to the landscape, imbuing each journey with an element of unpredictability. Fallen trees, icy bends and pregnant goats laugh in the face of English punctuality, regularly converting it into a local joke.

Spring

Spring is a pretty time of year, lending itself to a poetic turn of phrase: skies race with ragtag clouds and runaway rainbows and wet meadows shimmer with violets, buttercups and butterflies to match. And yet, despite the promise of more clement times ahead, the spring weather still offers little guarantee that Marion and I will make it to the Pulunpa School in Ituren before the 9am bell. This – just like most matters in Ameztia – is largely to do with the sheep.

To be honest, my slow awakening in the morning may contribute to the problem. While many are galvanised into action by the aroma of freshly brewed coffee or newly baked bread, in spring, as the yearlings nibble and tug at the mixed grasses below my window, I rouse all too leisurely to the divine smell of mint. However, the true culprits are the flocks of older ewes on the road at 8.50am, herded into the Zubialdea milking stalls by Isidro's sheepdogs while we stutter along in first gear at the end of the queue.

This does of course give me time to ponder our surroundings and the Zubialdea homestead in particular. Originally the stables would have been on the ground floor, with wooden partitions for each of the farm animals: sheep, cows, pigs, chickens and possibly the odd donkey or two. This would have made for a malodorous and noisy existence for the occupants sleeping in the *planta noble* above, each room with its individual aromas and acoustics. Apart from the rustlings of the odd mouse, cat, bat or barn owl, the hayloft at the top of the house would provide a more peaceful environment for the cheeses, hams and *txistorrak* dangling from its beams.

In more recent years Zubialdea has been modernised and the animals dispatched to a series of outbuildings on the other side of the road. Their former stables have been reappropriated and offer an open-plan kitchen and living area for the entire Zubialdea clan, of which there are currently four generations. Nevertheless, on pushing open the front door, it is the incongruous Thai cushions on the brown plastic sofa that first catch the eye.

Amatxi – just like her niece, Sagrario, from Sunbillenea – loves textiles and colour, and so I brought back these cushions as a gift from a brief trip I made to Thailand in 2006. But – unlike the lacy sewing box by the kitchen window – they have always struggled to blend in with the wooden yokes and horsehair whips hanging in the gloomy entrance hall. I amuse myself, however, by thinking that their brilliant colours, golden sequins and sparkle may just offer a second line of defence to any witch trying to enter the house – that is if they have successfully made it past the golden *eguzkilore* on the front door.

In a word of explanation, before my line of thought goes completely off-piste, I need first to tell you about the *eguzkiloreak*, a local design feature found on many Basque houses. Believed to symbolise the sun, daylight, and all good things, the *eguzkiloreak* (literally translated as 'sunflowers' from the Basque but known to us more commonly as 'silver thistles') are nailed to the doors and lintels of many Basque homes to repel evil spirits. Witches arriving at the dead of night – so legend has it – are now presented with a dilemma. To gain legitimate access to the house they need first to rid it of its lucky charms, which entails plucking out, one by one, each of the golden bristles from the heart of the flower. With only limited hours of darkness, the race is on and, if the first shafts of dawn light appear on the horizon before the last spike is removed, then the family can sleep easy for one more night. The stakes were higher, however, for any witches opting to slide down the chimney, for in addition to crosses etched in the ashes, vats of boiling oil were also left on the hearth to discourage progress. Even if they did make it into the kitchen, before they could get up to mischief – or spirit away the children – they would first have to navigate the crucifixes nailed above the table or the inevitable church-issued calendar hanging on the wall. However, some evil spirits seem to have sought out easier victims and I suspect it was a rather frustrated witch who, on finding her breaking-and-entering tactics continually thwarted, decided to turn her attention to my boots on the porch. On the only morning I ever accompanied a journalist to the witches' caves in Zugarramurdi, I discovered a large toad snuggled up in the toe of my walking boot.

Summer

In summer a different excuse accompanies our delayed arrivals at the village square. The month of May sees the valley sheep led up to the communal lands on the ridge, joining the sturdy *pottoks* (Basque ponies) that graze freely among the gorse and bracken.

Now the presence of sheep on the Ameztia road is replaced by slow convoys of tractors shunting ruddy-faced farmers and red-cheeked children between the high pastures of Ameztia and the farmlands on the floodplains on the valley floor.

Clasping wooden rakes and pitchforks, entire families dangle from the roll bars while infants jiggle in makeshift seating on the wheel hubs and plastic bags of sweaty sheep's cheese and chorizo sit wedged behind the gears. '*Iepa,*' they salute spiritedly as my car squeezes past, squinting in the sunlight as they look towards Mount Mendaur and the storm clouds gathering on the horizon. And then they are off, scuttling down the valley to bring in the hay while the sun still shines.

On my return home, I inevitably pause to take in the views from the top of my drive. In August, the typical farming scenes that greet me from Sunbillenea are as unfailing as the advent of summer itself. In a series of ever smaller dots, Lilliputian figures on the eastern spur tack back and forth across the fields behind the combine harvester. The larger dots of Sagrario and Ignacio forking the hay into east–west rows are followed by the smaller dots of the children, flicking up the last wisps of hay with slanted wooden rakes. Circling in the blue sky above this congregation – like Arabic vowels above a script – are two tiny specks. These are the red kites, birds of prey, ready to pounce on the field mice or grass snakes scuttling for cover. And then, at the end of the line, is Moriko, the family sheepdog, unsure of his role in the process but unfailingly loyal to the cause.

Autumn

If it wasn't for the autumn colours – the glorious kaleidoscope of tangerines, scarlets and golds that requires a photo stop at every turn – autumn would provide less of an excuse for unpunctual arrival at the school gate.

October is an especially happy, holiday month on the farms. It arrives after the bracken has been stacked in September and before the shepherds head up to the ridge in November to bring down the last of the sheep from the common lands and lambing resumes once again. As always, the farmyard of Zubialdea presents a perfect vignette of autumn traditions in the Basque Pyrenees. Old sheets are spread out across the courtyard and the walnuts are rolled out to dry, their green husks crinkling and blackening in the drying southern winds. Black beans are beaten with sticks to separate them from their pods and large pumpkins and squashes are strewn out along the farmyard walls to mellow in the last rays of the sun. But do not be fooled. Inside, in the kitchen, in wicker baskets, the more valuable loot is hidden from view. Mushroom gathering (of in particular the *Boletus edulis*, or in English, the 'cep') is a favourite autumn pastime, the location of good mushroom-hunting places being a jealously guarded secret and handed down from one generation to the next.

Freed from the tyranny of lambing and milking schedules, work routines are unusually relaxed in October, which is fortunate because this is also hunting season. Farmers dressed in camouflage fatigues stow lovingly polished rifles in the boots of their 4WD cars and race up to the spindly hunting platforms on the ridges where they pass the time of day in each other's company, catching up on local gossip, swigging wine from leather pouches with one eye on the skies. If they are lucky, with fate and the south winds on their side, the foil-wrapped bacon baguettes on the passenger seat on the way up are replaced by a couple of equally lifeless ring-collared pigeons on the way down.

Autumn is also a happy time for pigs, and just as the road appears miraculously uncluttered by either sheep or tractors and one is even contemplating a rare shift into third gear, a couple of runaways from the Zubialdea pig stalls appear around the next bend. Gorging themselves on windfalls of acorns, they are blissfully unaware that in a few weeks their ecstatic feasting will greatly benefit those further up the food chain.

Zubialdea is one of the most important pig farms in the area and the final destination of the ancient pig path from the village of Urrotz. In the past, the swineherds from Urrotz chaperoned their lady pigs up the mountain, past my door, towards Zubialdea where they were left to sojourn in the company of Zubialdea's prize boar. Naturally, even in Amatxi's experienced hands, the ensuing process was something of a hit-and-miss affair and, without telephones, the swineherds waited for a sign from Zubialdea to let them know when to return. In the distinctive mountain communication system used by farmers and smugglers alike, the signal would eventually appear. An old white bed sheet, hoisted to the top of a pine tree on the edge of the Zubialdea property, visible to the farms in Urrotz on the other side of the valley, conveyed that the sows were now happily sired and were ready to be escorted back home again.

Winter

Winter, with its sepia landscapes and acute shadows, arrives at the beginning of December and lasts roughly until the middle of March. It spans the dreary month of February, which seems to have little going for it when compared to December with its Christmas festivities, or to January with its spectacular, life-affirming Ituren carnival. In Basque, however, the name for February is *Otsail*, which commonly translates as 'the month of the wolf', indicating that it may have been a little livelier in times gone by. Sadly, neither wolves (nor bears) populate this part of the Pyrenees any longer, so we are free to keep our attentions firmly focused on the sun. Shuffling around the yard we chase the last of its sunbeams before finally scuttling off to our woodpiles for firewood and into our houses for warmth and broth.

On a more positive note, winter offers the most credible excuses for our late arrivals in the village square. Snow often bars our way down the mountain, until our snowplough (a communally owned appendage to my neighbour's tractor) clears the way. And even then, the ice on the 'goat bend' halfway down the mountain remains a formidable obstacle, lying in wait to catch out anyone who thinks of using their brakes rather than their gears to slow them down.

Yet every cloud has a silver lining. Although the villagers from downtown Ituren generally view Ameztia as a 'wild and woolly' outpost far from the reaches of civilisation, in winter this image earns us a certain prestige. When we do finally arrive in the village plaza, the car sporting a 30cm-thick coiffure of snow, 'wild and woolly' translates into 'intrepid and brave', and people are greatly impressed that we have made it down the mountain at all.

❖ ❖ ❖ ❖

However, it is during the final days of January that the real magic of our winters unfolds. Furtive shadows are detected around the back of the barns and heavy chests of old clothes, masks and wigs are pulled out from the back of closets. Sheepskins are draped over balcony railings, horsetail whips lie spreadeagled on benches, and the habitually solitary lights from farmhouse kitchens are now accompanied by a dim glow through attic windows. The holy trinity of bells, owls and braying donkeys that usually accompanies us through the night is now joined by a percussive symphony of manmade sounds. Ameztia is busy. Carnival time is here.

Infamous throughout Spain, the Ituren-Zubieta 'carnival' of the Joaldunak (bell wearers) dates back to pre-Christian times, finding its origin in an ancient Greek festival during which masters allegedly swapped clothes with their slaves and men dressed as women. Later the Church, politely – but ineffectively – hijacked these pagan celebrations of the winter solstice by rebranding them as carnivals, but the similarity is in name only.

As you would expect, many festivals at this time of year celebrate the fertility of the land, chasing away the cold, dark and disease of the winter months and heralding in the light, warmth and fecundity of spring. But matters are never that straightforward. Disconcertingly, it is not only the term 'carnival' which is misleading but also the festival's dates, coinciding with neither the traditional carnival period around Lent nor the full moon of the winter solstice. The Ituren-Zubieta 'carnival' takes place at the end of January, weeks before the land shows any signs of spring; once again, Basque pragmatism has played its part. During the later part of the twentieth century many young men from the valley worked as loggers in the Alps or high Pyrenees, leaving the village to return to their work as soon as the snows had melted. Having a festival dedicated to the forces of spring and fertility without the presence of the virile male studs from the community would have been senseless – and extremely dull – and so the dates were changed. Pagan ritual or religious rite, solstice or no solstice, Franco or no

Franco, Covid or no Covid, one way or another the Ituren-Zubieta carnival has been celebrated continuously since pre-Christian times.

One January morning, during my first year in Ameztia, I walked around to Zubialdea to visit Amatxi. Here, a strange pair of high conical hats – rather like miniature maypoles – were perched on the bench outside the front door. Poking out of the top of each was a pert, grey cock's feather, while flurries of yellow, blue and pink ribbons streamed down the sides, fluttering in the chill winter winds. Intrigued, I made my way into the kitchen to find Amatxi hunched over her sewing, warming her back against the wood-burning stove. She lifted her head briefly as I entered.

'*Ya llegan los carnavales*,' ('Carnival time is on its way') she smiled as her stiff, arthritic fingers daintily stitched a satin ribbon into the hem of a large lace petticoat.

'*Es pa' Imanol*,' she added. It appeared that this pretty petticoat belonged to her grandson, Imanol.

'*Ya sabes cómo son los carnavales*,' ('You know what carnival is like') she grinned.

Of course, the Ituren-Zubieta carnival was infamous. It always made the press, and not necessarily for the right reasons, but I had no idea what these celebrations really meant to the locals. This was my first year in the hamlet and I had yet to experience it for myself.

A few days later I headed down the road to Ituren to witness its carnival for the first time. Even before I left Ameztia I could hear the bells echoing through the mountains. This was not the skittish ring of sheep bells but a deep, primeval throbbing that ricocheted off the valley slopes from north to south and east to west. It was clear from the start that neither man nor beast would lie quiet this day.

Pulunpa… pulunpa… pulunpa…

Parking on the outskirts of the village I headed towards the square, picking my way between broken plastic beakers, clods of manure and a dubious entrail or two. I didn't stop to look. On the bridge, personifying the cruelty of winter, demons in miniskirts and chains with grotesque masks and bloodshot eyes writhed and screamed. Children with fluorescent wigs flung grey ash into the crowds while a pasty-thighed youth in G-string and fishnet tights lunged at me with a screaming chainsaw – the chain, mercifully, removed. Centre stage in the square, two mangled car chassis, fitted with antlers, butted each other like stag beetles, their engines screaming acrid black fumes into the winter air.

Stereotypes and norms were smashed to smithereens. This was absolute, unbridled chaos. Nothing in my life in England nor Denmark could ever have prepared me for such outrageous mayhem and it seemed I wasn't alone. In his red uniform, a solitary young policeman stood at a corner of the square seemingly trapped between his call of duty and his respect for tradition. He was evidently as out of his depth as I was.

But my incredulity got the better of me and, wiping the muck and gore from my clothes, I held my ground, thrilled, liberated even, by this flagrant repudiation of all the codes of conduct that I had taken for granted. At the same time, I felt a heightened sense of togetherness. Was this some fascinating paradox? One of those macabre twists of the human psyche that I had still to process and yet to understand? And then, as a second cowpat narrowly missed my freshly shampooed hair, I abandoned my philosophical musings, and the thought of some chicken broth – or a glass of wine – in the village *ostatu* became increasingly attractive.

Later that morning, a tractor from Zubieta turned up in Ituren village square. Pulling a trailer transformed into a cider fountain, it was an unparalleled work of art. A ladder covered in ferns had been fixed upright on to the back of the trailer and six men had woven their bodies through the rungs so that all that could be seen sticking out from the front of the ladder were six sizeable, naked bottoms and six pairs of black boots. The rest of their torsos remained hidden backstage by the ferns on the other side. The cracks were perfectly aligned, and I amused myself by thinking that we were being blessed with the same view a toilet seat may have had, had its occupant suddenly stooped forward to tie up his shoelaces. At the top of this tower of naked bottoms, a man wildly shook a bottle of cider before pouring it down the meticulously aligned cracks, forming a dribbling waterfall from one bottom to the next. On the floor of the cart, poking his head through the lowest rung of the ladder, were signs of a seventh protagonist. Aligned with equal precision, his upturned head poked through the bracken while the waterfall of well-aerated cider gradually disappeared into his open mouth.

Deserving of international artistic acclaim, this shocking image will at least go down in local history for its astounding and incomparable ingenuity.

But salvation was on its way. If you wanted it.

Pulunpa... pulunpa... pulunpa...

The Joaldunak were coming.

A band of children with accordions, tambourines and *txistuak* (one-handed whistles) struck up a melody on the bridge as we shivered in the thin rain, waiting for the Joaldunak of Zubieta to appear on the river path.

Pulunpa… pulunpa… pulunpa…

And then they were here. The Joaldunak stepped out of the mists, their magical presence bringing a spiritual element to the baseness and the madness of it all.

Pulunpa… pulunpa… pulunpa…

Sounding a ram's horn, the leader heralded their arrival, the shrill, eerie whine accompanying the troupe as they appeared, trance-like, out of the woods. With perfect military precision some fifty men or more marched in parallel along the river path, whips in hand, pointed hats strapped to their heads, their black eyebrows just discernible through frilly fringes. Sodden sheepskins lounged on muscular shoulders while coarse ropes strapped ten-litre copper bells to the embroidered skirts around their waists.

Pulunpa… pulunpa… pulunpa…

Accompanying the Joaldunak, a shepherd held the chains of a huge carnival 'bear' with ram-horn ears who, swiping at the crowd, sent children and parents screaming into each other's arms. But the march of the Joaldunak didn't stop and – as if there was still one supreme law that presided over the anarchy – the sea of monsters stepped meekly aside to let them pass. The arrivals were the good guys, dispersing the dark and disease of winter and ushering in the light and fertility of spring with the rhythmic lunge and flick of their hips, lace petticoats flirting with thick Basque thighs.

Pulunpa… pulunpa… pulunpa…

I have now lived in Ituren for more than two decades, longer than I ever lived in Birmingham, England, but I still struggle to understand the true weight and pull of my roots, and how they bear upon my identity today. As I seek out Marion's gaze among the mob in the square, the red highlights in her dark Basque hair provide physical evidence that my genes, at least, have mixed with theirs. Perhaps I have inherited part of her identity, or become part of this place in other ways too? This atavistic pounding of the bells does indeed pull at some primeval chord within me, concertinaing past into present, good into bad, human into beast, man into woman and now, after so many years, perhaps even Brummy into Basque. Perhaps.

BASQUE BORDERS AND THE COMET LINE
EGGNOGS AND PETTICOATS

Despite Franco's attempts to exterminate all expressions of Basque identity, the culture and language ultimately proved as resilient as the people themselves and, during the 1950s and '60s, clandestine Basque evening schools (*gaueskolak*) mushroomed furtively in hidden attics and basements throughout the Basque Country. Nevertheless, many of Franco's policies, particularly in the more populous towns, did succeed in undermining the Basque way of life. Deliberate steps were taken to further industrialise the Basque Autonomous Community, with big steelworks being built along the coast, and non-Basque-speaking immigrants from other parts of Spain were actively encouraged to seek work there. This was not only to bolster the workforce, but also to dilute the essence of 'Basqueness' in the communities around them. Unlike the mountain shepherds, Basque townsfolk were often too frightened to teach their children their language for fear of punishment. Today, because of this, there is a 'lost generation' of Basque people who, despite their Basque-speaking parents – and Basque genes dating back to prehistoric times – are unable to speak their 'mother tongue'.

This picture was slightly different, however, in the more remote mountain areas such as Basque Navarre, where intricate valley formations and steep-sided river gorges hid the villages, and their pocket-sized farming hamlets, from scrutiny. Compared to the cities of Bilbao or San Sebastián along the coast, the mountain farmers, with their livestock and home-grown produce, were able to live an uneasy but still relatively peaceful life – and in Basque.

Although there was a blanket ban on all traditional Basque celebrations, the mountain Basques, masters of clandestine activities, continued to celebrate their festivals in hiding. In Ituren and Zubieta, the sturdy oak doors and thick stone walls muffled the sound of village gatherings and the *pulunpa… pulunpa… pulunpa…* of a few irrepressible Joaldunak. Inside their houses, families continued to speak Basque in private, only switching to their few words of school Spanish as they reached for their overcoats and stepped out of the door.

❖ ❖ ❖ ❖

Franco's strategies to squeeze the population into submission were far-reaching and devious. One was to levy exorbitant taxes on goods coming over the border, while another subtler policy was to disable the watermills by clamping metal rings on to the milling machinery, leaving the locals without the means to grind their own flour and, hence, make their own bread.

But few people know their lands like the Basques do, and Franco and his police never found out about the existence of *Infernuko Errota* (Inferno Mill) in a remote valley to the west of the Baztan Valley. This tiny wooden mill was built into the rocks above *Infernuko Erreka* (Inferno Stream) which runs northwards towards the Atlantic through the caves of Zugarramurdi, infamous as a site for witches' covens. To grind their corn, local families would dispatch caravans of terrified children with heavily laden mules over the mountains into the night. Those unlucky enough not to live nearby had to make do with the universally detested 'grey bread' produced by a state-run chain of bakeries known as *panificadoras*.

Franco's heavy-handed restrictions had some curious consequences. One of these was to inculcate a national aversion to anything resembling wholegrain bread and another was to inspire a burgeoning trade in smuggling.

❖ ❖ ❖ ❖

I listened enraptured to the smugglers' stories with the glee of a runaway child, a runaway from Birmingham shopping malls and from the cold, impersonal winter streets of Copenhagen. And it was as a runaway child that I stole up the mountain paths towards the border with former smugglers from the villages of Lesaka and Etxalar. Although their backs were buckled from years of heavy loads, their eyes never forgot a turn, and their feet never missed a step. Scribbling down notes about their tricks and ruses, I committed their secret paths and hideouts to memory. In later years, this knowledge was to serve me well and, when the recent pandemic shut down borders, it served me very well indeed.

Leaving their various farms at dusk, the Basque Spanish smugglers would head nonchalantly to a designated meeting point on the French-Spanish border. Here they would hide in the woods in wait for their smuggling comrades to deliver the contraband from the other side. Copper, radios, brandy, lipstick, penicillin and a wide variety of other goods were then smuggled back into the village and – with the help of doctors, priests, beauticians and bureaucrats – distributed throughout the rest of Spain. Often, the smugglers would cover some 20 to 30km in one night with loads of over 30kg on their shoulders. In later years condoms, cows and even a pool table were smuggled over the border – the last surely being a fascinating story if only I could track it down.

Two main challenges faced the smugglers. The first and most obvious was to circumvent the *Guardia Civil* lying in wait along the border, while the second was to navigate the mountains in pitch darkness, heavy loads balanced on their shoulders.

In general, the guards were an easily surmounted obstacle. Although they had the backing of the law, they rarely shot to kill and had little knowledge of the local terrain. Mountain shepherds since childhood, the Basque smugglers knew their territory like no one else, giving them an indisputable advantage.

Smoking was a dead giveaway. As most of the guards smoked, they were easily detected from a distance, either by the glow of their cigarettes in the dark or – depending on the wind direction – by the smell. But even if they didn't smoke, they still smelt. Their thick regulation woollen capes gave off a distinctly musty smell which, just like the cigarette smoke, could be detected from afar.

Heading off along the paths to hide in ambush, the guards inevitably left trails, not only the inevitable footprints or snapped twigs and broken ferns but other clues too. The distribution of sheep within a field was often an object of scrutiny. If a path led along the top side of a field but all the sheep were found grazing on the bottom side, it was highly likely that the herd had been frightened by strangers walking by. On the other hand, cobwebs breaking across the smugglers' faces along an overgrown stretch of path implied the opposite; and they could rest assured that no one else had passed that way in the past few hours.

Even tomato plants disclosed valuable information. Franco's *Guardia Civil* were frequently from the south of Spain and were accustomed to raw tomatoes in their Mediterranean diet. The revelation that tomatoes could be eaten raw came relatively late to the Basque-speaking regions, hence the unexpected appearance of a tomato plant in the woods would inform the smugglers that they had stumbled upon one of the guards' regular latrines. The tomato seeds, on concluding their descent through the guards' digestive system, would take root in the freshly fertilised soil, blowing their cover even before the next crop of tomatoes appeared.

From strategic vantage points in their fields and mountain barns, the farmers kept an eye on the *Guardia Civil*, communicating their whereabouts to the smugglers with the help of a series of signs rather like Native American smoke signals. Here, however, it was not smoke billowing in the breeze, but something far less conspicuous: a white sheet – or a black apron – flapping in the wind from an upstairs window, ostensibly hanging out to dry.

By displaying various items of bedding or clothing at different times of the day, the locals created secret codes that were communicated across the narrow valleys and replicated from one farmhouse to the next. A black shawl pegged up outside the kitchen window one morning may have tipped off the smugglers to a new police patrol on the border, whereas a row of white petticoats hung over the balcony in the afternoon could have signified an unexpected change of plans. I can only hope that when the real washday arrived not too many mixed messages were given, and no smugglers were caught as a result.

Even cows entered the subterfuge. A farmer would lead the herd out to graze in a specific pasture, deliberately choosing the field according to the message he wanted to communicate to his fellow smugglers on the other side of the valley. Whether the same applied to sheep or goats I do not know but, given their tendency to escape through holes in fences, I can only imagine that they were a slightly less reliable communication method.

An inventive, quick-thinking mind was a vital asset in the smuggling fraternity, as was a deep understanding of botany and geography. With or without the *Guardia Civil* on their tail, a moonless night proved to be a double-edged sword. True, the total darkness would help the smugglers move undetected through the woods, but it would also put their own orientation skills to the test. However, professionals at clandestine night work (*gaulan*), the Basques had a heightened sensitivity to the natural world which, combined with their intimate knowledge of the landscape, gave them a huge advantage over the *Guardia Civil*. Even without the moonlight or stars to guide them, the breeze on their cheek became their compass, the colder winds blowing in off the north-facing slopes while warmer flurries lifted from the south. Like blind men reading braille, their expert fingers would reach out to the rough tree bark, checking their course by the damp patches of moss thriving on the cooler northern side.

In the spring, it was the soapy fragrance of the sweet chestnut blossom or the sharp citric notes of crushed walnut leaves that offered the smugglers vital clues as to their location. But by autumn, when the trees had shed their leaves, their attention turned to the soles of their feet and the texture of the foliage on the path: the springiness of dried chestnut husks, the crunch of fragile beech mast or the tough, unyielding acorns that would roll them downhill like a carpet of ball bearings. Just like wild animals, the smugglers became part of the landscape, blending into the woods and trusting the natural world to be their guide. Rarely were they caught.

When several bands of smugglers coincided in the woods on the same night, they needed a way to quickly identify themselves in the darkness. Their relationships were usually amicable, so it was to their advantage to communicate their presence to any other smugglers nearby lest their nocturnal rustlings be misinterpreted as those of the *Guardia Civil*. To this end, each group of smugglers would carry a sheep's bell and ring it to alert other smugglers to their presence, each bell having a different and easily recognisable ring. I suppose that carrying a sheep's bell around in a landscape full of sheep was not a particularly conspicuous thing to do, even if it did ring unintentionally. However, I do remember a very funny story where this was not the case. It was about a smuggler stealing across the border with a box full of alarm clocks.

In the unlikely event that the smugglers were caught, the *Guardia Civil* – out of their depth in these wild Basque hinterlands and often half-starved – were usually more than happy to extract a bribe. If the loot could be put to immediate use, such as bottles of cognac or cigarettes, they would simply carry it off for themselves. If, however, the contraband was of little interest – which was the case with herds of frisky steers (destined for Spain) or horses (destined for France) – then they would often be put up for auction. There, other locals would deliberately refrain from bidding, enabling the original smuggler to buy them back for a pittance and head off to another border crossing point on a different night, selling them on at a slightly reduced – but still significant – profit.

Given the colourful stories, and the passion with which these now 'unemployed' smugglers talked to me about their trade, I often took my Spanish-language students to meet them. I will never forget the image of my guests perched on the edges of their stools, enraptured by the smugglers' tales, pushing their Spanish vocabulary to the limit as they drank in the vivid details of these wonderful anecdotes together with several glasses of cider. No matter their age or place of birth on those days all my guests were runaway children too!

❖ ❖ ❖ ❖

One day, while sitting in a café in Elizondo, I found an article in a local magazine about a surprising diversification of smuggling activities in the Baztan Valley during World War II. Painstakingly, with the aid of a dictionary – which offers scant help in deciphering Basque sentences due to the language's infuriating tendency to place words in the most illogical order – I started to unravel stories about Basque smugglers working for a resistance network.

This network, known as the Comet Line (*Le Réseau Comète*), operated between 1941 and 1944, the brainchild of Andrée de Jongh, a surprisingly young Belgian nurse who was working at a Red Cross hospital at the onset of the war. Stranded behind enemy lines after the evacuation of Dunkirk in 1940, the Allied soldiers in her ward, once healthy enough to be removed, would be taken away by the Germans to spend the rest of the war in prisoner-of-war camps. The day de Jongh, just twenty-four years old, decided to throw a foul-smelling liquid over a young soldier in her care – repulsing the Nazi guards on watch and preventing them from marching him away – she committed her first act of defiance. It also marked the beginnings of one of the largest and most successful resistance networks of World War II.

Over the following four years, the Comet Line succeeded in saving the lives of some eight hundred people: soldiers, pilots and gunners shot down over occupied territories, and members of the resistance whose lives were in peril after their identities had been revealed. From safe house to safe house through the streets of Brussels, Paris and Bordeaux, the evaders – predominantly airmen – were escorted southwards through Nazi-occupied territories across the Basque Pyrenees to the relative safety of Spain.

Once in Spain, local Basque guides steered their protégés (code-named 'parcels') clear of Franco's pro-Nazi *Guardia Civil* and into the protection of British Military Intelligence (MI9) based in Bilbao. Then, with the help of the British embassy, they were escorted south to Gibraltar, from where they were able to catch a plane or boat back to the UK. Carried out in utmost secrecy, the numbers will never be exact, but it is estimated that some three thousand Belgian, French and Basque people – the majority of them women and children – risked their lives in service to the Comet Line and roughly a third were captured in the process. Some were shot by firing squad while others were sent directly to German concentration camps. The POW camps at least offered captured Allied soldiers a healthier chance of survival.

The work of the resistance was wide-ranging. Not only did it consist of establishing a network of safe houses but also, in a time of acute rationing, of sourcing food and clothing without raising suspicion. Identity cards and work permits also had to be forged to pass through the innumerable checkpoints on their route south to the Pyrenees. Trains were the main source of transport and guides, predominantly young women or girls – many in their teens – would escort small groups of evaders southwards towards the French-Spanish border. Andrée de Jongh (code-named 'Dédée') made the journey over the Pyrenees into Spain thirty-two times. It was as she was about to embark upon her thirty-third border crossing over the Bidasoa River, on a stormy evening on 15 January 1943, that she was finally caught.

The difficulties facing Dédée and the other French, Belgian and Basque guides were endless, but one of their greatest challenges was simply to make the escapees merge into the background. Pinning 'Deaf and Dumb' badges to their lapels was an unsophisticated way of overcoming the problem that very few of them spoke any French at all; ensuring that they blend in with the locals, however, was equally challenging. Even when dressed in peasant clothing, and the berets and espadrilles of the Basque people in the south, their appearance would betray their foreign origins. The well-nourished Allied evaders were often much taller than the local population and it was said that the Americans, in particular, had a certain swagger and confidence, with a habit of putting their hands in their pockets, that was difficult to hide. Despite these insurmountable difficulties, the Comet Line lost just two people, carried away by the turbulent waters of the Bidasoa on Christmas Eve 1943. On the other hand, one pilot, not content with being shot down once over occupied territories, repeated the experience a second time and needed to be rescued by the resistance twice.

Although the original escape route crossed the Bidasoa on the French-Spanish border near the Atlantic coastline, the article in my magazine described a lesser-known route. After Dédée's arrest in 1943, the original crossing came under Nazi scrutiny and local

Basque guides were forced to find alternative escape lines further inland. One of these passed through the Baztan Valley. The grainy black-and-white photo that headed the article showed Jauriko Borda, an old farmhouse nestled in a steep-sided valley near the border. There was also a photo of its owners, Xan Mihurra and his family, farmers who had risked their lives hiding Allied pilots in their hayloft and then guiding them westwards through the mountains into the Baztan Valley during the night.

In 2015, my fiftieth birthday was approaching and with only Marion to organise a surprise for me, I took the unprecedented step of organising an adventure for myself. At that moment nothing seemed more exhilarating than the opportunity to walk in the footsteps of the smugglers and resistance fighters of the Comet Line. With such exciting territory to explore on your back doorstep – and with such heroic and moving human stories to uncover – who would want to do anything else? I contacted the magazine and within weeks I was scrambling through the woods with Xan's grandson, Juanbi, clambering over fallen tree trunks and beating back the bracken on the old smugglers' trails as he recounted the stories he had heard from his father, and his father's father, Xan. Through my contact with Juanbi, I met an interesting mix of characters from both sides of the border: family descendants of the Comet Line resistance fighters, former smugglers and local historians – one of them being Juan Carlos Jiménez de Aberásturi Corta, whose meticulous documentation of every detail of the crossing has provided a valuable platform for my research.

After a couple of years of walking and documenting the various Comet Line routes, I began to hear from people as far afield as Australia, South Africa and Israel who would read my blogs and get in touch. They were interested in walking sections of the Comet Line for themselves; some wanted to follow in the footsteps of family and friends, while others were inspired by the stories of courage and sacrifice that resonated with their own family histories.

My research led me to the doors of two of the last remaining survivors of the Comet Line network, Maialen Larretche and Paco Iriarte. Both of them lived in former safe houses, on different sides of the border, and both their families had played vital roles in the resistance. During World War II, Maialen lived on her family farm in Urrugne, at the foot of the Pyrenees in Nazi-occupied France, while Paco lived some 26km away on his uncle's farm in Oiartzun, on the other side of the Bidasoa, in Franco's Spain. Both children instinctively understood the need for secrecy that had always been a vital part of life for the Basques on both sides of the border. Whether it was to protect the identities of the smugglers that stole past their farms during the night, or the World War II escapees hiding away in their attics and haylofts, they both implicitly understood the importance of their silence.

On 15 January 1943, as Dédée was about to attempt her thirty-third crossing into Spain, she was hiding out with three RAF pilots at the safe house in Urrugne. Bidegain-Berri was a humble farmstead run by a French widow, Frantxia, with two small children. Her safe house offered the last resting place before the final, gruelling crossing of the Endarlatsa ravines and the Bidasoa. The 14th January was a wild and stormy day. Torrential rain had swollen the river making the crossing far too dangerous and so Dédée took the fateful decision. She decided to stay at Frantxia's farmhouse one more night, but it was to be one night too many.

The next morning, while the RAF pilots were playing with the children in an upstairs bedroom, there was a knock on the door. It was the Gestapo. Rounded up at gunpoint, the group was marched off to the nearby fishing port of Saint-Jean-de-Luz. From here, the pilots were sent on to a POW camp while Dédée and Frantxia, as members of the resistance, were put on trains to Ravensbrück concentration camp in Germany.

That same morning, Maialen was returning home from Saint-Jean-de-Luz with her sister where they had been to sell the milk from their farm. Just twelve years old at the time, she still remembers the terror that she felt when she saw the Gestapo marching Frantxia, Dédée and the pilots down the lane at gunpoint in the opposite direction. Keeping her eyes firmly on the road, her gaze diverted, she pretended not to know them even though, tucked away inside her petticoats, was a message of warning for Frantxia from the Comet Line resistance in Saint-Jean-de-Luz. It had come too late. Despite their acute awareness of the risks, Maialen's parents still decided to take over Frantxia's work, offering their own farmhouse, Jatxou Baita, just 200m away, as the Comet Line's next safe house. Here, Allied pilots continued to be hidden in the loft above the kitchen until the end of the war.

I met Maialen and her nephew one day as I peered over the hedge of Jatxou Baita with a client, hoping to identify the back window through which the pilots used to escape. Graciously inviting us into her home, she offered us a glass of fortified wine and cheese *petits fours*, and in her softly spoken manner told us of the reign of terror under which she and her eleven siblings had lived during the war. She recalled one day in particular.

On the morning she had in mind, a group of Nazi soldiers had entered the farmhouse kitchen with laundry for her and her sisters to wash. She remembered them as surprisingly courteous, sometimes lingering in the family company and insisting on making an unusual drink for them all to sample. After talking with locals in Urrugne, I learned that the Nazis demonstrated an irreverence for French wine, and their unfruitful attempts to infiltrate 'eggnog' – a sacrilegious mix of raw egg and alcohol – into French cuisine are still talked about to this day.

Maialen was acutely aware that before dawn, that same morning, a group of pilots had been smuggled into her house and were awaiting nightfall before leaving to cross the Bidasoa River. She also knew that the slightest sound from the rooms above the kitchen, or any noticeable change in her behaviour, would have spelt death for her family. Fortunately, this time, the evaders weren't discovered and at dusk, Florentino Goikoetxea, the most famous of all the Basque Comet Line guides, came to guide them over the steep ravines of the Bidasoa River and on into Spain.

Born on the Spanish side of the Pyrenees, Florentino, like so many Basque republicans, had fled to France at the end of the Spanish Civil War and gone into hiding in the French town of Saint-Jean-de-Luz. Florentino came from an extremely poor farming family and, before the war, had spent his life working on the rivers: shovelling sand, hunting rabbits and smuggling. He knew the Basque lands, on both sides of the border, as intimately as his own back garden. A large, strongly built man of few words, and most probably illiterate, Florentino had a great love of French cognac, and his secret stashes of cognac and espadrilles, hidden beneath rocky tors along the border, formed an essential part of his logistic operations. He worked for the Comet Line until the end of the war and his knowledge of the mountains and the fickle Bidasoa currents was invaluable in guaranteeing the survival of every person in his care.

That night, as on many others, Florentino arrived at Maialen's farm to pick up his 'parcels' and lead them over the border to the next safe house in Spain. Monosyllabic as he was, he had apparently learned the English phrase 'two hundred metres' and, with these three words, the occasional glug of cognac and a possible change of espadrilles, he coaxed his charges along the 26km into Spain. Dodging the *Guardia Civil* patrols, they scrambled up and down mountain shoulders and mining tracks, arriving at Paco's farm by dawn.

As a young child, Paco had been sent to live and work with his uncle on their large and relatively prosperous farm, Sarobe. Sarobe (code-named *Xagu*) was situated on the outskirts of Oiartzun, just inland from San Sebastián, and the first evaders were smuggled into their attic when Paco was about eight years old. He still remembers Florentino's coded knocks at the door and the men being ushered quickly and silently into the kitchen where they were given warm milk, cornbread, sheep cheese and *txistorra*. He also remembers helping peel the espadrilles from the men's blistered feet, which were soothed in buckets of salted water by the fire. Talking about his childhood hero, Paco smiles as he recalls helping to pull thorns from Florentino's hands. He also remembers Dédée (whom they fondly nicknamed *La Pescadilla* [the little fish] for her numerous crossings of the Bidasoa), and the ten-peseta note she once pressed into his hand to keep his silence. But it wasn't necessary. The Basque farmers and their children knew implicitly not to talk; the silence that surrounded *gaulan* (night work) – whether it be smuggling goods or people – had been part of their culture for generations.

Sarobe operated as a safe house for the full duration of World War II, although towards the end the *Guardia Civil* had the house under surveillance, making it increasingly unsafe. While not as cruelly cold-blooded as the Gestapo, they were still capable of turning the pilots over to the Nazis on the border and sending the resistance workers to Franco's harsh prisons within Spain. Paco proudly remembers the day his uncle asked him to lead a pilot through the woods to another safe house further down the valley and how, despite his young age, he felt that he had been given sole responsibility for saving a life.

Over the years, I have tried to record as many details as possible of Paco's and Maialen's lives but the high point of my work on the Comet Line came in 2019. Seventy-five years earlier, Maialen and Paco had shared a common history. They both lived in fear of their fascist regimes and in awe of the enigmatic Florentino, and both had been involved in hiding the very same pilots – but always one day and 26km apart. Despite this shared history – and the numerous documentaries and books dedicated to their roles in the resistance – they had never met, and so I had the privilege to organise a meeting between the two.

One golden September morning, Paco, his daughter Itziar and I walked up the gravel drive to Jatxou Baita in Urrugne, a box of Spanish biscuits in hand. Maialen greeted us in a starched skirt and crisp white blouse, taking in our arrival with quiet dignity and inviting us into the kitchen, where she produced a bottle of fine Muscatel and her best crystal glasses. Paco sat down at her side, his rough farming hands and weather-beaten face contrasting with her fragility and delicate white skin, and slowly they revisited their childhood experiences.

Although they had lived their lives on opposite sides of a 'virtually impenetrable' border between two vastly different countries, there was much common ground. Maialen was officially French and Paco Spanish. Despite this, and some variations in accents and local vocabulary, the two of them passed the afternoon contentedly peering over photos and exchanging personal stories in, of course, their common language, Basque. While the inscrutability of the Basque language was undoubtedly an important factor in the success of the Comet Line, so too was the tenacity and innate sense of justice and honour ingrained within the Basques on both sides of the border. Having struggled for so long for the freedom to live in their own culture and speak their own language, their resistance to the Nazi occupation was just one more chapter in their eternal fight to free the underdog from oppression.

At the war's end, Dédée returned from Ravensbrück to continue her humanitarian work, this time with lepers in the Congo. Frantxia, like almost a third of the three thousand Comet Line network members, never made it home, and her orphaned children were brought up by her sister. Florentino, having narrowly avoided arrest with Dédée in Urrugne in 1943, was wounded and captured in 1944 while returning over the mountains from Spain with a message from MI9 for the resistance. But his French friends didn't let him down. Conjuring up the most audacious of escapes, they dressed up in Gestapo uniforms, commandeered an ambulance, marched past the guards at the hospital in Biarritz where Florentino was being treated, and simply lifted him from his bed and walked right out the door. From there he was ushered into hiding until the end of the war. It was not until Franco died in 1975 that the Spanish members of the Comet Line were formally recognised by the Spanish government and Florentino received a personal thank-you letter from Winston Churchill. In 1976, he was flown to England, where he was awarded the George Cross for bravery.

'What line of business are you in?' someone from the ceremony asked him. To which, in broken English and with a shy grin, he allegedly replied, 'I'm in the import-export business.'

MOTHER AND BABY

SNAKES, TOOTHPASTE
TUBES AND THE MOON

Just like Florentino, I was, in some manner of speaking, also in the import-export business, although *usually* by more traditional means, importing international visitors and exporting language skills. Borders make for a lively trade, and my interactions with the local Basque community, smugglers, resistance fighters and a stream of international guests opened up entertaining dimensions to my life. The diversion was welcome. There was always some exciting project to be developed or perplexing logistical problem to be solved.

However, when everyone had gone home it was life at Iaulin Borda, alone on an isolated mountaintop, that presented this girl from Birmingham with the greatest challenges of them all. It had always been the intangible aspects of my existence that had perturbed me more than the tangible ones, the twin fears of loneliness and purposelessness having hounded me relentlessly. But now two tiny fists claimed their filial rights, knocking loudly at my door, drowning out the solitude and the more egocentric caprices of my mind. Buoyed by constant company and an indisputable *raison d'être*, it seemed that the greater the demands of motherhood, the less complex my life was overall.

Even before she was born, in May 2004, Marion had already accumulated many months of mountain walking, as I continued leading my guests into the hills until I was seven months pregnant. At this point there had been a noticeable change of roles. Now, with every stile or slippery path, my clients would reach out to steady me, their concern culminating in tangible sighs of relief when they finally chaperoned me back in through the farmhouse door.

Very soon after her birth, Marion and I headed off into the hills once again, but this time she tuned into my beating heart through the drapes of a cotton sling, breathing pure mountain air into her ten-day-old lungs. Sadly, I have forgotten the names of my first guests that May, but one of them was a midwife. While we changed a nappy on an old feeding trough in a field, her expert reassurance imbued me with a confidence that made a notable difference to my first tottering steps into motherhood.

How I wish I had had her help three months later after I broke my wrist and was grappling with the geometric puzzle of breastfeeding with a plastered arm. I remember one fraught afternoon at feeding time when, no matter from which angle I approached, it seemed impossible to engineer a connection between her and either one of my breasts. We spent a good half-hour rolling around the bed becoming increasingly flustered and irate, all the while trying to avoid crushing either arm or baby in the process. Finally, in desperation, I called Sagrario, who came running immediately to align baby with breast and dry our tears.

On the whole, Marion was an easy child, although that first summer her hunger cries pursued me over hill and dale. I had hired a teenager to look after her while I was working, and we had organised for her to track me down in the hills at the critical hours of Marion's feeding regime. I, in turn, planned my walks in such a way that they would pass through a village with road access every three hours or so, with the idea that the babysitter could intercept us there. Emerging from the woods with my group of walkers, a crescendo of cries would approach us from a distance, culminating in a squeal of brakes in the village square. As a purple-faced Marion was hoisted from the car I would lift up my sweaty T-shirt, whereupon peace was restored to the valley for the next couple of hours. The birds sang again and my guests could all enjoy the sound of water tinkling from the village fountain as they filled up their bottles, waiting patiently for Marion to finish and their walk to continue.

That first summer, complicated by my broken wrist, was not our best, but when she was bundled up in a sling around my waist, we could take on the world. As for dummies, feeding bottles and other such paraphernalia, she never used them, and a pushchair would never have made it to the end of the drive.

So, once I had overcome the shock of being in charge of two disoriented creatures rather than one, motherhood seemed a surprisingly easy state of affairs. It chased away my fears of loneliness and gave me a far more meaningful cause than anything I could have concocted on my own.

One of the more difficult challenges was the apparently straightforward task of arriving at my front door which, without direct vehicle access, was fraught with logistical problems. Lugging bags of shopping and a small child down the narrow, muddy path from the road to the house could be complicated exponentially by the vagaries of ice, snow, wind and rain – and further complicated by the moon. Or to be precise, the lack of one.

On moonless nights locating the barn was only possible thanks to the fact that the path had no other objective in its sights and deviating from it would have meant tumbling into the waters of the stream below, which with an infant in my arms was not an option.

Opening the barn door then presented another obstacle and I would sometimes spend interminable minutes, battered by the elements, fumbling around in an attempt to locate the keyhole. Never having lived anywhere without artificial light before, the pitch blackness of the moonless nights here made me acutely aware of how useful and important the moon is in rural life. For the natives of Ameztia, the influence of the moon was a deeply integrated part of their daily routines with which they calculated and worked every day of their lives.

❖ ❖ ❖ ❖

Quite apart from the *matanza* – always programmed to take place during a waning moon – the phases of the moon played an important role in such varied activities as the planting of crops, the chopping of wood, the shearing of sheep and, according to Atautxi, who professed to be an expert on the subject, even the conception of babies.

Most vegetables, so I have been informed, including such staples as potatoes, tomatoes, beans and spinach, are better planted during a waning moon so that they can first deepen their roots before putting energy into their upward growth. When it comes to the cutting of trees for firewood, Atautxi assured me that the shape of their leaves plays an important role in determining the lunar phase in which the trees should be cut. Those with smooth, rounded leaves, such as beech and walnut, should be cut on a waxing moon, whereas those with more irregularly shaped leaves, or leaves with separate protruding fingers (such as oak, chestnut and ash) are better cut when the moon is waning – it is all to do with the rising sap, so I have learned, but what that has to do with the shape of the leaves, I am not sure. Personally, my relationship with wood is far less highbrow, although admittedly it could do with a little more thought. Stately woodpiles formed of meticulously aligned logs are a defining characteristic of the agricultural landscape, and no self-respecting Basque farmhouse could face the world without one. Just one look at my wood stack is enough to alert any passer-by to my foreign origins: a higgledy-piggledy stack of wood and kindling crammed beneath a tattered tarpaulin with an evil sense of humour. When I loosen the hooks on the cover to access a few logs on a stormy night, the rainwater – accumulated within the depressions on top of the tarpaulin – spies a sudden escape channel within the folds of plastic. With uncanny frequency and astonishing accuracy, it calculates its chances, and often makes its bolt for freedom by leaping down the front of my wellington boots.

But don't think that the moon's influence is limited only to the cultivation of vegetables and firewood. There are notably more clients at Amaia's hairdressing salon in Sunbillenea during a waning moon, as it is this moon that supposedly concentrates the energy into the roots (just as it does with vegetables), preventing the hair from growing back too rapidly. As the Basque word for hair, *ile*, is similar to the word for wool, *artile*, it should come as no surprise that these beliefs apply equally well to sheep and I remember one day, during a waning moon, when I turned up at Zubialdea just in time for a herd of newly shorn sheep to be ushered out of their pens. Following in their trail was a tiny shepherd of about three years old. By his looks he was obviously Basque, and his crew-cut hairstyle was typical of the way most boys wore their hair on the farms. But the wellington boots were vaguely familiar. That little boy turned out to be my barely recognisable daughter, Marion.

That morning I had left her on the farm with long, wavy hair and now here she was, as shorn as the sheep she had been shepherding down the lane. It would have mattered less had I not been expecting a photographer to arrive from *Living Spain* magazine and secretly looking forward to the rare opportunity of dressing her up in a pretty, brand-new dress sent to me from England. And, as a vague whiff of sheep emanated from her freshly coiffed hair, I did wonder what type of cutting implement had been used, as this was not a Monday, and Amaia's hairdressing salon in Sunbillenea was closed.

Atautxi also enlightened me as to the moon's influences on some more extracurricular activities. 'Did you know that if you conceive a child during a waning moon it will be a boy and during a waxing moon it will be a girl?' he stated, the gleam in his eye giving away the fact that he was honing in on one of his favourite subjects.

'Really?' I replied, my mind boggling at the ramifications this could have for the planning of families. And then I remembered that Amatxi and Atautxi had produced eight sons and just one daughter. Given the increased amount of farm work during the waning moon, was it possible that Atautxi had reneged on some of his farming duties?

❖ ❖ ❖ ❖

Moon or no moon, it was on entering the dark, cold interior of The Borda on wintry nights that I would reach a particularly low ebb, my home greeting me with a sullen welcome and the stagnant odours of yesterday's dinner. Bags and baby were dumped on the sofa as I hurried to light the fire, making a small wigwam from old bank statements and muesli packets, followed by a nest of kindling from the woods. Often, when Marion had fallen asleep during the journey home, it was easier to leave her in the warm car and dash inside to prepare the house alone. But fire-lighting is a notoriously fickle art and would sometimes take longer than anticipated, until – amid the cries of the owls in the woods – distant screams shamed me from the top of the drive. Sprinting out to the car, I would apologise profusely and bring her in.

I couldn't blame her. Abandoning babies in the mountains in pitch darkness went against the advice of all parenting handbooks. Personally, I have always felt safe outside in the mountains at night, preferring its animal smells and thick, velvety absoluteness to the shifting shadows within the walls of The Borda. Marion, however, has never agreed.

During the long nights, after putting her to bed, my piano kept me company. I had missed it. Since moving away from home twenty years earlier, I had rarely had a chance to play. But we reached out to each other, savouring a private, timeless harmony of thoughts and enjoying the peace – without the screams of 'Shut up, George!' that would echo down the stairs from my younger brother during my childhood. I am definitely not a big drinker but as I launched into one failed attempt after another to play Beethoven's Moonlight Sonata, I assuaged the inevitable defeat with the occasional glass of wine – that is if I could extract the cork.

One evening I remember standing in the doorway, bottle in hand, peering into the darkness to see if the lights were still on in Sagrario's farm and contemplating the idea of going for help to uncork the wine. It was my final bottle and, no matter how hard I pulled, the cork simply wouldn't budge. But in the end, I chose not to go. My neighbours would have found the whole scenario somewhat embarrassing. Not because I was too feeble to pull out the cork, but rather because the idea of anybody opening a bottle of wine just for themselves would have been considered a bizarre extravagance, anathema to their naturally frugal and sociable natures.

In any case, as a strategy to gain respect in the community, a knock at a door on a dark night, fancy bottle in hand, would not have been productive. Even if they had sympathised with the joys of a swig of wine over dinner, *bottles* of wine were only reserved for the very best occasions, such as carnival or fiestas, and their own evening tipples would have sloshed out of a five-litre plastic container with a screw top. Or not. This charmless modern container never completely won them over, Ignacio and Luis's preferred method still being to squirt a thin pressurised jet into their mouths from a crumpled leather wineskin passed around the table. This traditional drinking vessel is an upgrade from the sheep's stomach pouch of their ancestors – examples of which are most probably still hanging alongside the hams and cheeses in the spidery eaves of their fascinating attic.

Wine bottles with stubborn corks were a trivial obstacle in my path compared to other situations in which I simply had no choice but to ask my neighbours for help. And they would respond immediately, their battered Renault careering down the track to rescue the English damsels in distress once again. Over the years my dear neighbours have helped me to clean chimneys, stack wood, trap mice, shoot snakes, clean water tanks contaminated with duck pee, pull piano delivery vans from the mud, attach babies to breasts and so much more. But more than anything they have provided me with a model of humanity, community and decency – a kind of nobility, even. That quality is so infrequently encountered today that I don't know if it is even the right word, but when I think of my Basque neighbours it seems the perfect fit.

Of all the human vignettes that are engraved on my heart, there is one that stands out and, of course, it is to do with Amatxi. I remember one spring afternoon at the beginning of March, Isidro and Lourdes had harnessed the donkey to a small plough and were planting potatoes while Amatxi oversaw the operation from the seat of her walking frame at the edge of the field. But she wasn't idle. At ninety-three years old, she hadn't known an idle day in her life. Gathering some wisps of orange string that she had found in the yard, she tied them to the handle of her frame. Then slowly, painstakingly, with hands crooked like crows' feet, she started to plait them together – macramé style – to make a metre of stronger twine for use on the farm. And there, as I watched her, the parallel became clear. Just like the strands of string that she was weaving together, every last fibre of Amatxi's body was also doubling and twisting in lifelong service to her family – and to her home, Zubialdea.

❖ ❖ ❖ ❖

Slowly, within this warm and supportive community, Marion and I established our routines and settled into our rural lives. We watched *Bambi* and *Magic Roundabout* videos on an old VCR machine and read *The Gruffalo* and *The Tiger Who Came to Tea* at bedtime. She learned her numbers by counting the eleven wooden beams above our bed, and her colours from the empty gun cartridges we found on the ridge (and the colour-coded wrappers of the tampons she discovered in the bathroom drawer). Fascinated by empty toothpaste tubes, she would pursue me around the house on all fours, tube in hand, the sounds of patter, patter, patter, CLONK, patter, patter, patter, CLONK reverberating through the bedroom as she crawled across the wooden floor.

In addition to personal hygiene accessories, Marion has always loved dolls. I am not quite sure how it came about, and I swear that I had no influence in the matter, but Marion baptised her favourite doll 'Patxaran', after a local sloe and aniseed liqueur – tantamount to naming a doll 'Tequila Sunrise' or 'Gin and Tonic'. Hers were international dolls, showing a great deal of linguistic and cultural versatility. She would offer them cups of Earl Grey tea at home and *kafesne* (coffee with milk) when they accompanied her on her visits to the neighbouring farms. Credit cards and tea towels also caught her eye, and she would use the tea cloths to make little beds for the toothpaste tubes, cards and dolls, singing them all lullabies of '*guapa-guapa*' and '*lo-lo, lo-lo*' ('pretty, pretty' and 'sleep-sleep, sleep-sleep'). While her passion for tea towels was short-lived, her interest in credit cards is growing by the day!

Experience was her greatest educator and she soon learned that stinging nettles stung by crawling into them, that mountain banks were steep by falling down them, and that long grey hosepipes were not always what they seemed. Fortunately, Marion was too young to either remember or appreciate the full ramifications of the 'hosepipe' incident but having heard the story a thousand times, she will never take gardening equipment for granted again.

One sunny afternoon I decided to leave her for a siesta in the dappled shade of the hibiscus tree, placing her wicker basket down on top of a hosepipe that lay coiled amid miscellaneous objects on the warm terrace tiles. At first, I thought it was merely Marion stirring in her sleep that was causing her basket to quiver, and it was only when the basket started wobbling off in the direction of the field that I realised that it wasn't a hosepipe at all. In fact, on reflection, I didn't even own a hosepipe. It transpired that the first creature to bag the hibiscus tree for his afternoon nap had been a 2m-long grass snake.

The sound of bells from outside the door often inspired our first morning exchanges as we came down the stairs from the bedroom. While the higher-pitched bells of the sheep (*bee, bee*) were the easier ones to identify, the deeper-sounding ones were not so easy. But Marion got it right every time. She knew the difference between the horse bells (*txitxu, txitxu*) and cow bells (*mua, mua*) long before she could pronounce the animals' real names.

Around midday, after another slow morning routine, we would swap pyjamas for farm clothes and wander along the pig path to visit my neighbours – our repertoire of Basque onomatopoeias expanding at every step. *Pupua* (ouch), or *ñan-ñan* (eat, eat), Marion would exclaim proudly as she identified the spiky chestnut shells on the ground or the blackberries on the bushes, and *tto-tto* (doggie) as Moriko barked our welcome at the entrance to Sunbillenea. 'Mummy, *tto-tto, tto-tto!*' she would cry with glee.

Our vague and unrealistic intention was always to have visited both Sagrario and Ignacio at Sunbillenea, and Amatxi and Atautxi at Zubialdea, before lunchtime and their final flurry of activity at one o'clock. But I think we all knew the score.

For the hamlet, the sight of *Las Inglesas* approaching the farmyard just as the stews simmered to perfection on their stoves was most probably a source of amusement and, after the ritualistic 'I couldn't possibly', we were swept along into the house with the rest of the family. Marion and I spent many of our lunchtimes around our neighbours' kitchen tables where I finally learned how to drink from a wineskin without leaving a running stitch of red wine down the front of my shirt, and where Marion expanded her Basque farmyard vocabulary. Amatxi would always keep a stern eye on my mothering aptitudes and, suspicious of my ability to feed my daughter adequately, would be unable to restrain herself from giving my breast the occasional deft tweak. An instinctive reflex, I imagine, after a lifetime of milking sheep. After lunch my neighbours would go for a brief siesta and Marion and I would amble home replete and contented, a bag of *puskak* swinging at our side.

❖ ❖ ❖ ❖

The word *puskak* takes its origin from the tiny parcels of liver delivered from one farm to the next during the winter *matanzas*. After the pig had been slaughtered, each farm would dispatch one of its children to the neighbouring farms with – so Isidro and Lourdes informed me in considerable detail – 'a slice of liver, one pork fillet per adult, a couple of black puddings and a bone.' As the day of the *matanza* varied from farm to farm, this regular supply of *puskak* offered an important supplement to the local food supply during the winter months.

As the local throat-slitting expert, Isidro often helped out on various farms, returning home with a particularly full bag of *puskak* for his services. The example of honesty that he was, I am sure that Isidro never once thought of leaving the scene with an extra ration of prime pork cuts stuffed down the front of his wellington boots. It appears that someone from Zubieta, no names were ever mentioned, was not quite so scrupulous.

In the old days everything was recyclable and *puskak* were either wrapped up in a large cabbage leaf or a membrane taken from the pig's stomach. The term *puskak* eventually evolved to include a variety of edible offerings, such as small parcels of cheese or *txistorra*, which were also used to curry favour with the village doctor, teacher or priest.

However, in a nod to modernity, as Marion and I ambled back home after lunch, our *puskak* bounced along in a plastic supermarket bag. Inside might be a slice of sponge cake, slabs of bacon or a box of eggs – if the chickens hadn't eaten too many peaches which, according to Amatxi, stopped them from laying. If we were lucky the bag would also contain earthenware pots full of *mamia*, a smoky sheep's milk junket, best eaten with honey or a sprinkling of sugar. The constant stream of *puskak* that accompanied us home from our farm visits was perhaps as much due to doubts about my culinary abilities as it was to my neighbours' profoundly generous nature.

With these doubts in mind, Sagrario, mother of all waifs and strays from both sides of the Ameztia crossroads, took to pureeing the leftovers of their evening *menestra* (a plate of mixed vegetables), making them into a delicious vegetable soup. Early the following morning her brother-in-law Luis would leave the farm with a shepherd's stick in one hand and a plastic bag in the other. After delivering his sheep to my field, he would continue down the pig path towards my house, hanging the bag on our gate as he passed by. Several hours later, at an hour that we spent much of our lives trying to disguise – getting up late being seriously frowned upon in farming communities – Marion and I would wander out to the gate. In the bag, in a small Tupperware container, was another example of the constant stream of neighbourly *puskak* that came our way: a miniature portion of Sagrario's homemade soup, just in time for Marion's lunch.

CULTURE SHOCK

MAGGOTS IN THE TOY CHEST

Even though Marion and I had little experience with pushchairs, I have observed the behaviour of parents with pushchairs on zebra crossings with bemusement. It seems to me that the buggies – and their infant occupants – are often thrust out into the road to test the traffic conditions and only then, if the coast is clear, do the parents venture out behind. Metaphorically, my entrance into life in Ameztia was somewhat similar, and it was Marion who systematically ran ahead of me into the farmyards where my neighbours, wiping the muck off their hands, would scoop her up and hug her tight. As they carried her off to the kitchen, through stables permeated with the inevitable '*kolonia euskaldun*', I would simply traipse along behind.

In motherhood, I inadvertently fell back on many of the customs of my own British upbringing which, when living in Ameztia, occasionally gave rise to an amusing clash of cultures. The following farcical duel, entirely of my own making and resulting from my British obsession with hygiene and sterility, was a prime example. It concerned the race to wipe clean Marion's mucky nose.

Long before my neighbours reached into the pockets of their blue dungarees, I would detect the gleam in their eyes. Anticipating what was about to happen, I too would fish around frantically for a pristine paper tissue before their own crumpled handkerchiefs – used indiscriminately for all manner of farmyard emergencies – surfaced to the light. Over time I perfected my technique but even when I lost the race, I was always careful to keep my feelings to myself, well aware that generations of healthy, snotty-nosed children had grown up in the hamlet before her.

And then there was one day when my British fastidiousness simply overwhelmed all my efforts to adapt to rural life. One morning when Marion was about four years old, I made my way down to her bedroom, which had recently been moved from the attic to a corner of the conservatory. Her toy chest, full of dolls – and possibly the odd toothpaste tube – sat against the wall beneath an old oak beam and a join in the roofing. From a distance, my first impression was that it was snowing in her bedroom. But instead of forming a blanket of pristine ice crystals, the curtain of small white particles drifting down upon her dolls had covered them in a seething mass of maggots, distorting the expressions on their pink plastic faces and giving them a macabre almost zombie air. This was a scene straight from a horror film and, as if the house was under siege – which in my mind it was – I snatched her from her bed and ran screaming out on to the terrace. Here we camped out with emergency rations until my neighbour's Renault came careering down the drive to save us – once again. Later that day, in conversation with my neighbours, I was soberly advised on the disadvantages of using poison on water rats in the roof cavity.

❖ ❖ ❖ ❖

Pink is the colour I most associate with Marion's childhood. And I don't just mean her pretty pink dolls or the pink toy pushchair she used to trundle through the puddles of blood on my neighbours' farms. Pink was also the colour of the girly birthday parties that we held for her friends in Zubialdea's backyard. Pink 'Hello Kitty' beakers and napkins would complement the magenta stains on their wooden party table – a table used indiscriminately for family celebrations, mechanical repairs and the yearly *matanza*. However, one rose-tinted memory lingers longer than most.

When Marion was a few years old, my mother sent her a pink top with sequined lettering from a fancy high-street store. The following morning, as I was heading off to the valley to take my guests for a walk, I dressed my little princess up in her new sparkly top before dropping her off to be looked after in Zubialdea. As I sped off down the mountain, glancing in my rear-view mirror, I will never forget the vision of shimmering pinkness that met my eye. Marion stood in the yard waving goodbye in her immaculate T-shirt while behind her a freshly slaughtered lamb dangled from a hook in the garage, the blood staining its white fleece to an identical shade. Just at that moment, a ray of sunlight lit up the scene, setting the sequins on her top shimmering and the globules of blood twinkling as they dripped from the slash in the lamb's neck into puddles on the flagstones below. It seemed as if both pairs of eyes were fixed upon me, bidding their farewells – one more permanently than the other.

❖ ❖ ❖ ❖

Living in Ameztia, death is very much part of the landscape. And I don't mean just the glazed stare of a slaughtered lamb, or the occasional animal carcass picked clean by the vultures. I mean the death of local people. Death is a frequent topic of conversation here, often coming in just after the usual preambles of lambing, wood-cutting and the weather. Of course, its popularity as a conversation topic has much to do with the fact that everyone knows each other, which in turn has much to do with the fact that everyone is related. And here I digress once again.

Anthropologists analysing the genetic make-up of these isolated valleys would find a concentrated cluster of closely related families. This is reflected in the high frequency of repeated surnames such as Elizalde Elizalde or Mariezcurrena Mariezcurrena – names often taken directly from the house names themselves. In Spain, everybody uses two surnames, the first from the father and the second from the mother. Consequently, a repeated surname indicates a strong possibility that both the mother and the father have shared genetic origins, which in these Basque valleys of Navarre is too often the case. Despite my involvement in readdressing this balance, it still remains a fact that few foreign genes have ventured here from the outside world.

Weekly, it would seem, I hear of the death of somebody I am supposed to know: a neighbour's cousin, the butcher's mother-in-law or the bar owner's wife's great-uncle. Talk of death reverberates through these small communities and newspapers bearing expensive obituaries are pored over during the Sunday morning vermouth in the bar, the bilingual Basque-Spanish nature of the region not only doubling the word count in road signs and marketing brochures but also in tributes to the dead.

Frequent accidents occur on the N121 road which runs through tunnels and ravines, past hydro-electric plants and brothels, connecting Spain to France and Europe beyond. This road is the principal access to our valleys and its popularity as an international trucking route, combined with mountain bends and overconfident locals, creates a dangerous cocktail which regularly takes its toll.

Recent statistics confirm that it is the most lethal road within the entire 10,000-square-kilometre region of Navarre.

But the farms claim lives too. One death, in particular, left its mark on the views from my living room for an entire summer. I did not know the man directly, but he had been haymaking on the steep slopes of Urrotz on the other side of the valley. The use of machines in the mountains is an unreliable (and unforgiving) science. Although one year the farmer may have the measure of his land, the following year conditions could have changed; slightly more claggy soil than usual or a different angle taken across the contours can be enough to flip tractors and send the drivers to their death. This is exactly what happened to the farmer from Urrotz. His tractor tyres lost their grip on the land, taking him on a death roll to the valley floor. All summer the uncut swathe of the field was visible from my living room window and his epitaph was a teardrop of crumpled hay plunging down to the river below.

❖ ❖ ❖ ❖

Ultimately, there was no choice other than to relax into my chosen existence in Ameztia, accepting the death, gore and grime that are part and parcel of mountain life. Any struggle to uphold my suburban hygiene standards – for Marion's sake at least – was dealt a final blow one beautiful starry evening. We had just had dinner at Zubialdea and were walking home with our usual bag of *puskak*. There was a new moon and the stars were bright, and Marion had been silent for a while when all of a sudden she stopped and pointed at the sky.

'Look, Mummy,' she commanded. 'Look, look at the sky, Mummy.'

'Yes, sweetheart, what is it?' I replied, gazing upwards at the star-studded void.

'Look, Mummy, look, the stars look like fleas.'

And with that she took my hand and continued up the rise in her new, oversized wellington boots, unaware of the devastation her words had left in their wake. I came from a world where stars had always looked like diamonds and now my darling daughter, the one person to whom I wanted to give the very best this world could offer, was telling me that these beautiful jewels of the cosmos looked like fleas. There were no two ways about it, our reference points were now galaxies apart.

A FAMILY BUSINESS

HANGMAN AND THE UNFORTUNATE WORD

As a self-employed, single mother with a lifestyle business, my work and guests have formed an inseparable part of our family life, and Marion has never known a life without my tapping away at the computer or flitting around attending to the needs of the countless guests and friends who walk through our door.

I remember an amusing conversation I had with her one day while chatting with recently arrived guests enjoying aperitifs on the terrace. Tugging at my jumper, she seemed desperate to ask me a question, as if she had had a sudden revelation that she was eager to share.

'Mummy, Mummy, come here.'

'Wait a moment, darling, I'm working,' I replied dismissively. 'I'll be with you in a minute.'

She sat down on the steps of the terrace in the shade of the hibiscus tree and watched me at work.

After a while, when the guests had disappeared inside, she came over to me and tried again.

'Mummy,' she launched even more emphatically.

'Yes, darling, what is it?'

'Mummy, but is that your work?'

'Yes, darling, it is.'

'But Mummy,' she exclaimed in either shock or disillusion – I am not sure which – 'but Mummy, it's just like having a party!'

❖ ❖ ❖ ❖

My first office headquarters (in the days when the company was still known as Language Adventures) was a tiny desk in our attic bedroom. As an infant, Marion would wake to the sound of frantic tapping on my computer before she was whisked away to an internet café nearby. There, I would spend the morning replying to emails and sending press releases to journalists, all the while breastfeeding her on my lap to keep her quiet. Soon, naturally, the breastfeeding dried up, but the constant tap-tapping away at the keyboard never did.

'Mummy, the first word I ever learned was "emails",' she once reproached me, at an age when she was well aware of the power of her words.

'It wasn't, darling, it was *tto-tto* (dog),' I retorted, hurt, the missile having met its mark.

During the first years of building the company, it was slightly easier than it is today for an imaginative press release and a human-interest story to catch the attention of the tabloid press, and journalists from the *Observer*, *Guardian*, *Daily Mail* and even a BBC documentary producer made their way up Ameztia's hairpin bends to meet us. The last, unfruitful, episode prompted a tongue-in-cheek email to my client database entitled '*Almost* Stephen Fry'. It turned out that the Michelin-starred restaurants of San Sebastián had proven a more appetising background setting for a documentary on the Basque language than the far more original – but infinitely less sophisticated – Joaldunak of Ituren.

❖ ❖ ❖ ❖

By the time Marion was a few years old, Language Adventures had blossomed into Pyrenean Experience, and I was receiving some fifty to sixty guests a year. She embraced her role in the family company early on, adding to the general 'ambience' with shrieks of '*kaka kaka!*' (poo poo) at the top of her voice while I was talking to clients on the phone. Applying her artistic talents to my reservation book, she would cover my guests' vital details with scribbled princesses and dogs. But before long she moved out of the back office and joined my guests to head up the entertainment department, organising paper airplane competitions with Spanish verb sheets and commandeering fly swatters for fencing competitions. When she grew older, she entered the language faculty, teaching Spanish with the aid of tongue-twisters and hangman, the latter didactic technique ultimately bringing her teaching vocation to a dramatic halt.

As language students are aware, much of the fun of learning comes, in hindsight, from inserting a wrong word in a sentence, producing something totally unexpected, or perhaps using the right word but with an unintended double entendre. It was this ambiguity of language that was to blame for the demise of Marion's brief career as a language teacher.

At thirteen years old she had organised a game of hangman with my guests, one of whom, a birdwatcher, had proudly put forward a new Spanish word that he had learned that day. The word he chose was the name for a tiny bird that he had spotted on one of the walks, diligently jotted down in his notebook. The word was *chochín*, the Spanish name for the Eurasian wren. Marion asked him to draw the number of dashes on the whiteboard that corresponded with the number of letters in his word, but he was not to tell anyone what the word was – not even her. He then sat back and handed the pen over to Marion who, with his guidance, helped elicit letters from the rest of the class. Slowly, letter by letter, the mystery word appeared. No one else knew the word for 'wren' in Spanish and so it was only Marion who had any idea of the meaning of the word materialising on the board.

Unfortunately, the Spanish word for 'wren' is a homonym for a colloquialism which means something totally different, and my daughter – not known for her ornithological interests – was aware only of the latter.

When the word *chochín* appeared, a strangled scream came from the front of the classroom, provoking bemused laughter from my guests, none more so than from the man who had innocently used the word in the first place. There was a crescendo of infectious laughter as the class begged Marion to tell them what it meant, followed by more screams in a spiral of increasing hysteria. I ran to the teaching room to save the situation and literally had to throw a coat over Marion's head and escort her out of the door. Hangman has now been removed from her pedagogical toolbox, but the Spanish word for wren, *chochín* (an unfortunate homophone for a familiar Spanish word for 'little vulva') will remain forever engraved on the memories of both teacher and students alike.

THE BASQUE LANGUAGE

STRAWBERRY ICE CREAMS AND GREEDY PIGS

There was little doubt that Marion was destined to be a Basque-speaker, but the linguistic triangle within which she would grow was evident even before the umbilical cord was cut, and their cultural idiosyncrasies became an integral part of her identity. Or identities. Her progress, as she rapidly came to terms with her multicultural and multilingual background, provided me with an endless source of entertainment.

Culturally, the rhythms of our lives were mainly dictated by our Basque surroundings. After the beating of my heart, *pulunpa… pulunpa… pulunpa…* was the second rhythm she experienced as her father danced her around the maternity ward to the step of the Joaldunak. Nevertheless, many of the routines of our home life remained resolutely British, with the melodies of English nursery rhymes ringing through the house from an old CD player as I jiggled her on my knee.

In order to counterbalance the overwhelming Basqueness of our surroundings, our home in Ameztia has always been a bit of a shrine to the English language, stocked with English books and videos, extending to a repertoire of dramatised audiobooks in the car. We had our cups of Earl Grey tea, our Marmite on toast, and bowls of Corn Flakes or Frosties for breakfast. It was not at all in the spirit of an 'expat' that I had surrounded myself with all things British, but quite the reverse. I had situated myself so deeply in the bosom of Basque mountain life that, apart from my guests in the summer, the winters could pass by without our meeting any other English-speaking adult at all. While I missed the intimacies and cultural references that I could share with those who spoke my mother tongue, I accepted that this was the price to pay for living in paradise.

Enforcing a British household was simply the only way to ensure that Marion was ever going to learn English at all and reaffirmed my love for my sorely missed English language. Two kittens, Snowflake and Blackie, rescued from the stream and lured into our British castle with a tin of tuna and a saucer of milk, also signed up as new members of our English-speaking team.

When Marion came back from her Basque-speaking babysitters on the farms, she unconsciously changed the pitch of her voice and the set of her chin the moment she walked in the door, and it was evident which language she was going to speak even before she opened her mouth. She slipped out of her Basque wellington boots and into her English princess slippers as she changed between her public and private spaces, just as I imagine the local farmers alternating between Spanish and Basque during Franco's reign. But she would also come home with linguistic '*puskak*' from her Basque-speaking life, peppering her English vocabulary with the odd Basque word that she felt we could not live without.

❖ ❖ ❖ ❖

At home, my parents had always talked euphemistically about body parts and their functions, and so consequently, the more popular expressions for such matters didn't sit comfortably with me, never really entering my active vocabulary. Marion, and her knowledge of the Basque language, soon put an end to this tradition. These were exactly the words that she needed in order to express herself and so she enthusiastically filled the lacunas in my English vocabulary with Basque words such as '*kurroka*', '*kaka*' and '*pusker*' (burp, shit and fart). These Basque words quickly found their place within our household vocabulary, and it took her many years to learn their English equivalents.

Apart from an array of Basque – and later Spanish – expressions, Marion inserted other elements of the Basque language into her otherwise native English grammar. The first was the Basque suffix -ek. In retrospect, her insistence on using -ek words at two or three years old may have offered us one of the first signs of her bossy nature, as -ek is a suffix used to state and emphasise *who* is doing an action. For example, if I had asked *her* to fit a jigsaw piece into a puzzle but she had wanted *me* to do it, she would point at me emphatically saying Mummy-ek, Mummy-ek, Mummy-ek. On the other hand, if *I* was about to squeeze the toothpaste out of the tube and *she* wanted to do it, she would push me aside with a fusillade of Marion-ek, Marion-ek, Marion-ek as she wrestled to prise one of her favourite toys from my hand.

But the real trophy was the dazzling array of Basque onomatopoeias. How could one not fully embrace them and welcome them into the household too? We certainly had the linguistic space. So we walked (*ttipi-ttapa*) in the drizzle (*zirimiri*), splashing (*plisti-plasta*) through the puddles, and then returned home for a bath (*putxu-putxu*) and dinner (*ñan-ñan*). Then, following a bout of *kili-kili* (tickling) on the sofa, we headed up the stairs to sleep (*lo-lo*).

❖ ❖ ❖ ❖

Whereas Marion learned Basque at the farm – and later on at school – her Spanish skills arrived by a more circuitous route. Whenever we went to visit our neighbours together there would be a triangle of languages around the dinner table. I would speak to Marion in English and my neighbours would speak to her in Basque. However, when my neighbours and I conversed, we would use Spanish. So, eager to understand any plans laid – and any skulduggery afoot – she immediately learned Spanish. Naturally, as soon as she socialised outside the hamlet, the national language, Castilian Spanish, became a feature of daily life, as – contrary to the opinion of some – we do actually live in Spain.

Marion has lived in English, Basque and Spanish on a daily basis ever since she was born, and due to our proximity to France – and our occasional forays over the border for *moules à la crème* and *huîtres* – French has come easily too. As she often talks in her sleep, I have observed that she dreams in all these languages. One of her most entertaining nocturnal phrases combined a fluid stream of nine words from three different languages: French, Basque and Spanish.

'*Une glâce de fraise… txerri handi handia… ¡qué desastre!*', which translates as 'a strawberry ice cream… a big fat pig… what a disaster!' The mind boggles as to exactly what she was dreaming about.

❖ ❖ ❖ ❖

The Basque language (Euskara) lies at the very heart of Basque identity, so much so that the word used to define a Basque person, *Euskaldun*, literally means 'he or she who speaks Basque'. Euskara is the sole survivor of the ancient languages spoken in southwestern Europe before the invasion of the pre-Indo-European languages roughly five thousand years ago. It has been primarily a spoken language, and the first Basque book – a volume of poetry published by a priest – was printed in 1545. Nevertheless, personal names, toponyms and inscriptions reveal that when the Romans showed up in the region in around the first century BC, Euskara was spoken over an area roughly eight times the size of the Basque-speaking lands of today. Sweeping southwards with their Latin culture and language, the Romans would have encountered this odd-sounding language throughout the Pyrenees: stumbling into it, and overpowering it, in areas as far afield as Andorra to the east, Santander to the west and Soria to the south. In the territory now known as France, its reach appears to have extended as far north as the banks of the Garonne River and Bordeaux. Slowly, Euskara retreated into the more isolated mountain villages and these remote valleys of northern Navarre became one of its principal strongholds.

Despite numerous attempts to find similarities with other tongues, Euskara appears to be a language isolate whose origins – like that of the Basque people – are thought to hail back to prehistoric times. Its Stone Age roots are evident in the etymology of various words, notably in the frequent appearance of the word *haitz* (stone) and its permutations in the names of various tools, many of which – or so it appears – would have once been made of stone. Examples include *aizkora* (axe), *aizto* (machete), *aitzur* (hoe)… and even *aizturrak* (scissors). Although the materials such tools are made from have changed over time, the language has not, and for this reason the Basque language is sometimes referred to as a 'living fossil'.

Another possible indication of its prehistoric origins are the many references to giants in Basque mythology. One such figure is Basajaun (lord of the forest), a large, hairy giant who lived inside caves in the woods. Allegedly, Basajaun was far bigger than the Basque shepherds around him. However, according to certain legends, despite his intimidating and primitive looks, he often collaborated with the shepherds, watching over their flocks and alerting them to marauding wolves or bears. He is portrayed as an intelligent being, a toolmaker and occasionally even a savant. Although modern anthropologists tend to refute this idea, could these numerous tales imply that the Basques date back to a time in prehistory in which they cohabited with another large hominoid species? Are there any parallels here with the myths that surround Bigfoot or the Yeti, or the Chuchuna of Russian folklore? Are the Basques direct descendants of Cro-Magnon man? And could Basajaun have been a Neanderthal?

❖ ❖ ❖ ❖

After having survived for so long, the Basque language faced its greatest challenge at the hands of General Franco's fascist dictatorship. At the end of his reign in 1975, less than 600,000 people spoke Euskara, yet now – fifty years later – there are 900,000 speakers. After the Basque Autonomous Government was created in 1979, it implemented a huge variety of initiatives to revive the Basque language, creating television and radio channels, schools and universities, and even encouraging rap.

Basque rap, a highly prized local art form featuring spontaneous rhyming bards known in Basque as *bertsolariak*, has a strong following among all generations and all backgrounds in the Basque Country. These artists improvise long and humorous stories in rhyming verse, usually to the tune of a well-known Basque song or ballad, competing in tournaments and taking centre stage in many communal banquets. They often sing in pairs, the lines bouncing – every thirty seconds or so – between one *bertsolari* and the other, and it is a moving sight to see this unique art of storytelling uniting Basques of all ages. The silence before they launch into a new verse is intense, almost reverential, and their speed of thought is breathtaking, as rhyme after rhyme, twist after twist, sweep the audience along on a roller coaster of suspense, laughter and cheers. The almost cult following of the *bertsolariak* has undoubtedly been instrumental in preserving the Basque language, all the more precious because it is so fiendishly hard to learn. Ironically, a local legend says that it was too difficult for even the devil to manage, and anyone who has attempted it will understand why. Apparently, the devil tried to learn the language so he could decide which Basques should join him in hell. Yet, after seven years, he still couldn't understand it and gave up – as so many well-intentioned students do. Whether this meant that no Basques were sent to hell – or all of them – I may be able to tell you one day. But not yet.

THE VILLAGE CALENDAR

WHEELBARROW RACES
AND GRUMPY COALMEN

Unlike the devil, the children at the Ituren village school seem to have no problem with the Basque language. Daily, sixty to seventy children between the ages of three and eleven climb the school stairs to study everything from arithmetic to rap in this most demonically difficult language.

Pulunpa Eskola is the school's official name and it is indeed a strange one, even by Basque standards. In true Basque style, the name was chosen democratically by the pupils in a 'naming-the-school' competition a few years back, and now officially heads all written correspondence.

The children come to the school from the surrounding villages of Ituren (with its three satellite hamlets: Aurtitz, Latsaga and Ameztia), Zubieta and Elgorriaga. However, due to age-old rivalries between Zubieta and Ituren – exacerbated by the turbulent January carnival of the Joaldunak – some parents in Zubieta choose to avoid 'hostile territory' altogether. Gathering up their small progeny, they make a dash past the Ituren school gates for the more bourgeois school in Doneztebe at the head of the valley.

At school the children learn the usual range of primary school subjects in Basque, including *bertsolaritza* (the art of becoming a *bertsolari*). In addition, when Marion first attended the school in 2007, aged just three, she had three hours of Spanish and four hours of English each week. It seems startling that a school in Spain dedicates more hours to teaching English than Spanish but – turning a blind eye to politics – general opinion is that the Spanish language is absorbed by osmosis through daily exposure to Spanish officialdom and media. As far as the spoken word is concerned, this is generally true, but the locals' spelling of certain Spanish words can be atrocious. Thinking about it, their spelling in Basque, primarily a spoken language, can be even worse.

The day I helped out the children's English teacher in one of his lessons, elements of geography also appeared not to have curried favour with the school curriculum. After several renderings of *The Gruffalo* to a group of eight-year-olds, I decided to improvise conversation in the final minutes of class.

'Do you live in England?' I asked.

'Noooo,' came the answer.

'Do you live in France?' I continued.

'Noooo,' came the same reply.

I built up the momentum with one more question.

'Do you live in Italy?'

'Noooo,' came the reply again, before I asked the final, obvious question and waited, relieved, for the obvious reply.

'Do you live in Spain?'

To which they answered without a moment's hesitation:

'Noooo…'

At the age of eight, it was clear that the children had no idea that they lived in Spain, but whether this was due to a gap in the curriculum or to a certain bias on the part of the parents, I am not quite sure. In any case, this belief would have horrified the more patriotic Spanish society of Pamplona and the flatlands to the south. As far as the children from the Pulunpa School were concerned, they lived in Euskal Herria. Spain was somewhere you went to on holiday.

Marion's attendance at the Pulunpa School has probably been the most important factor in my integration into the local community. Suddenly, I was no longer an Englishwoman among Basques, but a parent among parents, and this shared identity gave me a heightened sense of belonging.

Unsurprisingly, the school is the hub of village life and both children's and parents' routines swing to the rhythms of the school timetable, seeing us careering into Ituren square, unpunctually, for the nine o'clock bell and then returning in a more leisurely fashion at around four. Sunny afternoons are spent in the village square, catching up on local gossip while the kids run riot or play *pelota*.

❖ ❖ ❖ ❖

Several times a year the Pulunpa School organises social events, and one of my favourites used to be the Christmas party. Ironically – and to the understandable bemusement of my neighbours, the Ameztiarrak – it may just be for my culinary offerings during these fiestas that the locals from Ituren, the Iturendarrak, remember me most. I amuse myself by thinking that perhaps, in years to come, some curious anthropologists might uncover mention of an English tapa (*pintxo*) called the *pintxo inglés*. And that they will sit back and scratch their heads, puzzling not only over its mere existence in this tiny mountain village but also by its flagrant lack of British ingredients. The *pintxo inglés* consists of toasted baguette, Italian pesto and melted French goat's cheese, crowned by the cosmopolitan cherry tomato. I first introduced it as finger food for the end-of-term Pulunpa School parties, proud of the fact that it sported the red, white and green colours of the Basque flag – which went totally unnoticed. In spite of competition from its well-established rivals, *tortilla* and *txistorra*, its fame took off, and the *pintxo inglés* has now been adopted by the more adventurous households in the village. I have never dared mention that the recipe is not English at all, having been copied from a Hawaiian friend in Copenhagen.

After Christmas, the next party on the school calendar is the famous Ituren-Zubieta carnival at the end of January. On the Friday before the valley erupts into mayhem, excited children enact their own mini carnival, dressing up as witches, demons and monsters. Others, with higher aspirations, dress up as the Joaldunak with tiny whips, sheepskins and bells all made to size. Pursued by proud parents laden with anoraks, smartphones and umbrellas, the children run amok through the village before they are herded back into the warmth for hot chocolate and sponge cake.

Afterwards we all slowly make our way home, stopping off for a final drink at the village bar. Maika, my lumberjack friend, and I form the hard core, while our happily neglected children play freely in the square. Or so we think.

Several years ago, our children were actually locked into the school with no way of raising the alarm, their tiny noses pressed against the windows of the second-floor classrooms while their parents partied on, unaware and totally insouciant, in the plaza below. Hours passed before we realised that they had disappeared, and that was only because the cleaner had entered the building and let them out.

Among the many advantages of living in a small community is the feeling of safety in the knowledge that everyone keeps an eye on each other's children. I have rarely worried about Marion's whereabouts, trusting that if she were out of sight, she would have been scooped up by a friend, a neighbour or one of her many distant relatives.

The summer solstice is celebrated in our area by jumping over bonfires at twilight. The school's end-of-year party falls in June at about the same time, but the principal protagonist of the school festivities is quite a different element; instead of fire, a big water fight in the village square launches the start of the holiday season. A noisy and boisterous affair, it is preceded by a friendly competition of traditional Basque rural sports, with teams made up of a mix of children, teachers and parents. Maika is inevitably the master of ceremonies, organising tugs-of-war and races in which participants run around the square with heavy sacks on their shoulders, conjuring up images of runaway smugglers with their loot.

Another popular game is *koxkor biltzea*, my personal favourite of all the Basque sports. While Marion attended the school, Maika invariably put my name down on the list, its need for speed and agility suiting me far more than the many other games that demanded sheer brute force. *Koxkor biltzea* is an unusual Basque sport involving running backwards and forwards placing corncobs at increasingly long intervals along a straight line and then picking them up one by one to be thrown into a basket on the touchline. This game, like most Basque rural sports, is directly derived from a farming activity, and in the same vein, grass-cutting and stone-lifting competitions are also frequently found throughout the Basque lands. In uncharacteristic deference to health and safety regulations, however, the more dangerous Basque sports such as *aizkolaritza* (log-cutting) or *orga-joko* (dragging carts around the square) are deemed inappropriate for the under-fives and, consequently, sidelined by the school board.

Several years ago, I remember one sunny sports day which, coming after several days of rain, coincided with perfect haymaking weather. In farming communities like ours, the only timetable more imposing than that of the school calendar is that of the land. Hay is harvested two or three times a year between the beginning of May and the end of August, and all other engagements are dropped whenever perfect haymaking weather comes along. On this occasion, Maika's carefully calculated teams were consequently short on numbers, and the only parents present were myself and Jeni, the village beautician, whose young body lies today in Ituren graveyard.

Faced with a dwindling number of participants, Maika spied my English and Swedish guests gathering discreetly at the corner of the plaza to watch the events and shepherded them into the arena where she eyed them up expertly and distributed them among the teams. To this day, we savour memories of John and David pushing Sonia and Birgitta in wheelbarrows at top speed around the plaza while the schoolkids cheered them on from the sidelines in broken English.

After the final tug of war, the sports day drew to a close and my flushed guests joined the now hysterical children, their flustered parents and a cohort of ecstatic teachers for the end-of-year banquet beneath the porticoes of the bar. This was followed by music and dancing which inevitably deteriorated into water fights and a jump in the river. However, most parents tried to avoid this final activity, saving all the energy they could muster for the two-and-a-half-month child-intensive summer holidays that followed.

❖ ❖ ❖ ❖

The day my guests helped boost the ranks at the school sports day was just one of the many spontaneous cultural exchanges between us and the local community that have occurred over the years. Somewhere in my photo album is a photo of Glen, a client from Wales, balancing precariously on top of one of Maika's bracken stacks, and Jane, a doctor, trying unsuccessfully to milk one of Sagrario's sheep. But perhaps one of the most amusing moments was Tom's lively and drunken rendition of 'She'll be Coming 'Round the Mountain' at a banquet with the Joaldunak, one potentially disastrous September day after I had made a mistake with the festival dates.

Little do most people know that the Joaldunak actually make an appearance several times a year, although it is only during the January carnival that they are accompanied by the unbridled mayhem and demonic incarnations that have made this event so famous. On Christmas Eve, the Joaldunak also appear out of the darkness, naked flame torches only metres from children's heads, as they accompany the Basque equivalent of Father Christmas (Olentzero) – a dirty, grumpy Basque coalman – down from the hills with a donkey laden with presents.

But there are other dates which are a little more complex to calculate. In Spain, as in all Catholic countries, every date has a saint's name. As many male names are also saints' names – for example José, Pedro, Isidro, Ignacio, and so on – this means that most men enjoy two birthday celebrations a year. Not only each day, but also each village, has a patron saint, and the annual village fiestas (often week-long affairs) are timed around their saint's day, culminating in great feasting and spiritual merriment.

In mid-September there is a rather fickle date when the Joaldunak appear in Ameztia. It is a complex date to calculate, as it falls on the weekend before the fiestas in Urrotz which, in turn, fall on the weekend closest to the feast of San Miguel. The complex timetabling of this event can pose serious problems for those of us planning tourist schedules and cultural activities a year in advance. When San Miguel falls on a Wednesday – equidistant between the weekend before and the weekend after – my planning is in trouble.

On this particular day, the Joaldunak make a pilgrimage to the farms of Ameztia in honour of my neighbours' ancestors. It is an intimate affair enacted purely for my neighbours at the Sunbillenea, Zubialdea and Sotillenea farmsteads, who hurry around preparing tapas and mushroom *tortillas*, uncorking bottles of warm cider and laying them out on multipurpose trestle tables in the farmyard. Ears straining to pick up the first sounds of the bells, we all hover excitedly amid the ash trees at the bottom of the drive, waiting for the Joaldunak to arrive.

As a foreigner, I feel it is a great honour to be part of this event and with my neighbours having always been so welcoming to my guests, I make the event the highlight of one of my Basque Mountain Experience Walking Weeks. The fame of the Joaldunak has spread, and I often have guests reserving a place for this week a year in advance.

When guests from all around the world have booked their flights to join me for this ceremony, the least I can do is to get the date right. So, you can imagine the horror when Juanito explained that despite my careful calculations I had got it wrong! How on earth was I going to face my clients after that?

What happened next was, without a doubt, one of the greatest honours ever bestowed on me during the two decades of my life in

Ameztia. As soon as I found out that the dates had been changed, I sprinted along the pig path to Sunbillenea to tell Sagrario my woes.

'Oh Sagrario, you won't believe it, they have changed the date of the Joaldunak,' I blurted as I ran into her yard, skipping the nicer preambles about the weather and the hay which usually preceded more personal conversations.

'And I have all these guests coming from all over the world, from Australia, America – what shall I do? What on earth shall I do?'

There was a faint smile on her lips and a few long seconds passed while Moriko, their sheepdog, pawed at my jeans. Sagrario was superb at problem-solving. It was an essential skill in the mountains, all the more so when a clueless English woman had moved in next door.

'I'll have a word with Juanito and we'll see what he says.'

Three weeks later, at twelve noon on a Saturday in mid-September, the leader of the troupe drove into Sagrario's farmyard with a brass horn under his arm and slung a bundle of sheepskins and bells, knotted with thick rope, into a corner of the yard. A few minutes later another van arrived with five more Joaldunak who, placing their tall lace hats on the bench, coloured streamers fluttering in the wind, headed over to shake Ignacio's hand and go through the usual preambles and greetings. From time to time, everyone's eyes flickered towards the ash trees near the garage where a lamb had been slow roasting on a spit since earlier that morning and old tables had been set up together with all the chairs the hamlet could muster.

There had been no choice but to come clean to my guests about the calamity I was in, so I apologised profusely, explaining that my neighbours were doing their utmost to remedy the situation. Their reaction was heart-warming. Instead of feeling that I had brought them to my mountaintop under false pretences, they appreciated the extraordinary efforts made by the community on our behalf and rose to the occasion magnificently. From that moment on, they took over my kitchen and busied themselves making apple pies and quiches to contribute to the festivities.

Back in Sagrario's farmyard, two more woolly bundles, retrieved from a dusty corner of their attic, had been added to the others. Neither Ignacio nor Luis had picked up their bells in twenty-five years and now they were about to wear them for me. My guests did not appreciate the full significance of the moment but the rest of the Joaldunak knew. After years of living alongside them, I also could imagine what it meant for these two brothers to put on their bells a quarter of a century after they had last put them down. Their honour and pride shone through in the unbridled emotion of Ignacio's green eyes and in Luis's shy smile.

More cars arrived from the village and this time musicians stepped out with accordions and tambourines, while trays of plates and glasses were carried to the garage on the other side of the yard. The men pulled on their sheepskins and turned to help each other tie on their bells. Placing a foot in the small of their companion's back to keep the first knot tight, they strained at the thick ropes to bring the second knot into line. In total, about forty people joined us that day and the small troupe of Joaldunak, with Ignacio and Luis bringing up the rear, marched around the yard, blessing the lands of Ameztia and all those who had ventured here.

The lunch afterwards in Sagrario and Ignacio's garage was a hearty affair, the exceptional circumstances heightening the emotions and camaraderie for us all. Afterwards, replete with roast lamb and apple pie, a couple of *bertsolariak* among the Joaldunak stood up and improvised songs about the strange foreign guests in their midst and that silly English woman who got her dates wrong. I laughed and blushed and cried all at once. It was one of the greater moments of my life.

Suddenly, Tom, a northerner, stood up and, swinging a glass of Patxaran dangerously over the heads of our hosts, started to sing. Within moments we had joined him, serenading the party at the top of our voices with a discordant and unprepared – if not entirely inappropriate – rendition of 'She'll be Coming 'Round the Mountain'. Reverberating and amplifying our merriment, this tiny, makeshift garage with its corrugated tin roof broadcasted the euphoria of that moment over the hills and into the night.

But not all the foreigners who 'come 'round the mountain' to live in Ituren have had such a happy time.

ITUREN CHURCH

STORIES FROM BEYOND THE GRAVE

The graveyard in Ituren adjoins the northern wall of the church of San Martín which is situated, unusually, on the outskirts of town. From the back of the cemetery, the sheer slopes of Mount Mendaur rise steeply to more than 1,000m, culminating in a series of ferrous rocky tors. Here, on clear days, La Trinidad – a tiny white chapel doubling as a mountain refuge – can be discerned from the valley below, beaming in the rays of the sun. The Christian community erected the chapel in the seventeenth century in an attempt to ward off witches from the summit, renowned as the location of frequent lightning strikes and legendary covens with the devil. Curiously, the word in Basque for a witches' coven is *akelarre*, which translates as 'the billy goat field'. It refers to the secret places where witches allegedly congregated to fornicate with the devil, who appeared to them in the form of a goat.

At first sight, the summit's rocky extremities and difficult access would seem to make it a totally unsuitable choice for an events venue. However, for those participating in secret *akelarreak*, it is perfect, as possibly the only living creatures with any chance of getting there in the dark are witches on broomsticks and mountain goats.

Mount Mendaur is an intrinsic part of our valley identity, and not an hour passes in its presence without our eyes drifting upwards towards its jagged peaks. It is our barometer, alerting us to the sea mists rolling in from the north or the rain clouds gathering in the west. The views of Mount Mendaur and its backdrop of prevailing weather conditions offer us a constant reminder of who we are, and of our mortal fragility and insignificance. Its gruelling three-hour ascent is the object of a yearly pilgrimage for the fitter villagers of the area, its name striking a note of fear among the children of the Pulunpa School.

Whereas more conventional school outings chaperone their children through botanical gardens and history museums, the pupils of Ituren's Pulunpa School are sent off to climb the precipitous slopes of Mount Mendaur. Infants as young as five are dispatched from the village square, tiny rucksacks on their backs packed with suncream, wedges of *tortilla* and bottles of water from the Hello Kitty fountain.

Mount Mendaur pitches upwards from the northern wall of Ituren's church and cemetery. That is to say, if ever you were to topple off the steps of La Trinidad, you would terminate your 1,000m descent, quite conveniently, at the graveyard gate, uttering your last Hail Mary's at the shrine of Saint Joaquin as you passed by on the way down. A direct line of sight links all three Christian shrines, and the cemetery at their end has witnessed its fair share of macabre witches' tales and real-life tragedies too.

❖ ❖ ❖ ❖

As you enter the graveyard through the stone archways at the back of the church, one of the first graves you come across is that of Zubialdea, the name of the house stamped in gold lettering on a black marble plaque. Below this is the name Manuel Bazterrica Elizalde, our beloved Atautxi from Zubialdea, and a photo of him in his Basque beret, the laughter lines sparking outwards like deep ravines from the corners of his eyes. Elizalde is a common surname in these valleys and means 'next to the church', which – given Atautxi's present location and most people's final one – is perhaps the most appropriate surname of them all. Atautxi died in 2012 leaving Amatxi alone as the matriarch of Zubialdea and of their large family of six children, sixteen grandchildren and thirty-eight great-grandchildren, enough family members to ensure that there are almost always fresh flowers on his grave.

If anthropologists dig deep enough among the humus of the flower beds, they may uncover the scraps of a child's drawing of Atautxi, his dog Txiki at his side, providing fragile evidence of the cultural exchanges that were part of his life in Ameztia. The card, written in English and Basque, is signed by Georgina and her daughter, Marion. Marion Elizalde Howard. Yes, Marion and Atautxi are actually related, making her a third cousin to Atautxi's grandchildren, and all of them distant descendants from the same mother house in Zubieta. It seems that Amatxi and I have more things in common than most people realise. Both our lives are eternally intertwined with the Elizalde clan, which may go some way towards explaining the complicity between us, and her protective motherly concern for my well-being.

A few graves further on, past the tombs of the Ariztegi and Zubizarreta families, a name stands out by its singular lack of Basqueness – Jenifer Salgado Pérez, 1976–2009. Jeni was thirty-three years old when she was murdered as she stepped out of her car in Pamplona. She knew that one day it might happen. The hitman, hired for a total of €8,000, completed the task with one bullet for every €1,000 he had pocketed. It was a revenge killing and it took place in front of her thirteen-year-old son.

Jeni was an attractive, charming woman who had set up a beauty parlour in her parents-in-law's town house in Ituren. Whereas Amaia's clients in Ameztia would stride out across the farm from her hairdressing salon in work boots, Jeni's clientele would mince along the pavements of downtown Ituren in chic sandals with pedicured feet and painted toenails. Her warm, outgoing personality had earned her the affection of the village and she was invariably one of the first mothers to put her name down for the family sports day at the end of the school term. She left behind four children: two boys, born to her first partner in Honduras, and the two girls that she shared with Marcos, a truck driver from Ituren. The youngest was five months old.

Jeni had been a single mother, living in a desperately poor district of Honduras when an earthquake destroyed her village in 1999. Had it not been for a wardrobe shielding a corner of the room from the avalanche of rubble, she would have lost her three-year-old son as well as her home. Pregnant with her second child at the time, she and her family found themselves living in a hut made of straw and animal dung where she scratched together a living working in local coffee and tobacco plantations and as a part-time beautician.

In January 2001, Jeni left her two young boys in her sister's care and boarded a flight to Spain with a promise of a work contract in a silk factory near San Sebastián. It seemed like a once-in-a-lifetime opportunity to lift her family out of poverty, but it would finally cost her her life. When she arrived in San Sebastián to meet her future employers, she was raped, her papers were taken from her, and she was forced into prostitution. The 'silk factory' turned out to be a brothel on the outskirts of a pretty mountain village not far from Ituren, situated on the N121, the major international trucking route connecting the Iberian peninsula to France and beyond.

Ten months later, while out partying with friends, Marcos discovered Jeni crying in a corner of a bar and they started to talk. The conversation was brief, but before he left, he gave her his telephone number and told her to call him if she needed help. Two weeks later he was planning her escape. The police were then alerted, the other women freed, the brothel was closed down and its owners were arrested.

Although Marcos offered to pay for Jeni's flight back to Honduras, she decided that the best way to help her family was to stay and look for work so that she could send money home. Marcos offered her the job of helping him look after his elderly parents, where her fun-loving yet caring nature endeared her to the whole family. They married the following year, her sons moved over from Honduras to join them, and Marcos's and Jeni's first daughter, Carolina, was born soon afterwards.

In 2002 the case went to court and Jeni testified against José Laredo, the brothel ringleader. He was given a twelve-year sentence, which gave him ample time to plot his revenge. And so it was that seven years later, from the confines of his cell, he arranged for her execution. By the time of the funeral, he had been condemned to life imprisonment, and Jeni's children to a motherless future.

'What a beautiful dress, Carolina,' I exclaimed inanely, at an absolute loss for words, before I joined hundreds of people for a five-minute silence in the square.

The girl did not reply, continuing to stare out above the village towards the slopes of Mendaur as she sat on the stone wall of the plaza in a blue satin dress.

I hesitated and finally walked on. What do you say to an eight-year-old child on the day of her mother's funeral? Perhaps, just like hundreds of other people that same morning, the only thing that came to mind was, 'What a beautiful dress, Carolina, what a beautiful dress.'

❖ ❖ ❖ ❖

Several years later, the village prepared for another funeral, although this was not a religious one. There was no church service and nobody was to be buried in the graveyard. This was a humanist ceremony, and the villagers of Ituren scaled Mendaur with an urn of Mateo Lertxundi's ashes to scatter to the winds. It is possible that one of the reasons that Mateo did not want a Christian funeral was because of the events he witnessed in the Ituren graveyard while working at the priest's side as a young choirboy.

On 16 September 1966, Mateo watched as Luisa Urroz's husband's coffin headed towards its final resting place in an imposing family crypt in Ituren. The Urroz family have one of the most impressive crypts in the graveyard, standing some 3m high. The dark stains seeping out from the seams around the lid streak down its white marble walls like tears and imbue it with an other-worldly air. Perched on top of the tomb, an angel blowing a trumpet cuts a ghostly silhouette against the flanks of Mendaur.

Instead of the decomposed remains of the Urroz family, the lid of the crypt slid aside to reveal two completely unknown bodies. In an interview with the newspaper *El Diario de Navarra*, Mateo confirmed that the bodies were lying back-to-back, bound by a rope and a tattered cloth; one faced north towards Mendaur and the other south towards the church. The mourners watched in shock as the bodies were laid out in the wet graveyard, and later even more sinister details began to emerge. Forensics determined that the bodies were those of a middle-aged man and a younger woman, and their rotting remains indicated that they had died some ten or eleven months previously. Both corpses appeared to have met a violent death. In the middle of the man's forehead, just above his left eye socket, was a bullet hole, but even more puzzling were the remains of a woman's high-heeled shoe found at their side: an impractical and unusual item of clothing in Basque mountain villages in the 1960s.

As soon as news of the bodies had filtered through to the outside world, journalists from the regional newspaper started to investigate the story. Almost immediately squadrons of *Guardia Civil* partitioned off the churchyard from the public eye, the corpses were spirited away, the villagers silenced, and the press threatened with closure if they dared mention the event. When the police were asked who had given the orders, they replied that the orders had come from the top, that they were the express demands of General Franco himself.

Forbidden to talk about the subject in public, speculation went underground, and discussions were held in whispered voices behind the solid oak doors of the farmhouses in the area. There seemed to be no immediate answer from within the local community, but the most convenient conclusion was to assume that they were the bodies of Portuguese refugees fleeing Salazar's dictatorship and making their way, slowly and pitifully, through Spanish territory towards freedom in France. But even the most colourful imagination couldn't realistically place a Portuguese refugee 1,000km into their flight through mud and rain in a pair of high-heeled shoes. And why would anyone want to murder them in any case?

In 2016, fifty years after the event, a national Spanish TV documentary and various press articles presented their own theories as to the identity of the two bodies. They argued that the male body could have belonged to the charismatic Moroccan opposition leader Ben Barka, friend of Che Guevara, and that the female corpse was his secretary. Ben Barka – considered a dangerous enemy by the French regime and their colonial governments in the north of Africa – had been preparing to chair the first international meeting of Third World liberation movements when he disappeared in France on 28 October 1965. He was known to have been tortured and eventually murdered by the Moroccan interior ministry in collaboration with the French authorities although his body had never been found. Fifty years later, some detectives thought they had traced the bodies to the Ituren graveyard, and TV documentaries and newspaper articles expanded on their theories.

It may never be known to whom these bodies really belonged, but the isolated location of the Ituren church below the rugged cliffs of Mendaur – just over the border from France – seems not only to have been an ideal hideaway for pregnant witches but for covert activities too. The fact that Franco himself gave express orders to close down any investigation into their identity continues to shroud the story with intrigue and mystery to this day.

HOUSE AND HOME

MUSHROOMS AND MARSHMALLOWS

When Marion started school, I also started a new project to resurrect the ruins of the original farmhouse just next to The Borda, on the other side of the terrace. It was a slow and dusty job that did marvels for my Spanish vocabulary but absolutely nothing for my patience. When the builders left in the early evening, we would crawl about the work site between empty beer cans and cigarette butts, imagining the home that it was destined to become. Hence, it came as no surprise when Marion, at four years old, returned from school to tell me that they had all been asked to choose a subject that they wanted to study and – amid cries of 'dogs', 'football' and '*pelota*' – she had proudly said 'construction'.

To facilitate the building process, I decided to create a parking area at the back of my house. Until then the only access to The Borda had been the narrow path that dog-legged back above the stream from the main track, giving us little option but to park the car at the intersection and traipse the final 100m or so down to the house. Inside this dog-leg was a sloping triangular patch of land with some rather scraggly cherry trees, *my* cherry trees – or so I had been told a thousand times – planted long before I had arrived.

Oddly enough, no one said anything as they watched Juanito's excavator lumber down the drive and gouge out huge walls of earth and stone from the bank behind my house, but apparently, this was not my land at all. Even though I had been told many times that the cherry trees were mine, I had no idea that the land on which they were planted was not. This is a common tradition – so I have since learned – and a reliable source of income to local lawyers embroiled in a constant series of petty land disputes. Often several parties can lay claim to the same piece of land, the trees belonging to one person, the grazing rights belonging to another, while the land itself is frequently communal and thus belongs to the town hall.

It transpired that the land where my cherry trees stood actually belonged to Maika and I had committed an enormous and irreparable error, the sort of thing that could cause blood feuds for generations. Looking at it objectively, I had just commandeered Juanito to scoop out a huge, gaping bite into land belonging to the Basque female axe-wielding, anvil-lifting champion.

But I didn't find this out until several months later when I bumped into Maika outside her farm and she gently broached the subject. At that time, in the first few years after my arrival, I knew Maika more by legend than in person, and I was mortified by the realisation of what had happened. But there was no going back; the damage was done. My property had now accrued a sizeable muddy car park and Juanito – who had been happy to accept all the stones that he could extract from the soil in exchange for his labours – had already cemented them into the walls of his new house.

Maika, fortunately, found it extremely amusing and apparently had land to spare. This was one of our first contacts and an early example of her generous nature and great sense of humour. It was also the first time I started to question the concept of ownership and realised that my rights to *my* land were more tenuous than I had previously thought.

When not observing the commotion of diggers, cranes and winches outside the door, Marion and I would sit in our conservatory and gaze at the skies, watching the changing cloud formations and colours. Our favourites were always the summer storms. Just in case the lights went out, which they often did, we would gather the Danish candles around us and huddle together to watch the lightning rage around the valley, counting the seconds before the thunder struck.

After these summer storms a wonderful smell emanated from the mountain as the moisture evaporated from the burnt grass and baked soil into the lazy morning sunshine. I believe the correct term for this smell is 'petrichor' and – although this word does not have the flair of Basque onomatopoeias – it is worthy of mention for its enchanting Greek etymology. *Petr-* finds its origins in the word *petra*, meaning rock, while *ichor* literally means 'the immortal liquid that runs through the veins of the gods'. Living with these heavenly views, surrounded by the marvels of the natural world, I was beginning to feel immortal myself. That feeling was to be short-lived.

Gradually, we gained a heightened sensitivity to the smells and fragrances around us and, although we had long been able to identify the different animals by the sounds of their bells, we now found that we could recognise them by their scents too. On arriving home, we could immediately smell the sheep, cows or horses that had passed our door earlier that day, and there was no mistaking the moment when mice took up residence in the cupboard under the stairs or Ginger Cat (a stray tom) returned to the terrace. We breathed in the bouquet of the orange blossom in the driveway or the jasmine on the patio – along with the occasional unmistakable sour stench of a blocked septic tank.

As for the muck-spreading that occurred several times a year, I could tell that the moment was about to arrive even before I could smell it. The muck-spreading took place religiously on perfect sunny days between two rainy spells – which were usually eagerly awaited washdays too. Just as the windows were opened to air the house and the washing had been pegged out to dry, the sound of the muck-spreader could be heard coming down the track. If I happened to be out that day, dear saintly Sagrario would come to the rescue, bringing our clothes into the house, and leaving them in neatly folded piles unlike anything they had experienced before or since.

Less than saintly was Isidro's wife, Lourdes's, grin. Spying me at the bottom of her field, she would point the nozzle of the muck-spreader in my direction and, with a mischievous glint in her eye, would shout the Ameztia battle cry '*kolonia euskaldun*!' as I fled off along the track.

I myself was responsible, inadvertently, for another fragrance entering the valley, deep in the oak grove where the cuckoo lives. But this was a slightly more sophisticated fragrance than most. From this moment Amatxi's Cuckoo Woods became known privately, between Marion and me, as the Treasure Hunt Woods, the name having been acquired during the annual treasure hunts that I used to organise in the area during the second week of May. The morning before Marion's birthday party each year, I would head off along the spur to hide tiny presents under the leaves or between the roots of the oak trees. That afternoon, after crisps and disembowelled sandwiches had been scattered over the terrace, a crowd of children would career around the oak grove to hunt them down.

Eventually, all the presents were discovered, and a winning team would be announced. All the presents except one. I remember once hiding a small sample bottle of expensive perfume in the grove which the children never found. As I don't have any recollection of where I hid it, it is probably still buried in the undergrowth to this day, infusing its ingredients into the soil and perhaps imbuing a new species of mushroom with its aroma.

In fact, *our* Treasure Hunt Woods have been the scene of *other people's* treasure hunts for generations, it being a local secret that the oak grove has always been a superb place for mushroom hunting. Just after dawn on damp autumn mornings, while the mist burns off the valley floor, one can spy Luis furtively rummaging under the roots and bracken for the prized *Boletus edulis* (commonly known as 'ceps' or 'porcini'). If I am awake at this hour – which is usually not the case – I may just catch a glimpse of him sneaking back home past my door along the pig path, a hazel walking stick in one hand and a plastic bag nonchalantly swinging behind his back.

One evening, over dinner with Luis, Ignacio and Sagrario in Sunbillenea, they told me the tale of a mushroom thief who, many years ago, used to drive some 30km from Irun just to loot the mushrooms from the Treasure Hunt Woods. The woman would arrive at the crack of dawn when Luis and his father were still milking the cows and, consequently, she often got to the best mushrooms first.

But the locals were not easily cheated out of their rightful heritage. Spying on her from the woods, Luis observed her tricks. He noted that if she found a mushroom which was too small to yet be picked, she would cover it with bracken to hide it, marking the spot with a tiny, protruding stick so that she could then collect it on her following visit. Of course, it comes as little surprise that when she returned, those mushrooms were no longer there.

Intrigued about this whole mushroom-hunting culture and its jealously guarded secrets, I approached Sagrario one day as she cut strips of red and yellow peppers for her salad. Like Amatxi, her aunt, she loved colour too. It was something that all three of us had in common.

'Did your grandparents hunt for mushrooms there too? Was it a family secret?' I asked, hoping to glean some anthropological insight into this supposedly ancient Basque tradition.

'I can't quite remember… in the old days I don't think they ate many mushrooms, frying them needed lots of oil… yes, and oil in those days was far too expensive for us.'

I mulled this over, slightly deflated.

'But I do remember,' she continued, 'my father used to singe the mushrooms on a stick over the fire.'

Just like marshmallows, I thought, but lacking the linguistic tools to explain 'marshmallows' in either Spanish or Basque, I kept my thoughts to myself.

Today, the *Boletus edulis* mushroom is still highly prized, and local knowledge is key to finding it. Merely by the colouring on the skin and the thickness of the stalk, some villagers can identify the species of tree where any one mushroom was found. Depending on the size and shape of the fallen leaves at the foot of the tree, the varying patterns of light apparently leave distinctive markings on the skin. I have no idea whether their diverse locations mean that the mushrooms smell different too, but one day the shepherds may discover an unusual cologne-scented variety, and I – and I alone – will know the reason why.

❖ ❖ ❖ ❖

Finally, two years after we started the building project, Marion and I moved across the terrace from The Borda into our new, bigger house. The two houses were linked by a large, covered porch across the back of the terrace which converted them – in theory only – into one structure with two separate wings.

The new house hadn't been particularly well built, but the whole of the south side of the building, upstairs and downstairs, had been encased in glass, and with such spectacular views at every turn, one could almost overlook the cracks in the plastering, the asymmetrical roof timbers, and the sagging floorboards upstairs. Ironically, for someone with such rudimentary cooking skills, its best feature was its enormous kitchen with a 3m-long granite kitchen counter and French-styled kitchen units. Equally odd for someone who had funded the whole project, the room in the house with the most structural problems, painted in mismatching whites from sheer lack of interest, was my own. Without a doubt life was easier in the bigger house but, after plastering The Borda's inside walls and eliminating the shadowy, spidery recesses between the stones, I realised that she – my first family home – would always have a special place in my heart.

In the new house, I moved my piano under the staircase in our large open-plan living room where it sat, forlorn and mute, year after year, bursting into song only when Marion wanted to show off her one musical accomplishment: 'Happy Birthday'. Slowly the piano disappeared beneath piles of children's books and office files, but its presence was reassuring, nonetheless. I missed those musical evenings and the intimate conversations with myself and the universe that they inspired, as the melodies rippled through me and floated out into the night. But with a business and a young child to look after, I never seemed to find the time – or the peace of mind – to play any more. Had I sat down at the keys and revisited those velvety moments of emotional dialogue, I often wonder what I would have said to myself or what, perhaps more importantly, the music would have said to me. Apart from a few false notes – what else would we have found?

Gradually, I had slipped into the unsophisticated, bumbling routines of motherhood and Basque rural life, slowly becoming part of the landscape (and most probably smelling a little like it too). Sometimes I would look nostalgically at a lace blouse or an outdated party dress, or pin my hair up high with my favourite tortoiseshell hair clip, but they were relics of a past era, in wait for who knew what, for another life to come. Perhaps.

❖ ❖ ❖ ❖

Over time the villagers started to consider me, more or less, just another Ameztiarra – albeit a slightly more eccentric version. This integration, however, was not without its hiccups, especially when it came to my cultural reserve around privacy, a concept not greatly important to my village neighbours.

The postwoman of Ituren uses a wide variety of formal and informal delivery methods. Usually, the further one lives from the main valley road and the hub of Ituren life, the more informal – and indiscreet – they become. On the few occasions when she musters sufficient courage to brave the ten hairpin bends of The Road That Doesn't Exist to Ameztia, she leaves our letters at Zubialdea, the very first outpost, before sprinting back to the safety of the valley below. In years gone by another postwoman did venture as far as Iaulin Borda but, apparently, slipped on our muddy drive and almost broke a leg. From then on anywhere beyond Zubialdea was deemed as Comanche territory and she refused to return.

At times, when taking the road to Ameztia was too much of a challenge, she would find all sorts of ruses to avoid the drive. I started to find my mail – including registered deliveries of passports and credit cards – scattered about the village in the houses of Zubialdea's distant relatives, the presumption being that at some point their filial ties would prevail, drawing them up the mountain for a family reunion, chocolates, flowers, letters and parcels in tow. As far as I know, the system has not failed, and everything has arrived intact and unopened even if several weeks too late.

Similar liberties are taken by the chemist, who has a variety of improvised distribution points for the medicines his clients order. And because he is entrusted with sensitive information, given the nature of his trade, indiscreet divulgences can be potentially even more embarrassing – especially for those who live in the same village. It is well known in the valleys that young men, embarking on their first romantic excursions, drive far afield for a packet of condoms in order to keep their anonymity – if not their honour – intact. Unsurprisingly, I was not so clever.

Josetxo runs the chemist on Ituren high street, 'runs' being the operative word as he is also a marathon runner and has been known to take off for a sprint during his lunch break to deliver urgent medicine to some ailing farmer in the hills. In his free time he turns up regularly in village bars and fiestas, observing the ups and downs and ins and outs of village life with an expert – and hopefully discreet – eye. One day I had ordered some medicine from him which I was due to pick up that afternoon. But just after lunch, he rang to tell me that he had been called out early and would leave my order hanging on the shop doorknob for me to pick up later.

Rushing down to Ituren to protect my dignity, I found it defended only by a transparent, flimsy layer of plastic, stamped with the name GIORGINA in nowhere-near-small-enough handwriting. As I retrieved the rather personal contents in the bag, I did wonder just how many people had strolled along the high street that afternoon.

GILBERT: AN IMPOSTER IN MY HOME

MUSIC BOXES AND MOUNTAIN SAVAGES

This bucolic lifestyle punctuated by minor inconveniences was not to last long. A few months before Marion's fifth birthday, my enthusiasm for her linguistic repertoire got us into trouble. Real trouble. To this day, many years later, this traumatic train of events is still legend in Ameztia.

Having heard rumours that there was a Frenchman in the village renting a room from one of Isidro's brothers, I wanted to meet him. I was intrigued to find out how another foreigner had shored up in these parts, and what exactly he was doing in *my* village. The windows of his apartment were visible from Ituren bridge, in a wing of the Zubialdea town house which, true to its name and – unlike its mountain farm in Ameztia – really was situated 'By the Side of the Bridge'.

As I swung into the plaza every morning to drop Marion off at school, I had a fleeting view of the inside of his apartment, which appeared to be lined wall to wall with books, an unusual choice of interior design in this neck of the woods. I was curious, and contrived to meet Gilbert, a slim, charming man of about sixty-five years old. At this first meeting, he was wearing slip-on leather loafers, a carefully ironed pink shirt and immaculate navy-blue trousers with his keys clipped to his belt with a small gold chain. He had intense, sparking blue eyes and a tastefully groomed head of salt-and-pepper hair (all the more notable because Basque men tend to go bald at a very early age). The effect would have been little different had a peacock walked into a pen of farmyard chickens. He embodied all that the Spanish – as frontier people with an ambivalent relationship with their cousins over the border – would have stereotyped as French. Which, of course, he was.

Ostensibly, he had been working on a renewable energy project for the Navarrese government and I took him completely at his word. Had I paused for a moment to look at his situation objectively, I might have found it unusual that a Frenchman *d'un certain âge* had come to live all alone in a rental apartment in an isolated Basque village with no apparent connections to anyone from the area. My suspicions should have been aroused but they weren't, no doubt because only a few years earlier I had found myself in an almost identical situation, albeit at a much younger age. But I was soon to learn, to my peril, that even in the twenty-first century the isolated location of this tiny village on the French-Spanish border presented advantages for people who had something to hide.

We chatted superficially for a few minutes and when the subject of work cropped up he aired his grievances about the lack of an internet connection in his flat. My knee-jerk reaction was to invite him up to The Borda and offer him the opportunity to use my newly installed Wi-Fi if he needed it.

The following weekend the phone rang in the side pocket of my rucksack while I was out with the mountaineering club from Pamplona. It was Gilbert. 'Where are you?'

He was standing outside my house and needed to ask me a question.

Later that week we met up and he told me that he had looked around the property – from the outside, I presumed – and had noted that the house had two separate wings. He wanted to know if there was anyone living in the cottage and, if not, could he rent it? The question took me completely by surprise, as Marion and I had only just transferred our chattels from The Borda to our new home across the terrace. He continued that he would be happy to move in right away – all I had to do was say 'Yes'.

He had found my weak spot and, as saying 'yes' always came more naturally than saying 'no', I found myself agreeing to rent The Borda to him for a few months. Within a matter of days, Gilbert was piling up his possessions on the terrace. Handing him the key I felt an unmistakable twinge of foreboding and regret, that ominous chill wind that sends shivers down your spine and accompanies critically bad decisions. But I comforted myself with the idea that a French neighbour would add another language to Marion's repertoire and that it would be fun to see how it all played out.

Stack after stack of box files and framed leaf pressings built up on the terrace as he shuttled his possessions up the mountain in his dark blue Peugeot. Trip after trip. He then set about erecting a coiled labyrinth of shelving throughout The Borda, blocking out so much of the light from the once sunny conservatory that it evoked the gloom of a mausoleum. From that moment on his movements throughout the conservatory could only be discerned in a pattern of flitting shadows. He placed his desk in the 'maggot corner' of the conservatory, and then spent the next week putting hundreds, if not thousands, of box files in their place. For someone moving from one temporary accommodation to the next he was not travelling light.

On the first evening, I set out a spread of tapas on the terrace to welcome him into the fold. During the following weeks, weather permitting, we would set up a table under the hibiscus tree, establishing a routine of evening aperitifs: a glass of Muscatel or a plate of *petits fours*. To be honest, I secretly welcomed this touch of sophistication and refinement into my somewhat hillbilly and at times lonesome mountain existence.

Gilbert was an easy and interesting conversationalist, quick to offer paternal advice and, with the constant uncertainties of running a business alone, I welcomed the company of a good listener and an enquiring mind. In turn, he shared the pitiful details of his acrimonious and costly divorce from a hysterical wife who had turned his children against him. It was easy to feel sorry for a man who seemed to have lost everything. Gilbert, in turn, made himself very much at home, doing odd jobs, cultivating a vegetable garden and hammering together wooden planters for the terrace. Slowly but surely he integrated into life in Ameztia.

Sagrario offered him fresh eggs or pots of homemade jam, Maika took him to play *pelota*, and when I went away for a few days, I left him my house key so that he could water my flowers and use my computer, as his – apparently – had crashed.

Spring came along sunny and bright that year, life was easier than it had been for a long time, and the tangles of a family court case – a subject best left for another time – were finally behind me. Marion was safe and healthy, and my life finally felt on an even keel. Now, an amenable neighbour was suddenly in our midst, accompanying me for aperitifs on the terrace, listening to my rambling thoughts and even removing the odd spider (or bat) from my living room.

Marion was already learning a few phrases of French and I rubbed my hands in glee at the linguistic prodigy that I was creating. On her fifth birthday, Gilbert gave her a tiny music box which snapped open to reveal a pink ballerina pirouetting to the delicate notes of a Strauss waltz. The first few bars of that music would echo through the house endlessly, each repetition followed by a resounding slap as Marion lifted the lid again and again and again. While the generosity was appreciated, slowly, as the months passed by, that tiny music box on Marion's bedside table began to symbolise his insidious encroachment into the most private recesses of my life. But it took me a long time to see this coming.

As the summer arrived, I introduced Gilbert to my guests, and even invited him to join us for the occasional music concert or dinner. It was at one of those events that he struck up a friendship with my Spanish teacher, Marina. The highly responsible and competent Marina was an invaluable help to me, going so far as to sleep overnight with my guests in our Baztan Valley rental house, freeing me up in the evenings to dash back to Ameztia, pick up Marion from Zubialdea, and put her to bed. On occasion I would pass Gilbert's Peugeot on the road as – bearing gifts of chocolates and roses – he would be driving off to visit Marina and my guests of his own accord. Seamlessly, he integrated into the nooks and crannies of my private and professional life.

I went jogging most days, giving thanks to the gods embodied in the glorious mountain landscapes around me. Due to the complications of my separation from Marion's father, serenity had eluded me for so long that I chose to ignore the telltale signs alerting me to the winds of change. It was only as the summer drew to a close that I could ignore the evidence no more.

Little details of the man behind the façade were indicative of the drama to come. (A film director would have drawn attention to these with sinister staccato minor chords and uncomfortable camera angles.) The first time that I remembered feeling distinctly uneasy was at the end of August, six months after Gilbert had arrived. I returned one evening from Casa Tristantenea to find that Gilbert had left a box of *marrons glacés* on the steps leading up to my front door, and had even entered my house to leave a vase of wildflowers on the kitchen counter. A few days later I thought I heard the distinctive creak of my back door and, when I came downstairs, a tiny plate of *hors d'oeuvres* sat on my table, confirming my suspicions.

As autumn arrived, my unease intensified, and I sensed him observing my movements from within the bowels of The Borda, darting away behind his bookshelves when I appeared on the terrace. My instinct was to start avoiding him altogether and gradually I spent less time on my terrace, moving indoors, where I was haunted by interminable repetitions of Strauss. Eventually, I hid the music box in the back of a cupboard and bought Marion a new doll.

Occasionally, on arriving home late, I found him hovering in the shadows of the terrace, scuttling out in the darkness to greet me as I opened the car door and offering me a hand to bring in the shopping. The more I avoided him, the more obsequious he became, and I was beginning to feel increasingly uncomfortable within my own home. Once captivated by the beauty and isolation of my mountain paradise, I was starting to feel captured and ensnared.

What on earth had I let myself in for now?

The afternoon that I discovered a makeshift curtain on the window of our communal terrace, which looks out over the drive at the back of the house, it became impossible to ignore my instincts any longer. It happened just days after I had driven down my track and caught a fleeting glimpse of Gilbert through the window, exiting my house on to the terrace and hurriedly turning the key in the lock. He assured me that he had put up the curtain as a favour, in order to block out the strong summer sunshine but, as the window faced north, it was obvious that its purpose was purely to cover his tracks. I desperately wanted to believe that he had been watering the flowers or doing some DIY – he had an obsession for thermal insulation – as I had, after all, given him the key in my usual '*mi casa es tu casa*' (my house is your house) spirit. My incorrigible desire to see good in everyone was starting to look very naïve indeed.

The post came and went, but his cheque from the Navarrese Ministry of the Environment failed to materialise. There was always an excuse not to pay the rent. Subtly, I would attempt to bring up the subject, retreating apologetically and feeling awkward: it could not have been dignifying to find oneself penniless at his age.

The final straw came over something as trivial as potatoes. Gilbert had driven to the village with me to help with the shopping and had thrown the few things he needed, toilet paper, chewing gum and a sack of potatoes, into my basket. As we laid out our purchases at the checkout his were last in the line. I expected him to hold them back and pay for them separately, but he just watched on as I settled the bill. He then packed his shopping into one bag and mine into another and, gallantly, picked up both our bags and placed them in the boot of the car. We drove home without another word. It was almost as if he were testing my limits to see just how far he could go. I plucked up the courage to mention the potatoes, and he dug into the pocket of his perfectly ironed chinos for a couple of coins. But the mood in the car had changed. We both knew that he had overplayed his hand.

One September afternoon, seven months after Gilbert had moved in, I returned home from a day with my guests in the valley to find him waiting for me on the terrace. His air was far less subservient than usual.

'I need to talk to you,' he stated coldly, without any of the usual amicable preambles, as I put my bags down on the terrace and went to unlock my back door.

'Oh, I'll come over now then,' I replied, feigning an air of insouciance to mask my assumption that the only subject that deserved such unnatural formality was the subject of money. Perhaps this was the moment, perhaps he was finally going to pay.

'No,' he barked officiously, 'not now. Tomorrow morning at ten on the terrace.' And, with that, he turned on his heels and marched back into his warren, slamming the door behind him.

There was a steeliness and aggression in his tone that I hadn't heard before and I realised that I was living with a totally unknown quantity. The worm had turned; I was petrified, and my stomach lurched.

Immediately I called Isidro and told him what had happened, asking him if he could join me the following morning for the meeting. It transpired that my neighbours had been worried about me for quite some time, and that night, for the first time in my life in Ameztia, I locked the doors when I went to bed.

At ten o'clock the next morning Gilbert was waiting for me on the terrace. In his hands he had a folded piece of paper and some money. He offered me one of the seven months' rent he owed me, some €300, and was just starting to unfold the piece of paper when Isidro's car crunched up the drive. Gilbert looked up aghast as Isidro entered the terrace and, in a moment of pure farce, he bent double, making retching noises as if he were about to be sick and, excusing himself hurriedly, scuttled back into the obscurity of The Borda and closed the door.

Isidro and I waited. Some time later Gilbert reappeared with the intention of simply excusing himself before heading back into The Borda for good. But Isidro intercepted him, luring him into conversation, informing him calmly that he would have to come up with the rent, but that we would give him a month's respite to get the money together. And with that, Isidro shook Gilbert firmly by the hand. As he turned to go, he looked Gilbert straight in the eye and added, 'Jorjina is family.'

A truly noble Basque man had shaken Gilbert's hand and had promised to wait a month before bringing up the subject again; the agreement had been sealed with the *euskaldun hitza*, that sacred Basque handshake, and so there was absolutely nothing I could do now but wait.

A few years later, when Marion was about eight years old, I remember the following conversation on the terrace.

'Marion, what does it mean if you don't keep your *euskaldun hitza*?' As usual she rolled her eyes with impatience at my stream of silly questions, especially if they had anything to do with her Basque culture or language.

'It means that you are Spanish, Mummy, not Basque!' she said, quickly pirouetting off around the terrace to the other side of the hibiscus tree.

But we were soon to find out that the act of reneging on one's word was not only attributable to the 'Spanish' – those strange and foreign creatures from the lands to the south – but to nationalities north of the border as well.

During the weeks that followed, Gilbert and I avoided each other and, apart from my demanding the return of my house key, we had virtually no contact until our meeting the following month. During this time, Sagrario drew my attention to two incidents that had occurred while I was out. The first happened shortly before the meeting in which Gilbert had paid me the paltry one month's rent. A woman in a French car had turned up at Sagrario's looking for my house. They directed her round the spur to The Borda, following her route with the binoculars normally used to observe the sheep in the fields during the lambing period. The woman had seemed nervous, even frightened. Apparently, she called in on Gilbert and some sort of transaction appeared to have taken place, the details of which they couldn't pick up with the binoculars. However, within a matter of minutes, the woman had sped back down the mountain and, presumably, back over the border into France. From this moment on, Gilbert seemed to have some money and the incident coincided with his paying me that one and only month's rent.

The second, even more recent occurrence was creepier, occurring just days after he had paid me the €300 rent. One evening Sagrario had registered that the lights were on in my house and presumed that I had already come home from my day's work in the Baztan Valley. But then, as she went to herd up the sheep, she saw my car coming up the road from the valley below, making it obvious that I had yet to arrive home. We deduced, simultaneously, that it could only have been Gilbert, who had let himself in with a clandestine copy of the key I had originally lent him.

Mid-October, the meeting with Gilbert was due. This time Isidro was joined by Ignacio, and the heads of the main Ameztia farmsteads sat patiently on my pink terrace sofas waiting for Gilbert to arrive. Injecting even more absurdity into the drama to follow, Marion – who hates to miss out on the action – was also present, roller skating round and round the hibiscus tree. When Gilbert appeared from The Borda, Isidro, in his characteristically equitable manner, gently launched into the subject of money. Gilbert observed us coldly, his virtually colourless eyes flickering between the three of us, sizing up the atmosphere before he reached into his shirt pocket to produce the same sheet of paper that had accompanied him at our meeting one month earlier.

'I have no money and, what is more, it is not me who owes *her* any money but *she* who owes me,' he sneered, his contempt obvious in the fact that he could not even bring himself to address me directly. And with this he unfolded the paper to expose a handwritten list and started reading:

- *Removing bats from Mademoiselle Howard's house, €1,000.*
- *Pruning the roses for Mademoiselle Howard, €1,000.*
- *Tending the vegetable garden for Mademoiselle Howard, €3,000.*

And so on.

The list went on and on, arriving at an absurd total of some €10,000 while Marion twirled around the terrace, crashing periodically and theatrically into my arms as her skates wobbled off course.

We were stunned by this ludicrous bill. Even Isidro and Ignacio didn't know how to react. They were hard-working men who had dedicated every hour of their lives to the humble tasks of tending their lands, raking in the bracken or shovelling manure, and this Frenchman was presenting a bill for €1,000 to cut back a couple of roses! We were speechless. The blood drained from my face as shock gave way to the acute and terrifying realisation of my utter vulnerability. I was a single mother with a five-year-old daughter in a foreign country, living in an isolated homestead almost a kilometre from the nearest neighbour, and I had a madman in my house.

'Don't worry, Gilbert,' was my instinctive reaction when I found my words. 'You don't have to pay me anything at all, just leave. It's OK, I don't need any money,' I stuttered, desperately trying to come to terms with the full implications of what he had said.

Rising from his seat, he shuffled round to my side of the sofa, towering over me, at which moment Marion, sensing danger, executed another pirouette and flung herself protectively into my arms.

He slowly bent over, thrusting his face to within centimetres of ours. His warm, fetid breath caressing our cheeks, he pointed at his eyes with forked fingers, forcing me to look deep into his icy, reptilian soul.

'Look me in the eyes,' he hissed. 'Look, look me in the eyes. If you don't pay me ten thousand euros, I will ruin your life.'

We were totally unprepared for the insanity and violence of his words. Nothing of life in Ameztia (or anywhere else for that matter) had prepared any of us for this, and with Marion frozen in my arms my reaction was immediate and instinctive.

'OK, OK, I'll give you the money, whatever you want, but please,' I begged, my voice failing me, 'please, please then just leave.'

'You have a week,' he croaked, and with that he straightened up and slithered off again into his lair.

Isidro's equally knee-jerk reaction was to offer to help me with the money, but within minutes we all concluded that it would be crazy to pay him anything at all. We were out of our depth and it was obvious that we either had to find a lawyer or go to the police.

Maika, who was always highly entertained by the dramas that followed in my wake, accompanied me to San Sebastián to see a lawyer called Beñat. He was a smooth communicator with a bouncy, effortless sense of humour and exuded warmth and confidence from the start. Evidently, it was lunacy to let Gilbert blackmail me, and his advice was to go immediately to Elizondo police station to make a statement. Which we did.

The police took note, admitting that – on the record – the only way forward was to fight Gilbert through the courts. However, the policeman's voice on the front desk lowered a little, 'Off the record, of course,' eyes darting towards the open door, 'if we were in your shoes, we would simply gather up his things and throw the bastard out.'

That week the oak grove on the spur witnessed an increase in nocturnal activity as the regional police kept an eye on us from the woods, their presence announced by a merry-go-round of lights leaping around the walls of my bedroom.

Legally, so Beñat informed us, the logical way forward was to sue him through the civil courts to prove that he had been living in my house without paying any rent, but this drawn-out process would have meant Gilbert continuing to live just metres from my door. Simultaneously, we had another option of charging him with intimidation through the criminal courts and trying to obtain a restraining order.

A few weeks later, Isidro, Ignacio, Sagrario, Maika and I all donned our best city clothes and drove through the mountain tunnels to testify in a court in Pamplona. As no fists had been raised, nor had direct verbal abuse been uttered, Beñat was unable to acquire the restraining order we had been hoping for and Gilbert escaped with a paltry fine of €80, which of course, he never paid.

At one point in the proceedings Gilbert referred to all the congregation of Ameztiarrak – of which I was one – as '*estos del monte*', which roughly translates as something akin to 'these mountain savages'. His contempt for us was unmistakable, even for dear Sagrario who had shown so much concern for his apparently penniless predicament, furnishing him year round with eggs, courgettes, jam and other preserves.

On previous occasions when I had witnessed displays of disdain or derision towards the Basques, I had been angry, but now, when it was directed towards my beloved neighbours, I was outraged.

At the end of Gilbert's court hearing, we all filed back into our cars and returned to the mountains and up the ten hairpin bends towards Ameztia. The convoy of cars was led by Isidro's 4WD, which transported the Ameztia farmers. I came next in my battered VW, then Beñat in his low-slung BMW, and bringing up the rear was Gilbert in his French Peugeot. It would have been cheaper simply to have hired a minibus for us all!

From this moment on, Ameztia was busy. Sagrario and Ignacio kept almost constant vigil, watching over The Borda from the other side of the spur and ringing me every evening to check that I was home safely. At times they even slept over at my house to make sure that Marion and I were safe – one of the very rare occasions in their married lives when they slept anywhere but in their own bed in Sunbillenea. By this time, their binoculars were a permanent fixture on the windowsill in their bathroom, from where they had the best views of my house. I gathered that the frequency of their nocturnal visits to the water closet had increased exponentially too.

Although Gilbert's behaviour had shaken them to the core, this dark cloud appeared to have a silver lining. Everyone was ecstatic that *Jordi La Inglesa* now had a man in her life as my relationship with Beñat gradually took on other dimensions.

'A lawyer for Ameztia,' Sagrario chuckled in glee, like a child playing a poker game and having just picked up a trump card.

From now on my neighbours enquired daily about Beñat, who would spend occasional weekends at the house; handing me family-sized *puskak*, they dispatched me back home with an eye on the clock, worried that I was reneging on my 'wifely' duties. My cooking skills had become a standard joke in the hamlet by now and I enjoyed their teasing. It was a sign of the true confidence and trust between us all.

Winter was fast approaching but Gilbert made no effort to leave. He had barricaded himself in The Borda and pinned a note to the door stating that he was not budging until I had paid him his €10,000. Having failed to get a restraining order, the only other legal course was to hold out for the case to come up in the civil courts to demonstrate that he had not been paying the rent. But this would mean a long and disturbing wait of months – maybe even years.

The police knew the story and understood the danger I was in, and much to Marion's delight they still occasionally drove up to the house. I will not forget the first time that Marion waved at them from the upstairs window and how, interpreting her waves as a call of distress, they came hurtling down towards the house to check on us. Marion, with a love for drama – and an eye for a good-looking man – leapt into an officer's strong arms in her pink nightdress while they flashed torches through the windows of The Borda.

The next morning, I detected a self-important note in Marion's voice:

'Mummy.'

'Yes, sweetheart, what is it?'

'You know what?'

'No, sweetheart, tell me.'

'Yesterday, I put my foot on the policeman's pistol.'

Off the record, the police continued to encourage me to consider a Plan B: to change the locks and throw Gilbert out, which I attempted and ended up charged with breaking and entering. This was the first of two charges made against me that winter, the second being even more serious than the first.

The Justice of the Peace from Doneztebe, Juan Ignacio, the owner of Apeztegia, the village hardware store, is an expert at lock-picking. Apparently, there are certain locks which can be opened from the outside, even if they are locked from within. These locks are usually intended for the carers of elderly people who, in case of emergency, need access to the house at all times. Apeztegia is an institution, a household name attracting clients and lock-pickers from as far afield as Pamplona and San Sebastián. They mend virtually anything and offer all sorts of creative solutions to a wide range of problems, exemplifying the very best attributes of private enterprise and Basque pragmatism. My emergency options, apart from my neighbours and Aitor, my plumber, are the following: 112 for police, fire and ambulance, and a trip to Apeztegia for everything else. That November afternoon, I left Apeztegia with a new lock and keys, a tube of superglue, and a carefully constructed Plan B which I was about to put into action.

I waited for an evening when Gilbert was out. As soon as his car had driven up the track, and the lights had disappeared over the rise, I was on the telephone to Manu, a Sevillian builder friend, begging him to come and help me break open a skylight in The Borda. Once inside, we set to work changing the lock on the door, swapping it for the two-way lock recommended by Apeztegia. Apart from the principal doorway through the conservatory, there were only two other possible entrances. The first was the original stable door of The Borda, whose key had been lost, meaning that it was permanently latched from within. Since Gilbert didn't want to be observed, he had never considered this door as viable access, as it would have exposed his activities to scrutiny from my kitchen across the terrace. The second was a back door leading out towards the stream.

While I helped Manu with the doorway through the conservatory, Beñat was sent off through the labyrinth of archives to apply superglue to the back door, out of his depth with the sudden twist in events and all too aware that being my lawyer, lover and supergluer could give rise to some potentially embarrassing situations. Which it did.

On entering The Borda, I noticed to my horror that some four or five electric heaters had been left on full blast, undoubtedly with the successful and spiteful intention of increasing my electricity bill. Unattended for hours on end, they also constituted a potential fire risk. I unplugged the heaters and hurried back to my house, securing the new lock behind me. I then went to bed in the knowledge that I wasn't going to be there for long.

At about two o'clock, I was woken by the familiar merry-go-round of police lights on the bedroom walls, followed by loud thumps at my front door and the sound of crackling voices on a police radio.

The police had had a complaint from Señor Charbonneau who had called to say that someone had broken into his home through the bathroom window and that he suspected his neighbour, Señorita Howard, to be the perpetrator of this crime. The mention of the bathroom window puzzled me at first, but I soon realised that it had been Gilbert himself who had smashed the window to gain access, on his return, to his newly locked and superglued abode. Evidently, the old window's single glazing posed less of a barrier than the double-glazed glass of the relatively new conservatory doors. Absurdly, it appeared that I had also been accused of stealing some of his box files, which – as Beñat pointed out – was an illuminating accusation. This indicated that they were obviously of significant importance to him (and that it was highly possible that one of them contained information that he had accumulated about me).

Once again, I was ushered down to Elizondo police station to make a declaration, nodding knowingly to the policeman on the front desk who had suggested the break-in in the first place. We went through the charades of the declaration in a sterile interviewing room while the sergeant unsubtly signalled to Beñat to take me to one side and encourage me to deny the accusation altogether. This would have given them the occasion to tear up the case and thus avoid considerable embarrassment for everyone concerned.

After previous experience I was terrified of the law, as this situation touched on the raw nerves of a prolonged family court case which had concluded just before Gilbert had moved in. I worried that if ever this charge were to go to court, and if ever I were to be cross-examined, there was no way I would ever have been able to lie. Well, not outright. So, I insisted on admitting to the charges, owning up to the crime as the sole perpetrator. Admittedly, this was a rather simplified version of the truth, but I felt a duty to protect everyone else, and at least it was closer to the truth than a blanket denial. Firstly, I wanted to protect Manu, my builder, as it was not his battle. Then, of course, I had to protect Beñat, who now sat uneasily at my side, praying for me not to expose his supergluing prowess and acutely aware that, had his hidden talents been discovered, he would have been unable to represent me as my lawyer.

That November morning, when I left the police station, I had been charged with breaking and entering into Iaulin Borda and this had gone on my record. I headed straight to quiz Manu on the precise technical details of prising open skylights and picking locks, so that were I ever to be grilled on my criminal activities, I would at least know exactly what they were.

Beñat returned to his more law-abiding metropolis of San Sebastián, and I headed home alone, picking up Marion in Zubialdea *en route*. As we drove down the drive, we could see that Gilbert had now placed cardboard over the broken bathroom window which from then on became his only means of access, slithering in and out of The Borda over its jagged glass edges. A demon had taken up residence in paradise, and as the wheel on the electricity meter spun in a frenzy, he machinated plans to further undermine me in every way.

Marion and I were becoming increasingly frightened. Every time we returned home, we dashed into the house, bolting the locks and checking to see whether the scrap of paper that we had wedged above the kitchen door had fallen to the floor, evidence of someone having entered the room before us.

Although I had picked up on certain signs, I had failed to recognise the darker currents in Gilbert's nature; in retrospect, though, they were there to be read. Among the flowers, chocolates and lazy aperitifs on the terrace, I remembered that feeling of being studied through the grimy windows of the conservatory and recalled certain snide remarks about some of my larger female guests. How authentic was the damning portrayal of his 'hysterical' wife and absent children? Was his interest in my family court case, or in the detailed running of my company, purely benevolent? Had his computer really broken, or had he just wanted an excuse to get into mine?

December was fast approaching, and the temperature was dropping steadily. Strains of French radio wafted out on to the terrace reminding me, like a scent carried on the breeze, of the feral creature in my midst. No longer did my heart leap with joy as I entered the top of my drive; now it palpitated with dread at the thought of what I might find. At home, we kept the curtains closed so that his piercing blue eyes couldn't stare in from the darkness of the terrace. Whether the danger was imagined or real, it made no difference; the fear was palpable all the same.

❖ ❖ ❖ ❖

Among '*these mountain savages*' as he had called them, Gilbert was the talk of the town. No one needed a television now, even the vagaries of weather and lambing were secondary to the 'what-can-we-do-about-Gilbert' discourses that occupied us late into the night – at times with surprisingly cathartic gales of laughter. These moments of solidarity and conviviality with my neighbours allowed us to momentarily hold at bay the flood of anxiety and fear in which we were living. In many ways, despite their obvious concern for Marion and me, having a common enemy provided our hamlet with a shared purpose. It united us all on a level far deeper than that of the mundane routines of daily life.

One improbable plan we hatched was to wait in hiding for him behind the woodpile on one of the steeper bends of the Ameztia road and, as he drove by, to jump out and give him such a fright that he would decide to leave of his own accord. Had the plan ever taken root, the idea was simply to intimidate him verbally, not physically, as my neighbours, even if they were 'mountain savages', were gentle ones at least. That said, I soon realised that they all had access to underground connections who were not quite so scrupulous. This was the Basque Country after all.

The date of the civil court hearing was still months away and it promised to be a long, slow process, but the criminal courts worked more quickly. As I waited, petrified, for the results of the breaking-and-entering charges against me, my friends at Elizondo police station urged me to take matters into my own hands once again. In for a penny, in for a pound, and a further plan, Plan C, rapidly emerged.

In defence of the actions that followed, I genuinely believed that apart from bankrupting me with exploding electricity bills, Gilbert was also putting my property at risk of being burnt to the ground. Cutting off his electricity supply therefore seemed to be a most justifiable course of action, and Sagrario knew just the man.

All Gilbert needed to do was pack his bags and go, so Sagrario's nephew took matters in hand. We knew that one set of cables provided the electricity for The Borda, and that the other set fed the electricity into my part of the house. Our objective was first to cut the cables to the whole house and then reconnect them only to mine, otherwise Marion and I – apart from a small wood-burning stove – would have been equally doomed to a winter without heat or light.

It was snowing and our work was hampered by numb, frozen fingers. I held the torch while Sagrario's nephew sifted through a spaghetti of blue-and-yellow wires inside a fuse box fixed to an outside wall. I handed him the wire cutters and as the wire snapped, the distant strains of French radio ground to a halt and the air filled with a tense silence as we anticipated Gilbert's reaction. The sudden silence was so loud that we could almost hear him thinking inside his lair. As he groped around for fuses and switches on the inside of The Borda, we frantically coupled together the wires to my house on the outside, freezing fingers fumbling in the cold. And then, as we predicted, we heard the prolonged squeal of reluctant shutters creak open on rusty hinges as Gilbert squeezed his body out over the broken glass. Appearing from around the back of The Borda, Gilbert crouched low, snapping photos of us as we fiddled with the padlock on the meter before we rushed back into my house, hearts pounding.

From now on Gilbert had no electricity and, consequently, no source of light or warmth, but I calculated that he probably did have a few jars left of Sagrario's preserves. If he had been dangerous before, he was now not only dangerous but vengeful. His living standards were now reduced to those of a tramp, or worse, a wild animal tormented by the smell of woodsmoke from our fire and the glow of our cosy kitchen lights.

One of the coldest winters I have known in Ameztia took grip that year and, with every drop of the thermometer, my own fear deepened as an increasingly desperate, tortured soul scratched around in the darkness outside. Meanwhile, questions gnawed away inside me. Was I an irresponsible mother subjecting my five-year-old daughter to this terrifying and potentially dangerous environment? Should I have fled my home and moved in with my neighbours until civil law had worked its course? Should I have walked out on everything I had fought for over the past years and left it in the hands of the devil?

Despite all my fears, I decided to stay, to hold my own, to defend my home and family. Once again, I found myself smothering Marion's small body in my arms at night as we lay in bed, listening in the darkness for rattling windows and creaking doors. And, as always, I found my strength in the smell of her black Basque hair, with its hints of freshly cut hay and farm-fried sausage.

December arrived and so did the snow. Gilbert's Peugeot stood snowbound outside the door and, after months of disuse, the battery lost its charge. At times, as we drove down the track, we surprised him outside the house, but when he caught sight of us he would scamper away, slithering back into the darkness of The Borda through the broken window. I had no idea what he had been doing outside but my neighbours commented that they had seen an extension lead draped across my terrace and I could only deduce that he must have been taking electricity from an outdoor socket near my back door. This may explain how he managed to charge his phone and make a call, several weeks later, that was to change the course of his destiny – and mine.

On 22 December, just before I was about to fly to Birmingham with Marion for Christmas, I was working late to clear the office work before leaving. Marion was at Zubialdea, enjoying her farewell meal with Amatxi, Atautxi, Isidro and Lourdes. The dark hollow-eyed windows reflected the noose of light around my desk and, as I tapped away frantically at the computer, racing through my last-minute emails, I heard a loud banging at my front door. I hurried downstairs and opened the door to a pair of armed *Guardia Civil*. These were not the friendly regional police in their red uniforms and berets who had kept a paternal eye on us from a distance. The national anti-terrorist squad was now in Ameztia. Given the political sensitivities in the Basque Country at the time, and the reputation these Basque borderlands had for harbouring wanted ETA terrorists and their sympathisers, any reported kidnappings – no matter how unfounded – were taken very seriously indeed.

'We have been informed that a Señor Charbonneau has been kidnapped and is being held hostage on this property,' the elder of the two policemen stated. 'Would you mind telling us what is going on?'

I was flabbergasted at the utter absurdity of the accusation which appeared to be directed, once again, at me. Then, when I gathered my senses, I set about putting the record straight. It transpired that they already had an idea of the real story, as they had got lost trying to find the house and had had to knock on various farmhouse doors to locate me. My neighbours, therefore, had had an opportunity to enlighten them to the true version of events before they arrived. Given their terrible sense of direction,

I was glad that I was not the one who had been kidnapped and in need of rescue!

They asked where Gilbert was, and I showed them to The Borda on the other side of the terrace. Drawing their guns, they ordered me to wait inside but, naturally, having waited for this moment for so long, that was the last thing I intended to do.

The men left, walking around the back of the house to enter the terrace between the two houses.

On facing The Borda, the first door they came across was the original barn door which was permanently closed, bolted from the inside. The other two doors had, of course, been disabled by the new Apeztegia lock and Beñat's superglue, and the broken bathroom window provided the only easy access to the property. Fortunately, the police did not know the place, and presumed that the original Borda door – the only one that could still be opened from the inside – was the main entrance.

One of the policemen stood back. Holding a gun with both hands he pointed it at the door while the other knocked loudly, shouting, '*Guardia Civil. ¡Salga inmediatamente con las manos en alto!*' ('Police. Come out with your hands up!')

While the drama unfolded on the terrace, I had disobeyed orders and crept after the policemen around the back of the house as far as the terrace window, which now, with the curtain removed, afforded me a clandestine view of the action inside.

There was the sound of many bolts being drawn from within The Borda, before the old oak door slowly opened and Gilbert emerged from the darkness with his hands in the air. I didn't catch the exchange that followed, but it amounted to the fact that if the door was easily opened from the inside, and Gilbert's car was outside the door, there were actually no grounds whatsoever for a kidnapping charge and that this was a total waste of police time. And then, as there seemed to be no grounds to evict him from the premises, they allowed him, once again, to step back indoors.

I dashed back inside my house and waited demurely for the police to return to report on the situation.

'We've warned him not to go near you; if he does, he will be in serious trouble. But, for any reason whatsoever, don't hesitate to call the police.'

As they made to leave, the elder of the two policemen turned round and looked at me sternly. 'I've been working in this business for over thirty years and I have to warn you that you have one very dangerous man in your house.'

And with that they got into their vehicles and drove away – presumably in the right direction. I, in turn, wrapped a few Christmas presents and started packing for our flight to the UK.

On 2 January 2010, I returned to The Borda to the faint, acrid smell of burning and the sight of Gilbert's car still in the drive. All sorts of terrors gripped me, but my worst fears proved mercifully unfounded. My neighbours had loyally watched over the premises in my absence, and it appeared that no ostensible damage had been done.

Early the following morning, almost a year after he had moved in, Gilbert emerged from The Borda carrying dismantled shelving, tailored jackets, picture frames, jam jars and all sorts of bric-a-brac out to his car. But no box files. I watched him from the terrace, emboldened by the fact that the end had, apparently, finally arrived, and indulged myself in a sense of jubilation that my home was soon to be my own once more. For the first time in my life, I gloated in victory, surprised and repulsed by the base emotions which he had engendered in me.

Gilbert looked at me with such undisguised contempt and loathing that I felt he would happily have killed me on the spot had he thought he could get away with it. But my instincts had been telling me for a long time that he was far too intelligent to do that, his actions being determined by cold calculation rather than dictated by impulse. Based on this naïve intuition alone, I had held my ground, staying in my house and – so some have said – recklessly putting both Marion's and my lives at risk. Fortunately, this time, my instincts had been right.

Soon a white removal van arrived with a French number plate, which I reported to the police. After Gilbert had loaded it up, it drove away down the hill, followed by Gilbert's car a few minutes later while all my neighbours watched from their different vantage points on the mountain, curious to see what he would do next. Maika's husband waited in his Suzuki for Gilbert's car to pass through Ituren before tailing it at a distance to see where he went, but Gilbert, after a lifetime on the run, made a zigzag through the busy streets of Doneztebe and managed to shake him off.

With immense trepidation, I entered my poor, sad, violated Borda, the cherished family nest which had cradled my daughter, nourished my dreams and once rung to the sound of children's nursery rhymes. Now, here it was, stripped and dirty, studded from head to toe with the rivets, hooks and screws that had fixed rows of bookshelves in place. Shards of glass still covered the bathroom floor but – to my great relief – there was no permanent damage that a lick of paint and a good spring clean could not resolve.

Walking around the back of The Borda towards the stream, I found the source of that acrid smell in the ashes of a large bonfire and the blackened remains of burnt papers and plastic files. I rummaged through the debris and looked for clues. Little had escaped the flames, but the odd charred remains revealed lists of handwritten numbers and calculations.

Gilbert never returned to Ameztia, but his legacy remained. That same year, my brilliant Spanish language teacher left the company with my client database to start up in competition, and ministry officials called me to interviews in Pamplona to sift through the fine details of my work practices. Over the next few years Marion often had nightmares about being snatched away from me and kidnapped, and it was not until her teenage years that she found the peace of mind to stay home alone.

It is a story that we often muse over in the hamlet. Of all the possible scenarios I had imagined for my life on a Basque mountain, I had never dreamt of being accused of breaking and entering, not to mention kidnapping. The ending could have been much nastier. We had been very lucky, and I have been scolded by friends who considered that I had put my daughter's life at unnecessary risk with my naïve actions.

At times I wonder what would have happened had the terrorist squad knocked on a different door, as both the main one to the glass conservatory and the back door had either been locked or jammed. This may have added more credence to the accusation of kidnapping and would have required further explanation. But how would it have been explained without involving the police from Elizondo, the Justice of the Peace from the hardware shop in Doneztebe, the builder from Seville and the lawyer from San Sebastián?

Sometimes, when we stand around in the farmyards in Ameztia and run dry of the usual mountain gossip, one question is likely to arise.

'And that Gilbert, I wonder what has happened to him? Where do you think he is now?' And, although it may just be the angle of the setting sun, I think I detect a glint of nostalgia in their eyes.

Sagrario smiles and shakes her head in disbelief. 'And you remember what he called us, don't you? He called us *estos del monte, sí – ¡estos del monte!*'

As far as my neighbours were concerned, to be called 'mountain savages' opened ancient wounds and, as Basques, this was probably one of the worst insults imaginable. For me, however, it felt like the ultimate accolade. Finally, I belonged. Thanks to Gilbert, I had been branded together with some of the noblest people I had ever had the honour of knowing. And so, with head held high, I followed my fellow 'savages' up the stairs to Sagrario's kitchen for biscuits and a cup of Earl Grey tea.

APRÈS GILBERT

TWO TREES AND A HEADLESS WOMAN

The winter sun streamed in from the south, baking my bones as I scrubbed away at eleven months of accumulated grime. Never again would I be so irresponsible. The hooks and nails that Gilbert had employed to hold up his labyrinth of shelving were prised from the plaster, the holes filled with putty and The Borda painted daffodil yellow. Tutti frutti watercolours smiled from the walls, and the old industrial carpet, rolled out when Marion started crawling, was replaced by bright terracotta tiles. Our beloved Borda was restored and beautiful once again. Its soul had proven far too strong even for the likes of Gilbert, his presence having now been eradicated from our lives. Almost. Never again would I rent out The Borda for more than a few days at a time. It was not that my incorrigible faith in humanity had been dented – surely it was not possible to meet more than one Gilbert in a lifetime – but I had come to realise the importance of The Borda in my life, practically and symbolically. Not only had it provided me with my first home and a crèche for my child, but it had offered a cradle for my dreams too. And, although it had failed me slightly at night in the 'creepy-crawly, wiggly-wiggly' dimension – if the Basques have these wonderful onomatopoeias why can't we? – by day the windows had let in the sun and inspired me with majestic mountain views. Since then, renting out The Borda to strangers has always been tinged with foreboding. It feels a little like putting a price on one's soul.

Ever since Gilbert left, I have lavished The Borda with small – and not so small – gifts, rather like the Buddhists adorning their shrines. The attic mezzanine, where Marion and I huddled together, sheltering from the enormity of our existence, has been partitioned off, now with its own separate door at the top of the stairs. In the kitchen, a leather wineskin hangs from a large hook above the sink (a hook, I suspect, left behind by Gilbert and a detail that I choose to ignore). Now it is me who enjoys the spectacle of observing my guests trying to squirt the thin stream of wine into their mouths, just as – so many years ago – Ignacio had amused himself watching me. A pot of Marmite and a box of Earl Grey teabags sit on the shelf above the kettle, while jars of Spanish red peppers and chickpeas jostle for space under the stairs (at times with the occasional hungry rodent or two). Held together with superglue, the last remaining cut-glass Danish candleholder sits in the middle of the table on top of my red-and-white check tablecloth, a cracked relic of the life I had many years ago.

Yet it is the terrace that best chronicles the passage of time, not only by the size of the hibiscus – its roots slowly cracking through the patio tiles – but also by the innumerable, impromptu dramas it has witnessed throughout the years.

The first, but by no means the most important, protagonists of terrace life have been our cats. For many years it was just Blackie and his sister, Snowflake. Affectionate, sociable creatures, accustomed to the numerous visitors at the house and anyone's friend in return for the lickings of a yoghurt pot. Blackie snores and loves pink, while Snowflake smells of sheep and opens the cat flap backwards. Puski – short for Leonardo de Pusketings Pipe-Cleaner Smith (if you want to know how his name came about, do ask) – is the new kid on the block, his confidence reminiscent of a seventeenth-century dandy from the Versailles Court. His glossy, panther-like form transforms the patio from a pretty backdrop into a live stage set as he poses and prances, obsessively vain, between the branches of the hibiscus tree. He is a skilled footballer player, too, entertaining guests as he careers around the terrace with a walnut while keeping me awake at night with his obsession with the red, glittery Christmas hats he likes to fish out from the bottom of my wicker drawers.

For many years all my cats lived in fear of Ginger Cat, a stray who was eventually caught – humanely – in Luis's badger trap to be exiled to pastures new and distant. Two weeks after his expulsion, he was back to terrorise the terrace once again, which was quite a feat for a cat with only three paws. And so Luis's badger trap was put into action once more, and Ginger Cat finally moved on to a farm further afield in the Baztan Valley.

The terrace is now bordered with flower boxes and is painted in a few too many colours by a few too many people and there is a large convivial outside sofa with crimson cushions.

A statue of a Grecian woman stands beneath the hibiscus tree, full of cracks after many falls. I suspect this voluptuous fountain is subject to some of Puski's more amorous advances when he comes to drink her waters, and we have had to retrieve her head from beneath the sofa on several occasions. Luckily, Peter, a student on one of my Spanish-language courses with a Fine Arts degree, came to the rescue. After a Spanish vocabulary lesson with the Justice of Peace in the Apeztegia hardware store, he spent a golden Saturday afternoon meticulously sticking her head together once again. This earned him the illustrious title of 'Pedro de la Fuente' (Peter of the Fountain) for the rest of the week, although the location of her right ear still remains a mystery.

While the hibiscus tree rains a purple deluge of flowers over the terrace every July, it is the laurel tree which has the greater sense of humour and, in appreciation of the shade that it offers on the south-facing terrace, it has been treated with unprecedented respect.Several years after Gilbert left, we added an extension of four more rooms below the house. During this construction, the laurel tree was given a private chamber of its own and now sticks out of the lower roof like a Tolkienesque chimney pot. In turn, it expresses its gratitude by dropping deceptively olive-like berries into our salads as we sit in its shade, distracted by the views. Fortunately, they taste so foul that few make it past the first bite.

Many years have passed since I first moved to Ameztia, and not all things have remained the same. Last year, Sagrario's son, heir to the Sunbillenea farmstead, bought in a flock of some five hundred sheep who infused more life into the hamlet and caused mayhem by inconsiderately lambing all at the same time. A new set of signposts escorts the traveller up The Road That Doesn't Exist and the pot-holes on the ridge road have finally been repaired. Even the faithful village of Urrotz, which has kept me company night and day from across the valley, has matured. Over the past two decades, its eight street lights have multiplied to eighteen, and a new purple sign at the entrance to the village states, in Basque, '*Urrotzan Ez Dugu Eraso Sexistarik Onartzen*' ('In Urrotz we do not condone sexist behaviour').

However, the pace of life seems not to have changed, and my life is still measured in the sixty-minute intervals marked by the chimes of the church bells, and by the almost hourly braying of the donkey in the fields below the village. This has provided me with two decades of inconclusive musings about a possible causal link between the two.

❖ ❖ ❖ ❖

Whether there was any authentic clairvoyance in the Australian fortune teller's prophecy, or whether it was just mere coincidence, I will never know. While she had foreseen that I would have two children and, technically, of course, I had just the one, perhaps – if I were to believe any of this at all – she had sensed the energy and passion I was to invest in my work? Pyrenean Experience, my calling, my life's creation, has certainly demanded as much patience and dedication as a child. And there is no denying that her prediction of 'a house… a big house, with lots of land around it' certainly has come true.

My beautiful Borda, my eagle's eyrie, my watchtower on the world, has now mushroomed – in higgledy-piggledy fashion – from a tiny mountain barn into a rambling country abode with an array of sloping roofs, all at different angles and all with their own assorted leaks.

The Borda is now by far the bigger and the more self-important of the two houses, and its freshly painted walls and matching bed sheets put those of my own house to shame. Loathing unnecessary waste, I have shunted The Borda's cast-offs across the terrace, and her chipped teacups, split lightshades and torn towels have now taken up residence with me. The accumulation of oddments on my own private porch has earned it the name 'the graveyard of unwanted furniture', while my yellow rose bush – planted at the same time as the magnificent specimen outside the new Borda rooms – struggles to bear me the odd paltry bloom.

As a tool of communication, my Spanish now serves me well, a rough-and-ready companion which can be taken most places although it has a habit of hijacking my English from time to time and putting the cart before the horse.

Of the two languages, it is Basque (Euskara) that steals my heart, never ceasing to surprise with its originality, counter-intuitive word order and outlandish bedside manner. Each word is a collector's item. Who can fail to fall in love with words such as *azazkalak* (nails) or *zirripi-zarrapa* (slovenly), or be seduced by the *pinpilinpauxa* (butterfly)? With absolutely no pretence that Euskara will ever have more than a utilitarian role in my life, the pressure is off, and my frustrated attempts to learn it are in the vein of a code-cracking exercise appealing to the smuggler and mathematician in me. I am, however, still one step ahead of the devil. My ability to fumble my way through a conversation in Euskara, and my occasional appearance on Basque TV – to Marion's horror – have undoubtedly earned me a few brownie points within the community. The act of speaking Euskara among Basque people offers a similar sense of complicity as the secret handshake among Freemasons.

Just as my Spanish language trespasses into my English conversations, so my business life has encroached upon my private one. My emails are constantly open on the kitchen counter, walking notes and bank statements overflow on the desk by my bed, and Prévert's dog-eared poetry book, *Paroles*, is now bullied into a corner of the library by a gang of Spanish dictionaries and Basque Country guidebooks.

Undeniably, my own house does, perhaps, need a bit of reordering and, as for me, well, that is another subject. Sometimes I feel that I have washed up on a bend in the river of life, out of breath, needing to find myself before the current carries me away again downstream. One day starts to resemble the next and, after getting up each morning and saluting the views from my bedroom balcony, I put on the same old working clothes. Well almost. There are two sets of clothes, an old one for mucking around on the land and, as a nod to corporate image, a slightly better ensemble when leading my guests off into the hills on their Pyrenean Experience.

Shorts, crumpled T-shirts, and old sweaters lie slung on a chair in my bedroom and, like my collection of maps, most of them are full of small rips and holes; battle scars from days spent beating down thorn bushes or scaling barbed-wire fences in pursuit of another perfect path. Or so I like to think. Secretly, I believe that it is the family of moths, enjoying a smorgasbord in my wardrobe, that deserves the blame.

Every night, before going to bed, I extricate the clip out of my tangled hair and latch it on to the frame of my mirror, where it spends the night in the company of two, sometimes three, maybe four, other hair clips. Often some go missing only to reappear again in a rucksack pocket or behind the cushions on the sofa and, in general, they make it back to base once a week or so. There are five clips in all. Four plain and one tortoiseshell, this one saved for special occasions as the colours reflect the highlights in my hair – or so I fancy. No matter how many clips choose to sojourn elsewhere in the house, the tortoiseshell clip remains in exactly the same place on the mirror. In standby for that special moment. It hasn't budged for years.

Occasionally, before retiring to bed, I open my wardrobe and flick through the rows of lacy summer dresses, wondering when, if ever, they will be worn again. Sometimes, just sometimes, I slip into one of the dresses and, squeezing untrained feet into narrow, high-heeled sandals, walk out to the full-sized mirror on the landing and contemplate my reflection. There is no denying the ravages of outdoor life on my skin nor the few grey streaks in my sun-bleached hair. But the clothes still fit, and the zip still closes on that tight-fitting designer dress purchased in Denmark some thirty years ago for a Spanish embassy party with Bernardo and Carmen.

And then the patter of rain on the skylight, that unrelenting gong of reality, shakes me from my reverie and I remember that the tarpaulin on the woodpile needs to be strapped down. Scattering my heels on the landing and throwing a dressing gown over my dress, I dash down the stairs, slip on my wellington boots, and bolt out into the night.

Climbing the stairs for the second time, I meet Marion, now eighteen, on the landing and our eyes meet in the mirror. Standing there in my threadbare dressing gown with dripping wet hair, I gaze at her in incredulity, wondering how we have got so far. *We did it, baby, we did it,* I want to shout. *Baby, we did it.* But her thoughts are elsewhere as she poses, beautiful and rebellious, in front of the mirror in her new party dress and my – yes, my – high-heeled shoes.

❖ ❖ ❖ ❖

And so, since 2015, I have finally been able to run my 'house parties' in my own 'house'. Throughout the summer, walkers and blossoming amateur linguists from all over the planet brave The Road That Doesn't Exist to join us at Iaulin Borda. Arriving, shaken and stirred in equal proportion by its hairpin bends and breathtaking views, they are then universally humbled by the mesmerising landscapes that unfold from my terrace. On lazy afternoons they can be found curled up with a book on a sofa sipping cups of tea or glasses of wine or dozing in the sunshine with Spanish verb sheets slipping from their hands.

The turtle on the tap now witnesses more ennobling scenes than that of an Englishwoman tripping over a pair of amorous toads on her nocturnal sprints to the water closet. Today, the turtle keeps vigil over my guests, listening in to the intimate conversations, laughter and debates that accompany our inspiring meeting of minds. Friends and local specialists – musicians, cooks, shepherds, millers, mushroom hunters, and the occasional disoriented smuggler or two – pay us regular visits, joining us on the terrace for an aperitif in the shade of the hibiscus and laurel trees.

Now that my guests stay with me in Ameztia, they have the opportunity to integrate into hamlet life, offering my neighbours an educational insight into their various worlds. As they wander by, map in hand, they greet the farmers with their few phrases of Spanish (or Basque), and help the hamlet's children drill their school English with carefully enunciated *Hello*s and *How are you*s.

My neighbours are both intrigued and welcoming, flattered by the interest that these newcomers show in their farming traditions and way of life. On frequent occasions, we are ushered into their farms for slivers of sheep's cheese and swigs of wine, but one of the livelier interactions I remember was actually over a simple coffee and biscuits in Amatxi's kitchen.

On this occasion, a friend of mine dropped by for lunch accompanied by a family of Senegalese women bearing homemade cakes and delicious pots of West African food. It was a surprise visit and I remember a moment of panic, wondering how to justify the introduction of this cohort of French-speakers into what was ostensibly a total-immersion Spanish-language week. But I need not have worried. Once the tinfoil had been lifted from the steaming stews, and the cakes had disintegrated into crumbs on the tablecloth, languages seemed irrelevant. My students had implicitly understood that the ultimate, nobler aim of learning any language is to break down barriers and communicate across cultural divides. Which they did, magnificently.

And then it was Amatxi's turn.

After lunch we all drifted down the road in a sea of colour, brightly patterned robes and headscarves billowing in the mountain breeze. After a brief exchange with Isidro and Lourdes we floated into the Zubialdea kitchen for coffee with Amatxi who – equally surprised by the visit and far less accustomed to such exotic guests – served us all coffee and biscuits without batting an eyelid. After some animated conversations and hilarious misunderstandings – translated to the best of my abilities – we glided back out into the yard where Isidro took me to one side.

'*Jordi*,' he grinned, 'you know, with you in the hamlet, who needs a television!'

If Atautxi had still been alive, he would have had a ball.

As for my dear, beloved Amatxi, she never fails to amaze me, rallying the ranks, kissing each of my guests on the cheek, and always interested to know how everyone is getting on. With a stern but maternal eye, she never fails to enquire about the food, checking whether my cooking skills – or those of my cook – are up to scratch. If I had a publicity sign with 'Pyrenean Experience' written on it, Amatxi would be holding it up for me. That is if she wasn't clinging to her Zimmer frame instead.

Amatxi, you are the best.

THE END… almost.

EPILOGUE ONE

HEADING NORTH AGAIN

Over the past two and a half decades, I have returned to Denmark to visit my friends several times, my stomach twisting into knots as the captain's slow, accented voice asks us to buckle our seat belts for the descent into Københavns Lufthavn. It always seemed that while I had physically broken free, the feelings and fears of my final frustrated years there had not. Traipsing through the cobbled streets from one friend's house to the next, it seemed to me the Scandinavian stones themselves had absorbed my memories, remaining to haunt me, ricocheting between one hard, grey façade and the next.

But the last time I visited something had changed. Even before I disembarked from the plane, a Danish man was picking up my coat, which had slipped on to the floor, and placing it on my shoulders. Then, on the crowded commuter train into town, a young man spontaneously offered his seat to an elderly gentleman standing in the aisle.

Finally – and as always – I enjoyed a wonderfully liberating few days visiting dear friends, reminiscing about old times and catching up on personal news. Chatting late into the night, we enjoyed the best of Danish *hygge*, hunkering down in their cosy, candle-lit homes, and crumbling more cinnamon biscuits into their slightly less pristine IKEA sofas. My Danish was rusty now and, as I tried, unflatteringly, to navigate my way through Danish vowels and glottal stops, my English accent made my friends laugh more than ever.

To be honest, I sympathise with those English-speakers who choose *not* to learn Danish but perhaps the euphemistic biases of my own English upbringing have much to do with this. Not only do most Danes speak excellent English, but learning their language, from my totally subjective point of view, is a singularly unromantic endeavour. It is full of ungainly sounds and ill-fated words – the words *fart*, *i fart* and *fartkontrol* chaperoning one everywhere from elevators to motorways. Nevertheless, once one has risen above these unfortunate false friends (*falske venner*), the English and Danish languages, in their written form, are actually remarkably similar.

❖ ❖ ❖ ❖

Time flew by and, a few days later, I found myself once again in Hans Knudsen's Plads waiting for the 6.47am bus to Københavns Lufthavn. I waited alone at the bus stop until another traveller joined me, coat collar turned up against the winds and lambswool scarf wrapped around his nose and mouth. Looking up unexpectedly, his soft grey eyes crinkled into a smile, and he greeted me with a muffled *god morgen*. It occurred to me that something had changed, something was different. Was it Denmark that had changed? Or – as with the endings of so many good stories – was it me?

I sailed through the wonderfully efficient Copenhagen airport departure hall, sparkling stylishly with champagne glasses and crystal candleholders. Peeling my nostalgic gaze away from the displays of pickled herrings, smoked salmon and creamy horseradish sauce, I scanned the list of destinations on the flight information screen, searching – as always – for evocative names of faraway places. And there it was – it really was. Just after the flights to Stockholm and Helsinki, there was an Air Greenland flight leaving for Kangerlussuaq. Just the name: Kangerlussuaq. Just the thought.

I sighed. A sudden draught of cold Nordic air made it into the undoubtedly well-insulated airport, giving me goosebumps as I recalled that magnificent icy wonderland and that helicopter journey that had in many ways changed the course of my life. One day, I had promised myself. One day.

And then I was off through muted corridors towards my plane, the baggage trolley whizzing along effortlessly on perfectly aligned wheels. Settling myself down by the window, I peeled back the greasy paper serviette that covered the Danish butter cookies my dear friend had baked that morning. There was no doubt that a piece of my heart still lingered here, and yet my home, my work, my community – and of course my daughter – were all Basque. As for my soul, there was no denying that it was still wandering around the enchanting mountains of Ameztia.

As the plane took off into the dawn, the sun etching its signature on crazy-paved, crackle-glazed dawn skies, I peered out of the window, cookie in hand, body and soul suspended between my northern life and my southern one.

There, to the west, beneath the clouds, lay a large island and the only truly inextricable identity I had. Whether it was the nationality stamped on my Spanish residency card, my amusing English rendition of Danish vowels, my Basque nickname, *Jordi La Inglesa*, or simply the jars of Earl Grey tea and Marmite on my kitchen shelves, my identity was still inextricably tied to the British Isles. Down there, on the edge of the North Sea, were my fellow countrymen, my family home, my childhood and my cultural foundations.

Incongruously, I seem to have made my home among the Basque farmers of Ameztia, a people whose identity is so deeply anchored within their own land, culture and language that it becomes impossible to ignore the importance of roots. And yet I had rarely given mine a second thought. Until now.

The pursuit of freedom has always been the name of my game and I have all too often equated roots with ties. Roots were little more than rigid bonds that needed to be severed in order to truly embrace the thrills of travel: of adapting to different cultures, of living in foreign languages and of making cosmopolitan new friends. Or so I have thought.

That island below me, cradle of my culture, home to those torn and tattered roots that I had left behind, was also the guardian of my dearly loved, sorely missed English language. My mother tongue – possibly the only remaining umbilical connection to my past – is the unique key to the uninhibited expression of that complex tapestry of emotions that stir within me. It is the sole language that I will ever really understand and the only one that has any chance of understanding me. And while I wait, eternally on tenterhooks, for my mountains to impart their wisdom – for I know they have their secrets, and I know they have their answers – I feel a desperate urge to reach out to my language, to write again, to painstakingly choose word after word to unravel the knots and twisted threads of this strange existence, and to make some sense of it all.

With fingers still sticky from the Danish cookies, I reach into my bag and pull out my British passport.

'*Buenas tardes*,' ('good afternoon') I beam at the Spanish passport controller at Bilbao airport. '*Arratsalde on*,' I correct myself in my best Basque.

'*Ongi etorri*,' ('welcome') he grins.

And with this, I walk out into the sunshine and catch the bus home.

EPILOGUE TWO

HEADING HOME

With the traumas of marketing, motherhood and kidnappings behind me, I can now almost say that I belong to Ameztia, that this really is home. Almost. Thanks to Gilbert, I have finally been granted the highest accolade of them all and risen to the rank of 'mountain savage' – just like the rest of my dear neighbours. Yet, although I live here and have put down deeper roots than anywhere else in the world, I am increasingly aware that even here my belonging is tenuous. It is a borrowed existence.

This all became clear one day when I saw Ignacio peering over the wall into my field. It was one of the first times he had strayed from Sunbillenea since a knee operation had confined him to his home. The leaves were just changing colour and the hamlet was busy, and while Sagrario and Luis were out on the ridge making bracken stacks for the winter, Ignacio had limped around the spur towards my house.

He did not see me at first, and I surprised him on the path. He was leaning up against the wall, gazing soulfully at my field where invasive clumps of nettles and mint were infiltrating their way into the previously perfect pastures that he and his family had lovingly tended for generations. He didn't turn as I approached, remaining motionless, staring out over the land as if in a trance. But he knew I was there.

After a long silence, he spoke, as if to himself. 'It breaks my heart to see the land like this. I can't take care of it the way I should… the way it deserves. I simply can't.'

I looked up and saw that his green eyes were welling with tears. And then, still without looking at me, he turned and stumbled back along the pig path, through the chestnut grove towards his farm, head bowed, broad shoulders swaying on his spindly crutches. A father who had failed his child.

It dawned on me then how strange this sounded: *my* land but *his* child?

My driveway formed part of the communal pig path from Urrotz, and the land on which *my* cherry trees grew actually belonged to Maika. *My* stream had once been Sagrario's tadpoling stream and *my* Treasure Hunt Woods had always been Amatxi's cuckoo woods and Luis's and Ignacio's mushrooming haunt – and *their* father's before that. All these places had been wooed and tamed by my neighbours and the generations before them long before I arrived. Long before I was even born.

Admittedly, I have left my own footprints on the Basque landscapes around me and woven my threads into their rich tapestries – *my* Iaulin Borda, *my* landscaped gardens, *my* chimney-pot laurel tree – but slowly I have come to question whether, in fact, *any* part of this beautiful slice of Mother Earth is actually *mine* at all?

Just like a cat that has climbed over the wall into somebody else's garden, I have curled up in a gloriously sunny spot and, dozing to the sound of the birds, have made it my home. Yes, I have fallen in love with these lands, I have eulogised their beauty, I have sat here with my cold cups of tea caressing every contour of this landscape with my mind. I have run out to take pictures of its rainbows, its morning mists and storms. I have marketed it, packaged it, bought it, sold it, loved it and lamented it, but it is still not *mine*.

This land belongs to them: to my neighbours, their ancestors and their fellow men and women who have broken their backs and hearts on a billion unacknowledged tasks, pitting soul and sinew against the gods of nature to keep their children and their children's children warm and safe. Hundreds of forgotten generations who have disappeared into oblivion like the banks of chestnut husks which shore up every autumn on the pig path.

Having made my way back to Iaulin Borda, I shake off my wellington boots and pop inside for a quick shower, hesitating just that second longer in front of the mirror. Perhaps this is the moment. Perhaps.

Reaching out defiantly for the tortoiseshell hair clip, I fasten it resolutely into my hair and, grabbing a blank sheet of paper, pad back outside to the terrace barefoot. There, to the sound of the church bells in Urrotz and the donkey braying in the valley below, I take up my pen and write down the words 'My Life on a Basque Mountain'.

ENDNOTE

In 2023 two of the matriarchs of Ameztia, major characters in this story and in many others, passed away: Sagrario, at just sixty, and a couple of months later, her aunt, Amatxi, aged ninety-six, her heart heavier as the years passed by, the spark in her eyes defiant to the end. Where wars and pandemics had been unable to check the comings and goings of life in Ameztia, the deaths of these two remarkable women did. The animals did not go out to graze on those days, the hum of the farm machinery was silenced, and Luis's cries of '*tox*, *tox*' to the sheep on the ridge were not to be heard.

Amatxi, Sagrario, we miss you very much.

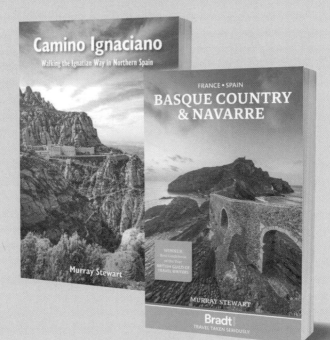

THE BRADT STORY

In the beginning
It all began in 1974 on an Amazon river barge. During an 18-month trip through South America, two adventurous young backpackers – Hilary Bradt and her then husband, George – decided to write about the hiking trails they had discovered through the Andes. *Backpacking Along Ancient Ways in Peru and Bolivia* included the very first descriptions of the Inca Trail. It was the start of a colourful journey to becoming one of the best-loved travel publishers in the world; you can read the full story on our website (**bradtguides. com/ourstory**).

Getting there first
Hilary quickly gained a reputation for being a true travel pioneer, and in the 1980s she started to focus on guides to places overlooked by other publishers. The Bradt Guides list became a roll call of guidebook 'firsts'. We published the first guide to Madagascar, followed by Mauritius, Czechoslovakia and Vietnam. The 1990s saw the beginning of our extensive coverage of Africa: Tanzania, Uganda, South Africa, and Eritrea. Later, post-conflict guides became a feature: Rwanda, Mozambique, Angola, and Sierra Leone, as well as the first standalone guides to the Baltic States following the fall of the Iron Curtain, and the first post-war guides to Bosnia, Kosovo and Albania.

Comprehensive – and with a conscience
Today, we are the world's largest independently owned travel publisher, with more than 200 titles. However, our ethos remains unchanged. Hilary is still keenly involved, and **we still get there first**; two-thirds of Bradt guides have no direct competition.

But we don't just get there first. Our guides are also known for being **more comprehensive** than any other series. We avoid templates and tick-lists. Each guide is a one-of-a-kind expression of an expert author's interests, knowledge and enthusiasm for telling it how it really is.

And a commitment to wildlife, conservation and respect for local communities has always been at the heart of our books. Bradt Guides was **championing sustainable travel** before any other guidebook publisher. We even have a series dedicated to Slow Travel in the UK, award-winning books that explore the country with a passion and depth you'll find nowhere else.

Thank you!
We can only do what we do because of the support of readers like you – people who value less-obvious experiences, less-visited places and a more thoughtful approach to travel. Those who, like us, take travel seriously.

Bradt GUIDES
TRAVEL TAKEN SERIOUSLY